IN THE PATH OF
HIZBULLAH

Modern Intellectual and Political History of the Middle East
Mehrzad Boroujerdi, *Series Editor*

Ahmad Nizar Hamzeh

IN THE PATH OF
HIZBULLAH

SYRACUSE UNIVERSITY PRESS

Mohamad El-Hindi Books on Arab Culture and Islamic Civilization
are published with the assistance of a grant from Ahmad El-Hindi.

The paper used in this publication meets the minimum requirements
of American National Standard for Information Sciences—Permanence
of Paper for Printed Library Materials, ANSI Z39.48–1984.∞™

Page iii: Ashoura Day march in southern suburb of Beirut, Lebanon,
March 2004. Courtesy of the *al-Intiqad* newspaper.

Library of Congress Cataloging-in-Publication Data
Hamzeh, Ahmad Nizar.
  In the path of Hizbullah / Ahmad Nizar Hamzeh.— 1st ed.
     p. cm.—(Modern intellectual and political history of the Middle East)
  Includes bibliographical references (p. 177) and index.
  ISBN 0-8156-3053-0 (hardcover (cloth) : alk. paper)
  1. Hizballah (Lebanon)   2. Islam and politics.   3. Islam and state.
I. Title.   II. Series: Modern intellectual and political history of the Middle East
JQ1828.A98H6245 2004
303.6'25'095692—dc22   2004021012

Contents

Ahmad Nizar Hamzeh is associate professor of political science at the American University of Beirut. He is the author of many journal articles on Islamic movements and coauthor (in Arabic) of *The 1998 Lebanese Munici-pal Elections.* His teaching and research interests include political theory and methodology, Islamic politics, and international law.

Illustrations

FIGURES

Preface

This book has been an unhurried project. Its origin dates back to six years ago when I decided to write a book on Hizbullah. For a long time, I have been researching and writing on Lebanon's Islamist movements, in particular Hizbullah. I intended neither to write a book that serves as a medium for academic promotion, nor to treat Hizbullah's phenomena from a journalistic perspective. Four years and four drafts later, the present work is the result of my efforts.

One reason it took so long to write this book is that I spent a lot of time working out a conceptual model to lean on and to guide the analysis. The book fills what I believe to be an important gap in the literature. Although there are some books on Hizbullah, almost none draw heavily, as I do, on the sophisticated organizational structure and functions of this Islamic group. Moreover, I have tried to write this book as a mode of inquiry, intelligible to any literate person interested in the subject. My aim has been to be reasonably clear without being simplistic, and to be somewhat original without being merely idiosyncratic. I believe that the result, though slow in coming, is unique.

Studying one of the most complex organizations of all Islamist movements in terms of structures and functions, rather than ideology, has allowed me to develop a conceptual framework of crises and responses that are solidly based on widely accepted theories. The conceptual framework specifies linkages between crisis conditions and responses in terms of ideology, organizational structures, and modes of action. I found it hard to understand Islamist movements, Hizbullah or others, without the aid of conceptual touchstones found in the traditions of Islamic theology, history, and writings of the group's ideologues or fountainheads.

The measure of my success will be the degree to which I can contribute to the understanding of Islamist movements. Understanding Islamist movements is more than a worthwhile feat in its own right; it is a pathway for understanding the regenerative capacity of groups such as Hizbullah and their ominous challenge to contemporary politics.

Throughout the exciting but exhausting process of research and analysis, I was fortunate to have the devoted support of Professor H. Richard Dekmejian of the University of Southern California, whose wholehearted efforts made this book possible. I am also particularly grateful to Mary Selden Evans, executive editor of acquisitions for Syracuse University Press, for her invaluable support and encouragement throughout the review process; and to Sally Abi Khalil, Nathan Train, and Rudy Jabour for their invaluable work in preparing the manuscript. In addition, I wish to acknowledge the financial support for my research provided by the officers of the Fulbright program; I do not know what my colleagues or I would do without their assistance. Finally, I am deeply grateful to my family for their love and support.

IN THE PATH OF
HIZBULLAH

1

The Hizbullah Complex

Of the many Islamist groups that have emerged within the Muslim world since the mid-1980s, perhaps none has had as great an impact on Middle Eastern and international affairs as Hizbullah—"the Party of God." This group of mainly Lebanese Shi'ite Muslims has gained both infamy and fame by its resort to militancy. Yet Hizbullah's oscillation between militancy and political pragmatism in the pursuit of its goals has left most scholars and policymakers perplexed.

Existing studies that discuss the Hizbullah of Lebanon are mainly concerned either with Hizbullah's militancy or with the contradiction between its fierce ideological stance, as displayed in its "Open Letter" of 1985, and its responses to the shifting landscape of regional as well as Lebanese politics. Jaber, Ranstorp, and others have focused on Hizbullah's militancy, regarding its politics of violence, terrorism, and hostage taking as a one-way street, largely dependent on external factors, notably Iran's Islamic Revolution and Syrian policies under President Hafiz al-Assad.[1] Norton, on the other hand, has focused on Hizbullah's transformation from revolutionary group to tame political consultant. Although he acknowledges that Hizbullah has pragmatically confronted political reality, he asserts that the party's transformation is incompatible with its ideology.[2] His viewpoint is echoed to varying degrees by Picard, Abu Khalil, Zisser, and others, who stress that Hizbullah's goals are contradictory.[3]

Kramer and Sharara have looked at the evolution of Hizbullah, with Kramer focusing on the extent of violence in Hizbullah's jihad and Sharara analyzing the evolution of Hizbullah's local society.[4] Yet none of these writers has paid much attention to Hizbullah's organizational structure or its choices of modes of action, as sanctioned by the party's ideology. In

1

fact, as early as 1993, I was one of the first to argue that Hizbullah's choice between militancy and political pragmatism depends on the circumstances and does not contradict the party's ideology.[5]

In this book, I examine Hizbullah's emergence, ideology, organizational structure, and modes of action, focusing particularly on the evolution of Hizbullah's modes of action and their implications for Lebanon and the wider region. I base this structural-functional analysis on a considerable body of empirical and textual evidence, relying mainly on primary Arabic sources, in particular Hizbullah's own published and unpublished material, in an attempt to project Hizbullah's politics more accurately. I have also made extensive use of interviews with Hizbullah's leaders and members and assembled other primary and secondary sources to provide a general account for understanding the complexity of Hizbullah's evolution.

THE CONCEPTUAL CHALLENGE

Understanding Hizbullah requires a multifaceted conceptual framework that combines theories of crisis, revolution, leadership, personality, social class, and political parties. To this end, the inquiry is cast in a broad framework that combines crisis conditions, responses of ideology and leadership, and operational choices affecting the feasibility of the Islamic order. The conceptual interconnections among the components of the theoretical framework are outlined in figure 1.1.

Crisis Conditions in an Islamic Society

The heightening of Islamic consciousness mainly has been characterized as Islamic fundamentalism. The scope and intensity of the fundamentalist reaction, as argued by Dekmejian, "depends on the depth and pervasiveness of the crisis environment."[6] Similarly, the emergence of Hizbullah is perceived in this conceptual framework as a response to acute and pervasive crisis conditions characterized by at least four crisis attributes:[7]

- Identity crisis
- Structural imbalance

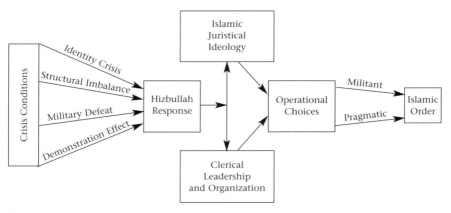

Figure 1.1. Conceptual Framework

- Military defeat
- Demonstration effect

Hizbullah's Responses

Hizbullah has a variety of ways to respond to crisis conditions:

• by developing and disseminating *Islamic juristical ideology*. A figure of Islamic doctrinal authority—the *wali al-faqih* (the jurisconsult) or the *marja' al-taqlid* (the highest religious authority among Shi'ites and the model, or source of emulation, for their religious practice)—will channel and interpret the final revelation of the word of God. Since Shi'ites regard such figures as carriers of divine testimony and succession from the Prophet and the imams, the *wali al-faqih* or the *marja'* may legitimately elaborate, mold, or alter salvational prescriptions of beliefs and practices to fit changing circumstances;

• by establishing a *clerical leadership and hierarchical organization*, within a political, social, and military executive apparatus, committed to establishing an Islamic order under the guardianship of the jurist; and

• through *operational choices* influenced by ideology but depending pragmatically on the circumstances, as sanctioned by the jurisconsult or the party's clerical leaders. Hizbullah may apply two modes of operational choices separately or jointly. The *militant mode* advocates the resort to armed jihad (struggle) as a means to establishing an Islamic order. Put hypothetically, the more favorable the circumstances—in particular the power equation—the more likely that Hizbullah will resort to militancy and armed struggle to achieve its goals. The *gradualist-pragmatic mode,* or what might be termed political pragmatism, employs nonmilitant means to build an Islamic order. In this mode, Hizbullah operates in some measure within the confines of legality, as defined by the government. Thus, the less favorable the circumstances, the more likely that Hizbullah will abandon militant tactics in favor of more peaceful methods, such as seeking seats in the legislature or investing in other elected bodies as a way to seize power in the long term. Whatever its operational choice, however, Hizbullah's ultimate goal is the same: to seize political power and establish an Islamic order.

The Islamic Order

The future of Hizbullah's Islamic order depends on state policies, on the unity of the party's leadership, and on external factors. Although Hizbullah's evolution can be variously interpreted, the advantage of this conceptual framework is that it combines themes from Western social science with Hizbullah's own diagnosis and treatment of the society's crisis conditions.

Subsequent chapters are structured according to the components of the conceptual framework. Chapter 1 introduces the reader to Hizbullah and the conceptual framework. Chapter 2 examines the crisis conditions that acted as catalysts for Hizbullah's emergence. It focuses on the attributes of identity crisis, structural imbalance, military defeat, and demonstration effect whose convergence was critical to the formation of Hizbullah. Chapter 3 analyzes the components of Hizbullah's ideology. Responding to crisis catalysts, Hizbullah developed an Islamic juristical ideology that contains salvational prescriptions and primordial values, beliefs, and practices. Such ideology provides not only a source of Islamic legislation but also flexibility in the face of changing circumstances. Chapter 4 systematically analyzes Hizbullah's leadership and organizational structure as impacted by the party's ideology. The chapter focuses on the political, social, and military and security apparatus of the party. The analysis also sheds light on the controversy over the classification of Hizbullah as a conventional political party. Chapter 5 provides an in-depth analysis of Hizbullah's operational choices. It focuses on the militant and gradualist-pragmatic modes as employed by the party in response to specific circumstances. It also analyzes the means of each mode and how the party has benefited from each mode, whether applied separately or jointly, in approaching its aim. Chapter 6, the conclusion, provides a summary of Hizbullah's evolution and modes of action, and discussion of the trends and prospects of the party's Islamist venture in Lebanon and the region.

2
Crisis Catalysts to the Emergence of Hizbullah

The systematic study of Hizbullah necessitates an inquiry into the crisis conditions that have acted as catalysts for the party's emergence, beliefs, and actions. Thus the aim of this chapter is to examine which crisis catalysts had the most immediate impact on the rise of Hizbullah.

Substantial scholarly and reportage works on the rise of Islamist groups and movements in the Arab-Islamic milieu have revealed the existence of protracted crises encompassing sociocultural, economic, political, and spiritual realms.[1] However, the relative causal influence of each *microcatalyst*—a term used by Dekmejian—depends on the crisis conditions in different national settings. More specifically, despite significant cross-national similarities among crisis conditions in the Arab-Islamic society, the microcatalysts found in a specific national setting might differ. This does not prevent the fact that crisis conditions in a national setting or in subnational groups might encompass catalysts peculiar to the national setting or a subset and catalysts stemming from the cross-national environment.

The long-standing crises of the Shi'ite community in the Lebanese context are well described by a number of studies. The bulk of these studies address issues of culture, mobilization, economic development, modernization, social protest, or describe events that led to Shi'ite politicization and fundamentalism.[2]

However, a diagnostic examination of the Shi'ite crisis environment reveals four sets of crisis catalysts, arising either from crises peculiar to Lebanon's Shi'ite community or from catalysts stemming from the larger

Arab-Islamic society. The dynamic interaction of crisis catalysts operating in a mutually reinforcing pattern has led to the emergence of Hizbullah (see figure 1.1).

IDENTITY CRISIS: OPPRESSION AND PERSECUTION

The term *identity crisis,* as defined by specialists, involves a crisis of the soul and personality. Such a crisis is often characterized by acute alienation and feelings of normlessness, powerlessness, insecurity, and self-derangement. In extreme circumstances, an individual might develop feelings of *anomie* (a term coined by Emile Durkheim and signifying an erosion or absence of standards or values), leading to a growing "sense of psychological distress, heightened aspirations, and vulnerability to mass appeals."[3] Although these characteristics are essentially important indicators of identity crisis, it seems that the incidence of identity crisis rises as the individual or group is increasingly at odds with other people's identities. The identity crisis then results in the formation of a struggle group and sets the scene for conflict.

The historical pattern of the Lebanese Shi'ite identity crisis stems from the larger identity crisis of the Arab-Islamic society. One major consequence of the progressive decline of the Islamic community *(ummah),* reaching back to the era of the prophet Muhammad, was the crisis of individual and collective identity among the Muslims. Because Islam constituted an all-encompassing life system that included religion *(din),* state *(dawlah),* and law *(shari'ah),* the task of finding a substitute framework of identity was to prove difficult, if not impossible. Hence, the outrages of the identity crisis surged as Islam was placed on the defensive by Western powers and their ideological influences. Yet within Islam itself the enormity of the crisis produced another identity crisis of micro nature for a group of Muslims known as the Shi'ites. The legacy of Shi'ism is more than fourteen hundred years old. It is a legacy of martyrdom, persecution, torment, suffering, powerlessness, and insecurity, resting on a religiously sanctioned belief that Islamic history was derailed when political power passed from the hands of the family of Prophet Muhammad (died A.D. 632) in the seventh century.

The most outstanding aspect of the Shiʿites' belief system is their conviction that their community, because of its lineage from the Prophet through the imams, is the legitimate interpreter of Islam. In fact, the Shiʿites believe that the Prophet designated their first imam—ʿAli, the Prophet's cousin and son-in-law—to succeed him as the head of the Muslim community.[4] This belief pitted the Shiʿites against the majority Sunnis, who asserted the *ijmaʿ* (consensus) of the community that Abu Bakr (d. 634) should become caliph upon the death of the Prophet. The partisans of ʿAli—the Shiʿites—argued that only members of the Prophet's family to whom he had granted the sacred powers of interpretation could correctly divine the meaning of the Qurʾan.[5] The disagreement over the succession revealed a more fundamental difference between the Sunnis and the Shiʿites over the interpretation of the Qurʾan and the Prophet's tradition, a difference that soon developed into a serious schism.[6]

ʿAli finally did succeed to the caliphate in 656 after he was passed over for succession by Caliphs ʿUmar (d. 646) and ʿUthman (d. 656). Upon ʿAli's succession he was opposed by Muʿawiyah, the Umayyad leader, and the Prophet's youngest wife, ʿAʾisha. The religio-political dispute between ʿAli and Muʿawiyah led the Kharijites—proponents of an insurrection movement that stressed that any strict follower of Allah's rule was worthy of becoming caliph—to denounce both ʿAli and Muʿawiyah as unfit for the leadership. While the Kharijites succeeded in murdering ʿAli in 661, their attempt to assassinate Muʿawiyah failed, and he emerged victorious as a Sunni caliph. Muʿawiyah then had ʿAli's son, Imam Hasan, poisoned in 670.[7]

Muʿawiyah passed the caliphate to his son Yazid, who had ʿAli's second son, Imam Husayn, murdered in the desert of Karbala in southern Iraq in 680. At this time, the split between the Sunnis and the Shiʿites became paramount, with the Shiʿites refusing to accept the legitimacy of the Sunni caliphate. They chose instead to follow the leadership of descendants of the Prophet: ʿAli, Hasan, Husayn, and a line of nine succeeding imams. Thus, Twelver Shiʿism consists of twelve imams beginning with ʿAli and ending with the twelfth imam, Muhammad Mahdi al-Muntazar, known as the Mahdi. It is said that he went into occultation in 874, eventually to return as a messianic restorer of Islam to establish a just rule.[8]

Shi'ism was particularly dominant in the Muslim world in the tenth century, at a time when the Shi'ite Twelver dynasty of the Buyids was ruling in Iraq and Iran, and the Fatimids—Shi'ite Ismailis or Seveners—in Egypt, North Africa, and Syria. However, with the downfall of the Fatimids and the conquest of Syria by Salah-al-Din-al-Ayyubi in 1171, it proved impossible to reverse the extinction of the Abbasids, who soon fell prey to Mamluks—Turkish warlords—and were destroyed by the Mongols under Hulaghu in 1258.[9] These events began centuries of oppression and persecution of Shi'ites everywhere. The Lebanese Shi'ites, most of whom belonged to the Twelvers, were no exception.

In fact, the pattern of the Lebanese Shi'ite settlements from the eleventh century onward reflects this history of persecution; the Shi'ites found refuge in redoubts in the area of Jabal 'Amil, known now as South Lebanon, and the plain of the Biq'a Valley.[10] Initially, the Shi'ites settled in the lower parts of Mount Lebanon—Kisirwan and the coastal cities. However, with the downfall of the Fatimids, the military expeditions launched by the Mamluks between 1291 and 1305 expelled the Shi'ites from these areas. First, the Shi'ites were replaced by the Sunnis because the coastal cities constituted vital trade centers for the Mamluks. Second, the Mamluks turned to expel the Shi'ites from the mountains, in particular from Kisirwan, which overlooks the coastal roads. Subsequently, the Mamluks substituted the Shi'ites in North Lebanon by Turkman clans to keep watch over the coast and secure the mountain roads that led inland to Damascus.[11]

Under Sunni Ottoman rule over Lebanon (1516-1922), the Shi'ites lost almost all land and authority to the expanding Maronite and Druze communities. The Maronites pushed south from the northern part of Lebanon and settled in Kisirwan, completely driving out the Shi'ites from the region. Shi'ites who sought refuge in the Druze area of Mount Lebanon were driven further south when, in 1585, the Ottomans appointed Fakhr al-Din Ma'ani II to administer the two *sanjak* (districts) of Beirut and Sidon on their behalf, leaving it to him to establish control over coastal cities and the mountains overlooking them.[12] After the Safavid established Shi'ism as the official religion of Iran in the early sixteenth century, the Ottomans became suspicious of the loyalty of the Shi'ite community within Ottoman territories. When Jabal 'Amil's Shi'ite *'ulama'* were invited to visit Iran, the Ottomans' suspicions about the Shi'ites grew. As the relationship between the Savafid and the Shi'ites in Jabal 'Amil improved, the Ottoman-Shi'ite relationship deteriorated, prompting the Ottomans to expand the authority of Fakhr al-Din to cover the sanjak of Safad. This gave him direct control over the Shi'ites of Jabal 'Amil, which was the *nahiya* (subdistrict) of Safad in Palestine.[13] This in turn provoked a war between the Shi'ites and the Druze. The persecution of the Shi'ites by Fakhr al-Din was documented by Shaykh Ahmad Rida of Jabal 'Amil as follows:[14]

> The ruler of Ma'an's family squeezed all of the resources from Jabal 'Amil. The area of Kawthariyya, which was the center of 'Ali al-Saghir's family [an early Shi'ite leader], was occupied by Prince Fakhr al-Din al-Ma'ani. Fakhr al-Din's soldiers killed and plundered there for three days. The Mutw'alis [Shi'ites] suffered great losses. In 1638, Milhim Ibn Ma'an entered Ansar during an attack in which fifteen hundred Mutw'ali men were killed. This situation made the Mutw'alis ask for independence. They announced their independence from Lebanon during the rule of Prince Ahmad al-Ma'an. However, the Ma'ani prince opposed the Shi'ites' move and attacked Nabatiyya, where many people were killed.

The persecution of the Shi'ites by the Ottomans was accompanied by a long-standing policy of discrimination. Unlike the Sunnis, Christians, and Druze, who were allowed by the Ottoman millet system to have their own personal status laws and courts, the Shi'ites were considered heterodox by the Ottomans. As such the Ottomans placed them under the direct jurisdiction of Sunni courts in personal status matters.[15] Moreover, the Shi'ite 'ulama' were conscripted in times of war, unlike the Sunni 'ulama'.[16]

In 1916, during World War I, Sharif Husayn—emir of the Arabs and the last of the line of Hashemite Sharifians that ruled Mecca, Medina, and Hijaz from 1201 to 1925—was persuaded by Allied promises of an independent Arab state to lead an Arab revolt against the Ottomans, who were supporting the Central Powers. After the breakup of the Ottoman Empire in 1922, however, the Allies reneged on their promises, creating a fragmented Arab world under French and British hegemony. The French wanted to incorporate the Shi'ites into a Greater Lebanon led by the Maronites. In general, the Muslims viewed the Maronites with great suspicion, as they were the only community to demand separation from the rest of Syria and seek protection from France. Nevertheless, the Maronites' hopes were realized in September 1920 when France established Greater Lebanon. The Muslims and the Maronites had different visions regarding Lebanon's future. The Muslims saw Lebanon as an integral part of Syria under King Faisal's rule, while the Maronites sought to create an independent state with French assistance.[17] For their part, the Shi'ites were committed to Faisal because Sharif Husayn's family were Hashimites; also, the Shi'ites had to show support for the general Sunni attitude in supporting Arab claims for independence. More important, the Shi'ites were suspicious of a French-supported Maronite state that might sentence them to oblivion. The contradictory views of the Shi'ites and Maronites regarding Greater Lebanon and a united Syria were irreconcilable. In late 1919, the rising tension between the two communities developed into armed clashes, particularly in Jabal 'Amil, where the Maronites constituted the second-largest population after the Shi'ites. On the Shi'ite side, some groups, such as those headed by Sadiq al-Hamza, Adham Khanjar, 'Ali Bazzi, and Mahmud Fa'aur, were supported by Damascus. The two major Maronite groups were headed by Ibrahim Fransis and 'Aid al-Hawrani.[18]

The armed clashes between the Shi'ites and the Maronites in Jabal 'Amil provided the French with an opportunity to increase their protection of the Maronites and put an end to the Shi'ites' forces. A French force of nearly four thousand soldiers, assisted by Maronite volunteers, crushed the Shi'ite forces. French warplanes and artillery bombarded Shi'ite villages and centers such as Nabatiyyah, Tyre, and Bint Jbeil. In June 1920, the French authorities forced the Shi'ite 'ulama' and notables to sign a document holding them responsible for the armed clashes. The downfall of the Shi'ites made it easier for the French to incorporate Jabal 'Amil and the northern Biq'a into the new State of Greater Lebanon, which was formally proclaimed on 1 September 1920.[19]

Clearly, the oppression of the Lebanese Shi'ites throughout their history gave rise to an identity crisis. This crisis has its origins in the killing of their eleven imams, in particular the martyrdom of Imam Husayn, which stands as the major paradigm of the suffering and persecution of the Shi'ites. Following the persecution by the Mamluks and the Ottomans, the Shi'ite sense of acute alienation and psychological distress increased immensely. When Lebanon became independent on November 22, 1943, the Shi'ites felt that they were the despised stepchildren of a state governed by a Maronite-Sunni alliance. Overall, the feeling of Shi'ite suffering and persecution as a tragic experience presented Hizbullah in 1982 with a community vulnerable to mass appeal.

STRUCTURAL IMBALANCE: POLITICAL AND
ECONOMIC DISFRANCHISEMENT

The Shi'ite identity crisis was reinforced by a growing political and economic structural imbalance. Within Lebanon's confessional system the Shi'ites were not accorded a political and economic role commensurate with their numerical size; they had increased from being the third largest community in Lebanon to being Lebanon's largest single sectarian grouping.

Politically, Lebanon's structure was based on the National Pact (al-Mithaq al-Watani) of 1943, which vested legislative and executive as well as military positions in rough proportion to the demographic size of the country's eighteen recognized sectarian groupings. The Maronite Christians, then the largest of the religious sects, according to the official census of 1932, were accorded the presidency. The Sunni Muslims, the second-largest community, were given the premiership. Finally, the Shi'ite Muslims, the third-largest sect, were given the speakership of the Parliament, a relatively weak position compared with those granted the Maronites and the Sunnis.[20]

In addition, underrepresentation of the Shi'ites was also reflected in the bureaucracy. Studies show that in 1946, 40 percent of the highest posts in the civil service were occupied by the Maronites, 27 percent by the Sunnis, and only 3.2 percent by the Shi'ites. Although the number of Shi'ites in the bureaucracy grew larger, Shi'ite gains continued to fall short relative to those of the Maronites and the Sunnis until at least 1982.[21]

In the second half of the twentieth century, however, a steep rise in the Shi'ite population put Lebanon's confessional system into political dead-lock. Although the Shi'ite population had risen from 100,000 to 250,000 between 1921 and 1956, it had remained proportionally stable at about 19 percent of Lebanon's total population. Between 1956 and 1975, how-ever, the Shi'ite population tripled, from 250,000 to 750,000, boosting their proportional size to almost 30 percent of the total population.[22] The regime's inflexible formula for political representation was not designed to accommodate sudden demographic changes, not only for the Shi'ites but for any of Lebanon's sectarian communities.[23] By the 1980s it was widely believed that the Shi'ites had become Lebanon's largest single confessional community with almost 1,400,000 people, surpassing the Maronite and Sunni populations, which were each estimated at nearly 800,000. Despite the fact that the Ta'if Agreement of 1989 made the Shi'ite representation equal to that of the Maronites and the Sunnis, the Shi'ites still believe that their representation is not commensurate with their numerical size.

Paralleling the political imbalance, the Shi'ites were economically disfranchised. Although Lebanon experienced economic growth in the 1950s, the growth was lopsided and resulted in slow socioeconomic devel-opment. Although the Shi'ites do have a wealthy elite of traditional families such as al-As'ad, Usayran, al-Zain, al-Khalil, and the Hamadih, the political leaders of these families had taken little interest in the plight of the broader Shi'ite community. Overall, the Shi'ite community experi-enced what Deutsch calls "double-trouble."[24] In other words, the Shi'ites belonged to the most disadvantaged social group, and most of them lived in the least developed geographical regions of Lebanon. In comparison with the Maronites and the Sunnis, who were overrepresented among the urban elite sectors of commerce, finance, and real estate, the Shi'ites were overrepresented among the poor working classes in the underdeveloped sectors of agriculture and industry. Almost 85 percent of the Shi'ites lived in the rural region of South Lebanon and the Ba'albek-Hermil district of the Biq'a.[25] In these two regions most Shi'ites could not subsist on what they earned from selling tobacco to the state monopoly or growing vegeta-bles.[26] The state, however, provided little help for rural development. In addition, the Shi'ite population in South Lebanon was caught up in the military fighting between Israel and the Palestine Liberation Organization (PLO).

To escape the harsh economic conditions and the PLO-Israeli struggle, many Shi'ites were forced to migrate. While a large number went to Beirut, others left for Africa, the Arab oil countries, and the United States. The wealth of Beirut attracted many immigrants from the underdeveloped regions. The increase of people living in the urban areas between 1943 and 1963 was as high as 146 percent, with the Shi'ites the most rapidly urbanizing community.[27] A majority of immigrants ended up in shantytowns in the southern suburbs and the Nab'a area of the eastern suburbs of Beirut. These two areas, known as the "belt of misery," became the breeding ground of Shi'ite militancy in the 1980s.

The Lebanese government became aware of regional inequalities in particular after the 1958 civil war, during which the Muslim population demanded more political power in proportion to their demographic size. However, Lebanon's modernization process under President Fouad Shihab did not produce the expected results. The spread of education and urbanization brought greater mobilization of the disfranchised Shi'ites. However, their heightened expectations were not met, as educational and urban advancement did not match employment opportunities and the state's level of institutionalization remained low compared to the high level of Shi'ite mobilization.[28] In other words, there emerged a gap between the aspirations of the members of the Shi'ite community and their real situation. The Shi'ites were not able to close the political and economic gaps as they were excluded from both the political and the economic structure of Lebanon's confessional system. To add to the fuel, the Lebanese civil war of 1975 magnified the Shi'ite political and economic discontent. The collapse of the state and the resulting violence took a tremendous toll on the Shi'ite community, producing another cycle of demographic, social, and economic dislocation that dwarfed the simple discrimination suffered by Shi'ites elsewhere. Hundreds of thousands of Shi'ites were made into destitute refugees, in a country without a functioning state. Their socioeconomic and political distress provided fertile soil for the rise of the charismatic leader Imam Musa al-Sadr, who in the early 1970s made it his chief cause to activate the politically quiescent Shi'ites of Lebanon. As will be shown later, Musa al-Sadr's politicization process made the Shi'ite community the most receptive to siren calls issued by Iran, which culminated in the formation of Hizbullah.

MILITARY DEFEAT: THE ISRAELI INVASIONS OF LEBANON

When identity crisis and structural imbalance are reinforced by military defeat, a society's militancy potential increases markedly. Military defeat followed by foreign occupation opens the way for militant movements fostering political organization or employing guerrilla warfare and enjoying widespread grassroots support.[29] In Lebanon, the Israeli invasion of 1978 and its occupation in 1982 served as a crisis catalyst, triggering the emergence of Hizbullah and its guerrilla organization.

The creation of the state of Israel in 1948, and the Arab-Israeli wars that followed, led to the exodus of Palestinians to Arab countries, in particular Lebanon and Jordan. Later, following the civil war in Jordan in 1970–71, tens of thousands of armed Palestinian guerrillas moved to South Lebanon. Taking advantage of the 1969 Cairo agreement, which allowed the Palestinians to carry out armed struggle against Israel from the 'Arqoub areas in South Lebanon, the PLO challenged the authority of the Lebanese government and established a state-within-a-state encompassing South Lebanon, much of the Biq'a, and West Beirut.[30]

Initially, the Shi'ites had sympathized with the Palestinian cause, and many of them joined the Palestinian revolutionary movements. In fact, in the aftermath of the 1948 Arab defeat, Sayyid Abdul Husayn Sharaf al-Din organized a guerrilla group from al-Ja'fariyyah, his school in South Lebanon. This group, consisting of tens of Shi'ite and Palestinian students, was trained to launch attacks at the Lebanese-Israeli border.[31] The PLO hegemony over South Lebanon, however, made the Shi'ites fear that the organization would take control of their area and transform it into a Palestinian homeland. On the Israeli side, the Palestinian military presence in South Lebanon was a direct threat to Israel's northern settlements. In response to the Palestinian presence, Israel invaded much of South Lebanon in 1978. It occupied areas as far north as the Litani River for the purpose of creating a "security zone" that would prevent direct attacks by the Palestinian armed groups.[32]

While some of the Shiʿites welcomed the Israeli invasion as a prelude to forcing the Palestinian groups out of South Lebanon, the results of the invasion widened the gap between the Shiʿites and Israel. Operation Litani, as it was called by Israel in 1978, aimed to destroy the PLO military structure in South Lebanon. However, the operation was not a great success, and the Shiʿites received the heaviest casualties. More than one thousand civilians died, many of whom were Shiʿites. A quarter of a million refugees poured into the squalid southern suburbs of Beirut, and hundreds of homes and properties were destroyed. The Shiʿites felt that Israel was targeting them as a community.[33] On March 19, 1978, the UN Security Council adopted Resolution 425, which called for the unconditional withdrawal of Israeli troops and the deployment of the United Nations Interim Force in Lebanon (UNIFIL) along the Lebanese-Israeli border. The PLO agreed to cease its military activity, and Israel partially withdrew, handing over the area to its ally, mainly a Maronite proxy militia, the South Lebanese Army (SLA).[34]

By 1982, the storehouse of Shiʿite grievances had overflowed. The invasion of 1982, which Israel chose to call Operation Peace for the Galilee, certainly was intended to uproot the PLO from Lebanon; but its greater objective was to dissociate Lebanon from the Syrian influence and control that had been building since 1976. The two-month operation, from June 3 to August 12, including the invasion of Beirut, led to the killing of eighteen thousand individuals and the wounding of thirty thousand.[35] In addition, Syria lost 102 aircraft and 61 pilots in the first three days and saw the destruction of its surface-to-air missile system, which had previously provided some security from the long reach of the Israeli air force.[36] While the Syrian forces retreated to the Lebanese-Syrian border, the PLO was forced to evacuate in September 1983 under the supervision of the Multinational Force (MNF), mostly American marines and French troops.

In fact, Israel had hoped that a Lebanon freed from Syria and the PLO, with a Christian-dominated regime, would bring peace and closer connections between the two countries. Israel tried to achieve this objective by helping Bashir Gemayel, a Maronite leader of the Lebanese Forces (al-quwat al-Lubnaniyyah), to be elected president. One month after his election, however, Gemayel was killed in a bomb explosion. With the succession of his brother Amin to the office of president, the Israeli army entered Beirut. To revenge Bashir's assassination, the Lebanese Forces, in collaboration with Israel, massacred more than one thousand civilians, including Shi'ites living in the Palestinian refugee camps of Sabra and Chatilla.

Yet the invasion of 1982 and the subsequent Israeli occupation of South Lebanon helped bolster the fortunes of Hizbullah. First, there was a conviction among many Shi'ites that they stood to become the victims of history once again. The loss of life and the damage wrought on Shi'ite areas was much greater than in the 1978 invasion. Second, the Lebanese-Israeli accord brokered by the United States and signed on May 17, 1983, was tailor-made to leave South Lebanon under the control of Israel.[37] The emerging alliance between Israel and Bashir and Amin Gemayel, who supported the SLA, threatened to place the Shi'ite majority under the control of a pro-Israeli regime. Third, Israel's protracted occupation of the south led quickly to a violent Shi'ite-Israeli confrontation. Hizbullah's resistance, which was nurtured during the confrontation, would eventually lead to the most effective guerrilla warfare ever waged against Israel. In this context, many Shi'ites were convinced that the time had come for armed *jihad* (holy struggle). Fourth, Shi'ite disillusionment with the PLO, combined with their disdain for the PLO's military performance during both invasions, opened an opportunity later for a Hizbullah-led war of liberation, where the Sunni cause of Palestine began to merge with Hizbullah's own cause.

The Israeli invasion, ironically, promoted the fortunes of Hizbullah by providing a politico-military environment that legitimated the group and gave a rationale for its guerrilla warfare. Similarly, the presence of the Western foreign troops in Lebanon, particularly of the U.S. Marines, also boosted the fortunes of Hizbullah, which considered fighting such forces to be as legitimate as fighting the Israeli occupation.

DEMONSTRATION EFFECT: IRAN'S ISLAMIC REVOLUTION

The term *demonstration effect* suggests that a revolutionary event in one place may act as a catalyst for a revolutionary process in another place at approximately the same point in time.[38] Indeed, the extent of the demonstration effect depends on a number of factors, most important being the success of the initial revolution, the cross-cultural reference of the ideology characterizing the revolution, and the effectiveness of communication networks.

Many examples confirm that the demonstration effect functions as a catalyst for analogous revolutionary movement or activity elsewhere. The success of the American Revolution, for example, is often cited as contributing to the outbreak of the French Revolution. The French Revolution in 1789 was immediately followed by revolutionary activity in central and northern Europe. The victory of the Bolshevik Revolution in 1917 inspired communist revolts in central Europe.[39] The demonstration effect of Iran's Islamic Revolution is no exception.

The success of the Islamic Revolution in Iran that followed the fall of the shah in January 1979 became the primary demonstration effect for Islamic activists, Shi'ite and Sunni alike. Iran's Islamic Revolution first inspired and targeted the Shi'ite populations of countries adjacent to Iran, across the Persian Gulf, and as far as the Mediterranean: Iraq, Kuwait, Saudi Arabia, Bahrain, Afghanistan, and Lebanon. Yet Iran's revolution had its greatest impact in Lebanon. Despite the fact that Lebanon is not adjacent to Iran, the Lebanese Shi'ites were the most receptive of all Shi'ites to Iran's Islamic revolutionary message.

The cross-cultural relationship between the ideology of Iran's clerical leadership, in particular Ayatollah Khomeini, and the Lebanese Shi'ite clergy dates back to periods before the Iranian Revolution. The circles of learning *(al-hawzat al-'ilmiyyah)* in Qom in Iran, and before that in Najaf in Iraq, acted as a magnet and meeting place for Shi'ite clerics from Iran, Lebanon, and Iraq. These hawzat laid the basis for similar—though not always identical—ideological views and a network of kinship and personal friendship and politico-religious structures that were to have a significant impact on Hizbullah's ideology. However, the paramount roles of Ayatollahs Ruhallah Khomeini and Muhammad Baqir al-Sadr as chief ideologues and inspirational leaders of the Shi'ites' Islamic movement is beyond question. In fact, it was Baqir al-Sadr's hawzat in Najaf that became the epicenter of Shi'ite activism and the home base of the Party of Islamic Call (Hizb al-Da'wah al-Islamiyyah), which sought to propagate its revivalist message throughout the Shi'ite communities of Iraq, Lebanon, and the Persian Gulf in an effort to trigger revolutionary activities.[40] Reportedly, during his tenure in Najaf's hawzat after being expelled by the shah in 1964, Ayatollah Khomeini and his Iran-based colleagues were at the center of the religious and political resurgence. In 1978, however, Khomeini was expelled by the Iraqi regime as a consequence of his anti-shah activities.[41] Soon after Khomeini's victorious return to Iran on February 1, 1979, he became the unchallenged leader and chief ideologue of the Shi'ites inside and outside Iran. Ayatollah al-Sadr's declaration of absolute support for Iran's Islamic regime prompted Saddam's Ba'th regime to execute him along with his sister in April 1980. Then the Iraqi regime turned to close down the Da'wah's and other hawzat, expelling most foreign Shi'ite students, including several hundred Lebanese.[42] At this junction, the epicenter of Shi'ite activism shifted from Najaf to Qom, where many of Hizbullah's clerics developed close ties with militant Iranian clergy.

The relationship between the Lebanese Shi'ite clergy and Khomeini and al-Sadr before and after Iran's revolution helped to establish an effective network that would subsequently facilitate Iran's demonstration effect in the Lebanese political arena and be the godfather of Hizbullah's future leaders. The early Lebanese Shi'ite clergy who emerged from the Najaf-Qom network were Imam Musa al-Sadr, Ayatollah Muhammad Mahdi Shams al-Din, and Ayatollah Muhammad Husayn Fadlallah.[43] Among Hizbullah's founders were Sayyid Abbas al-Musawi, Shaykh Subhi al-Tufayli, Shaykh Muhammad Yazbak, Shaykh Na'im Qasim, Sayyid Ibrahim Amin al-Sayyid, and Sayyid Hasan Nasrallah.[44] Yet it was not until the disappearance of Musa al-Sadr in 1978 that these militant *shaykhs* emerged with a network that was under Khomeini's direct influence and leadership. This network of shaykhs, emboldened by the success of Iran's revolution and influenced by Khomeini's ideological worldview, considered the idea of establishing an Islamic state real and even urgent.

THE FORMATION OF HIZBULLAH

As the foregoing crisis catalysts converged, Hizbullah was finally formed. However, the formation of Hizbullah and Shi'ite militancy as a manifestation of Islamic fundamentalism should be considered the culmination of a process of politicization initiated by Imam Musa al-Sadr.

Musa al-Sadr's Politicization Process

The arrival in Tyre, Lebanon, in 1960 of Imam Musa al-Sadr as a trusted deputy of Ayatollah Mohsen al-Hakim, an Iraqi marja' al-taqlid, ushered in a new era in the history of the Lebanese Shi'ites. Al-Sadr had been born in the Iranian city of Qom in 1928, the son of a leading Lebanese Shi'ite scholar, Ayatollah Sadr al-Din Sadr. During the late 1950s he had studied with Ayatollah Mohsen al-Hakim in Najaf.[45] Rather than adopt the Islamic fundamentalist view of al-Hakim, al-Sadr took up a more reformist ideology comprising a potent combination of traditional values and modern concepts. Thus, he set out to activate the politically quiescent Shi'ites and organize them as a formidable political force in Lebanon.

With the change of the demographic balance in Lebanon in favor of the Muslims, the Muslim community demanded a restructuring of the political institutions to reflect the new situation. However, the Muslim demand initially took only Sunni interests into consideration because the Sunnis had an established, officially recognized institutional structure under the leadership of the grand mufti of the Lebanese Republic.[46] The Shi'ites lacked such an institutional body to represent their interests. In 1969, however, following massive Israeli bombing raids on Palestinian bases in South Lebanon, Musa al-Sadr's efforts led to the establishment of the first such organization in Lebanese Shi'ite history, the Supreme Islamic Shi'ite Council.[47] He was elected its first president and soon became the symbol of the new, politically aware Shi'ite presence in the multireligious sectarianism of Lebanon.

The Shi'ite Council, a democratically elected organization entrusted with the responsibility of representing the Shi'ite interests and religious endowments, was conceived primarily as a forum for the emerging Shi'ite middle class, who were effectively blocked from political power by traditional Lebanese Shi'ite leaders *(zu'ama')*. The council provided the Shi'ites with a concrete expression of their identity as a distinctive sect, which Musa al-Sadr offered without rejecting the particularism of Lebanon's history. Of central importance in understanding Musa al-Sadr's meteoric rise is the fact that the Shi'ite tradition of submission and political in-difference, encouraged by some of their quiescent religious leaders, had contributed significantly to the political marginalization of the Shi'ite masses.[48] Al-Sadr recognized this and strove to reinterpret the tradition by drawing upon selected moments in the Shi'ite past, elevating them to po-sitions of prominence infused with political meaning, and claiming that political activism was now not only necessary for preserving Shi'ite iden-tity in Lebanon but equally important in keeping with authentic Shi'ism.

In his successful efforts to organize a Shi'ite mass movement, origi-nally conceived to be nonviolent, to campaign for social justice, he ritually and symbolically appropriated the historic religious experience of the Shi'ites' belief in martyrdom and occultation. Shi'ism in Lebanon, as in Iran and Iraq, provided the imam's followers with religiously expressive categories. Instead of interpreting the sufferings of Imam Husayn in Karbala as a warrant for political quietism and submission, however, Musa al-Sadr presented the event as an identity-shaping episode of political choice and courage. Under oppressive circumstances, Musa al-Sadr taught, martyrdom suffered for the lofty ideals of a just and equitable public order on earth became plausible and, if the occasion demanded, desirable through violent revolution.[49]

This aspect of the Shi'ite activism of Imam Musa al-Sadr attracted a mass following in 1974 when he launched the Movement of the Deprived (Harakat al-Mahrumin). Later in 1975 this movement developed into a military movement known by its acronym, Amal (Afwaj al-Muqawamah al-Lubnaniyyah, or Battalions of the Lebanese Resistance).[50] Amal and the Shi'ites were caught up in a bid between the Druze and the Christians dur-ing the early stages of the civil war. They joined the ideologically left-wing coalition of the Lebanese National Movement (LNM), formed by the Druze leader Kamal Jumblatt to challenge the Maronites' ascendancy. As a result of their participation during the 1975–76 civil war, where the Shi'ites suf-fered the heaviest casualties—more than any other single confessional group—and were encircled from East Beirut by the Maronite militias, al-Sadr broke with the LNM. He then supported the Syrian intervention against the LNM and the Palestinians in June 1978, effectively aligning the

Shi'ites with the forces of the status quo.[51] The relations between Amal and the Palestinians worsened further during the 1978 Israeli invasion of South Lebanon, when Shi'ite villages and homes were completely destroyed. All the crisis conditions necessary for the Shi'ites to revolt violently seemed to be in place, including the desperate hope that violent methods would at least earn the attention of the international community and thus publicize the injustices committed against them. The role of Imam Musa al-Sadr at this juncture is not clear and remains a matter of speculation. On one side, he had encouraged his followers to pursue, as far as possible, nonviolent methods demanding justice. On the other side, he saw violent revolution as a last resort. In August 1978, however, al-Sadr disappeared on a visit to Libya. His disappearance, reportedly attributed to Libyan foul play, turned him into a national hero for Lebanon's Shi'ites and a symbol for their suffering and martyrdom.[52] Since al-Sadr's disappearance, he has been popularly regarded as the "Hidden Imam" *(al-imam al-gha'ib)*. His deputy, Ayatollah Muhammad Mahdi Shams al-Din, filled his position until Shams al-Din died in 2002. The position is currently vacant, and Shaykh Abdel Amir Qabalan has functioned as deputy president of the Supreme Islamic Shi'ite Council. However, al-Sadr's sudden disappearance, combined with the Islamic Revolution in Iran in 1979 and the Israeli invasion in 1982, provided the impetus for the emergence of the Shi'ite militant movement known as Hizbullah.

THE EMERGENCE OF HIZBULLAH

Given the importance of the role of religious leadership in guiding the cause of an activist movement in Shi'ism in the era after the occultation of the twelfth imam and in the face of crisis conditions, it is worth noting that in both the historical and contemporary post-disappearance situations the Shi'ite faithful split into factions. The splits were due at least in part to varying interpretations of the anticipated messianic imam, al-Mahdi's final restoration of justice. This splintering produced a range of moderate and fundamentalist interpretations of the final restoration, represented by various religious leaders and organizations, each with its own program. Like the Shi'ites in Iraq and Iran, the Lebanese Shi'ites experienced this pattern.

In the wake of al-Sadr's disappearance, Amal experienced factionalization and militancy. The younger generation in Amal was, after 1978, attracted to the sense of religious identity generated by an activist interpretation of Shi'ite ideals under the fundamentalist leadership of Ayatollah Sayyid Muhammad Husayn Fadlallah, to whom a measure of al-Sadr's influence and power had passed. Fadlallah, erroneously described as the spiritual leader of Hizbullah, was the product of the hawzat al-'ilmiyyah of Najaf. These circles were very much influenced by the Iraq-based Hizb al-Da'wah al-Islamiyyah. The Da'wah ideology represented an activist brand of religio-political revivalism inspired by the charismatic ayatollah Muhammad Baqir al-Sadr.[53] Under the spiritual leadership of Sayyid Fadlallah, who returned to Lebanon in 1966, the Da'wah Party established several hawzat and self-help organizations to propagate its activist ideology. Fadlallah himself also established Jam'iyyat Usrat al-Takhi (Society of Brethren Family) and Jam'iyyat al-Mabarat al-Khiriyyah (Charitable Philanthropic Society) and his own hawzat.[54] In sharp contrast to Musa al-Sadr's commitment to Lebanese identity, Fadlallah's nascent movement stressed its loyalty to the emerging transnational ideology of Shi'ism with roots in Najaf. In his writings Fadlallah set down the circumstances under which force could be used against Islam's enemies.[55] His stature as a ranking *mujtahid* (jurisprudent) was not felt until after Musa al-Sadr's disappearance.

Suffering from the loss of the charismatic Musa al-Sadr, both the Supreme Islamic Shi'ite Council and Amal, under Husayn al-Husayni and later Nabih Berri, were incapable of containing the new Shi'ite militants.[56] The hitherto nearly complete domination of the Shi'ite constituency by Amal gave way as its more militant members gravitated toward the message of militancy issued by Ayatollah Khomeini. As a result, Sayyid Husayn al-Musawi, a member of Amal's command council, broke away in June 1982 and founded Islamic Amal, which was to become embodied in Hizbullah.[57] Amal under Berri remained a sectarian movement without assuming a revivalist character, and was ideologically and structurally inclined to concede a role to the militant Shi'ite clergy. The militant shaykhs and members, however, led by Ayatollah Fadlallah, Shaykh al-Tufayli, and Shaykh Raghib Harb, increasingly found common ideological ground with Islamic Iran and looked beyond Amal for an Islamic Shi'ite ideology of martyrdom and self-sacrifice and to achieve an Islamic state.

At approximately the same time in August 1982, Ayatollah Khomeini met a number of Lebanese Shi'ite 'ulama' who were participating in the Islamic Movements conference in Tehran—the First Conference for the Downtrodden *(mustad'afin)*. Among the participants were Sayyid Muhammad Husayn Fadlallah, Shaykh Subhi al-Tufayli, Shaykh Muhammad Yazbak, Shaykh Afif al-Nabulsi, Shaykh Husayn Kurani, Shaykh Raghib Harb, and Sayyid Ibrahim Amin al-Sayyid, chair of Amal's office in Tehran before he joined Hizbullah. During the meeting, Khomeini urged the 'ulama' to go back home and mobilize the people to fight the Israeli occupation and to turn the mosques into bases for their jihad activities.[58]

Shaykh Subhi al-Tufayli, Hizbullah's first secretary-general, describes the early stages of Hizbullah's formation as a field filled with noise and dust, similar to that of a "scuffle of camels" in the desert. He adds, "The situation was extremely complex as religion, politics, and opportunism were mixed. Even some of the shaykhs were political traders. However, the instructions of the leader—Imam Khomeini—were to create a movement that springs from pure Islamic fundamentals; a movement that shakes the current situation."[59]

Those Lebanese Shi'ites who openly rallied behind the banner of radical Islam in the summer of 1982 against the enemies of Islam—Israel, the United States, and their Lebanese supporters—revolted and took up residence in the Biq'a Valley. Hundreds of Shi'ites were led by several fervent young Shi'ite clerics who came from Hizb al-Da'wah, such as Sayyid Abbas al-Musawi and Shaykh Subhi al-Tufayli; from Amal, Sayyid Hasan Nasrallah, Sayyid Ibrahim Amin al-Sayyid, Shaykh Na'im Qasim, Shaykh Muhammad Yazbak, and others;[60] from the Islamist wing of Harakat Fatah, Imad Mughniyyah and Abu Hasan Khudr Salamah; and from the Lebanese Communist Party, Abd al-Hadi Hamadih.[61] When Iran's emissaries and a contingent of fifteen hundred Pasdaran (Revolutionary Guards) arrived in the Biq'a under the instructions of Khomeini, these young clerics and others rushed to pledge their loyalty to Khomeini and assume positions of leadership in Hizbullah. The contingents that had come to do battle with "the enemies of Islam and satanical forces" were stationed in Brital, Nabisheet, and Baʿalbek,[62] where the militant clerics and lay people began to participate in training under the command of the Revolutionary Guards. By the end of the first training session in Janta, forty kilometers from the city of Baʿalbek, they seized a Lebanese army barracks and transformed it into a camouflaged military headquarters ringed by antiaircraft guns and missiles. Bursting with the vision of an Islamic Lebanon and liberated Jerusalem, Sayyid Abbas al-Musawi addressed the crowd in the barracks, saying, "We are ready to fight Israel, we are martyrdom seeking *(shahadah),* and we will fight them even from the graves."[63]

In the beginning, several names were debated for the new organization, such as Islamic Amal, the Islamic Movement, Islamic Jihad, and the Revolution Committees. When no agreement was reached concerning the name, a committee of nine, headed by Shaykh al-Tufayli and Sayyid al-Musawi, traveled to Tehran to seek the opinion and permission of Khomeini, the supreme jurisconsult (wali al-faqih), over the new name. Khomeini's instructions were to adopt a new name that would unite all Islamists. The new formation took the name of Hizbullah—the Party of God—after a verse in the Qurʾan: "those who accept the mandate of God, his prophet and those who believed, Lo! The Party of God, they are the victorious" (*Surat al-Maʾida,* 5:56).

Hizbullah thus emerged from a marriage between the Lebanese Shiʿite militants and Islamic Iran, and grew to become the most influential Shiʿite militant movement in the region. For its part, Iran's new presence in Lebanon afforded the first direct point of contact between the Islamic regime and a major Shiʿite community in the Arab world—the largest such community outside Iraq. Henceforth, Iran would become a leading player in the Lebanese Shiʿite community and use it as a potential base for projecting its influence into the heart of the Arab-Israeli conflict. Accordingly, this base opened for Iran a more substantial regional role. Furthermore, Iran's presence in Lebanon helped it to break out of the narrow geopolitical confines of its war with Iraq and reach a wider constituency in Arab society. Equally important was Iran's hostility to the expansion of the U.S.

and Western presence in Lebanon. Iran's struggle with the United States was an integral part of the slogans and practices of the revolution, as witnessed in the taking of the U.S. Embassy hostages in 1979 in Tehran and later by the U.S. "tilt" toward Iraq.[64]

During the time of Hizbullah's formation the interests and outlook of Iran and Syria began to converge. In its campaign to drive the Israelis out of Lebanon, Syria was willing to accept any help against the "hostile" Israeli and Western forces entrenched in its Lebanese backyard. Syrian concerns about the possibility of regional isolation and the dangers of separate bilateral Lebanon-Israel deals were then, as now, a primary determinant of its foreign policy. In this respect, the May 1983 Lebanese-Israeli accord brokered by the United States fed Syrian suspicions. Equally important, a hostile Lebanon could become the base for internal subversion, leading to the breakdown of internal stability within Syria itself. Under these circumstances, strengthening its ties with Iran was the only way for Syria to ease its isolation. Also, for the momentous task of reshaping the strategic landscape to its advantage, Syria relied on Iran's economic help, in particular its oil, and political help in the form of a ready-made local constituency that was anti-Israeli and anti-Western in outlook, while it remained at a sufficient distance to avoid becoming too dependent on Iran.[65] Thus, the Syrian-Iranian alliance boosted the fortunes of Hizbullah. Syria allowed a supply line of support to run from Iran through Syria to Hizbullah.

Working invisibly under Iranian sponsorship and with Syria as a willing accomplice, Hizbullah waited until February 1985 to declare the birth of its organization publicly, through a communiqué called "al-Risalah al-Maftuha" (The open letter). This letter marked both the first anniversary of the assassination of Shaykh Raghib Harb in February 1984 and the second anniversary of the Sabra and Chatilla massacres. Hizbullah had emerged in response to a crisis environment to deal with the needs of its adherents. Yet it also demanded ideological commitment and obligation, which are the topics of the next chapter.

3

Islamic Juristical Ideology

The ideology of Hizbullah was not fully revealed in its "Open Letter" of 1985, as commonly thought.[1] This letter is a programmatic document rather than an explanation of the components of Hizbullah's ideology. The letter, as Hizbullah's deputy secretary-general Shaykh Naʿim Qasim explains, is "a program that didn't intend to address in a detailed way Hizbullah's ideology and its modes of action in particular, but what one can do under certain circumstances."[2] As such, the "Open Letter" is a manifesto to evoke a broad appeal rather than a systematic doctrine of Islamic activism and government.[3] However, to understand Hizbullah's actions in the context of its ideology, one has to make an in-depth analysis not only of the "Open Letter" but of Hizbullah's ideological doctrine as well. This doctrine is rooted and patterned after that of Ayatollah Ruhallah Khomeini's ideology, Ayatollah Ali Khamenei's similar themes, and the elaboration of Hizbullah's main ideologues, in particular, Sayyid Hasan Nasrallah and Shaykh Naʿim Qasim. Although Sayyid Muhammad Husayn Fadlallah had initially contributed to the formulation of Hizbullah's ideology, Fadlallah subsequently clashed with Hizbullah over its acceptance of the marjaʿyyah of Khamenei as supreme marjiʿ, after he succeeded Khomeini in 1989. This has made ineffective Fadlallah's *ijtihad* (authoritative interpretation of Islamic law) for the party's rank and file.

Hizbullah's response to crisis catalysts manifests itself through an Islamic juristical ideology. This political-legal-religious doctrine, which is distinctively Shiʿite, contains a salvational prescription of primordial values, beliefs, and practices that are to shape the actions and the future of the intended Islamic order, as interpreted and mandated by the jurisconsult (wali al-faqih). This chapter systematically analyzes the components of

Hizbullah's ideology—that is, the necessity of an Islamic order, rooted in a restored theory of guardianship of the jurisconsult *(wilayat al-faqih)*, in which the Islamic masses bear the banner of holy struggle (jihad) against their local and foreign oppressors and for the liberation of Jerusalem and the spread of social justice.

THE NECESSITY OF THE ISLAMIC ORDER

In keeping with Khomeinist ideology, Hizbullah subscribes to the doctrine of the necessity of an Islamic order. For Hizbullah, the Muslim's primary mission is not only the worship of God *('ibada)* but also the establishing of an Islamic order as the expression of God's just society *(mujtama' al-'adl al-illahi)* where God's rule *(hukm Allah)* prevails over all mankind.[4]

The proof that God is the source of all sovereignty, authority, and wealth is provided by God's revelation through the prophet *(nabi)* Muhammad and his rightful designated successors (the imams) to guide the Muslims to establish a just Islamic order. Accordingly, man is freed from servitude and exploitation by other men. For God chose not to abandon the people and instead provided them with Islamic revelation, that through obedience to God's will, the faithful will accomplish God's just society and its equitable public order that embodies the will of God. According to Nasrallah, "Divine justice demands that God does what is best for humanity, and divine truthfulness has generated such a faith. God's promise will be fulfilled, if humanity keeps its covenant of working for God's just society."[5]

This indispensable connection between divine guidance and the necessity of establishing an Islamic order according to Hizbullah's ideology makes Islam a total system of social existence. The sources of God's Law *(Shar' Allah)* are God's book (al-Qur'an), the traditions *(al-Sunnah)* of Prophet Muhammad, the imams, and the interpretation (ijtihad) of the 'ulama'.[6] As such the authority (hukm) is inherent, according to Hizbullah. Sunnis, however, do not accept that rule as inherent. Instead, they accept the validity of consensus (ijma'), the Qur'an, the Sunnah, and ijtihad, which give the law, and the Islamic state, which enforces the law. Unlike

Christianity, the separation of religion (din) and state (dawlah) is inconceivable in Islam.

According to Hizbullah's theology, the Islamic order restores culture and political and religious unity, which have been destroyed by the various philosophical doctrines of Western culture. Hizbullah contends that Western culture has encouraged Muslims to pursue their own interests, to satisfy their egos rather than God's commands and the spiritual needs of the community. Only by returning to the rule of God (hukm Allah) are people relieved from a vision, law, and philosophy that are alien to Islam.[7]

Although Hizbullah urges the adoption of an Islamic order, nowhere does the party, or its ideologues, insist that this should be imposed by force. On the contrary, the question of implementing the Islamic order has carefully been tied to the concept of majority. As argued by Shaykh Qasim: "If Islam becomes the choice of the majority, only then will it be implemented. If not it will continue to coexist with others on the basis of mutual understanding, using peaceful and political means to reach peaceful solutions. And that is how the case should be to the non-Islamists as well."[8]

Hizbullah's concept of majoritarianism (majority) does not necessarily mean democracy. Hizbullah may find democratic means such as freedom of choice and an electoral system based on proportional representation of the people—as opposed to the present Lebanese confessional system based on single-member districts—very useful tools in achieving the Islamic order, but it does not support democracy as an ideal. Since the Shi'ites are supported by the largest single community, the establishment of an Islamic order depends on the freedom of choice of the majority. It is this connection between majority rule and demography that makes Hizbullah hopeful that Islamic order can be established by "peaceful and democratic means" rather than force.

Equally important, it is well established that majoritarianism in general implies a low level of pluralism and encourages a process of homogenization of the society. In this sense "majoritarianism sees the political system as a melting pot based on a universal criterion for power distribution, rather than on group-specific qualification."[9] Majoritarianism also implies a secular political system and emphasizes a process of nation building.[10] However, Hizbullah's criterion for power distribution is its demographic majority, not the melting-pot thesis. Therefore, Hizbullah considers that Lebanon's confessional system contradicts the principle of power distribution among the Lebanese sectarian groups and is incompatible with equal rights and the realization of majority rule. In addition, Hizbullah's majoritarianism does not imply a secular political system, nor does the party's process of homogenization of society mean national integration on the basis of secular laws. For Hizbullah, national integration is neither the sum of politics designed to promote democratization nor a magic formula that will accommodate every single Lebanese grouping.[11] Rather, it is the sum of a majority that accepts the implementation of Islamic law while ensuring that "people of the book" *(ahl al-kitab)* or "the protected people" *(ahl al-dhimmi)*—that is, Christians and Jews—will be able to coexist with the Muslim majority and will be treated fairly, without any use of violence or coercion.[12]

Nevertheless, fear of Hizbullah's Islamic order, whether achieved through demographic majoritarianism or forceful imposition, has prompted not only Christians but also mainstream Sunnis and Druze to support Lebanon's reemerging confessional system. For them, such a system will be the only way to prevent the creation of Hizbullah's Islamic order or the achievement of the more general ideological goals of Islamic fundamentalism in general. Such opposition has not caused Hizbullah to abandon its commitment to the necessity of the Islamic order or its demand for majority rule. Establishing an Islamic order will always be a demand of Hizbullah's, for the party cannot abandon what is religiously sanctioned. However, the means it will employ to achieve its aim could vary from forceful imposition to political tactics, depending on the makeup of society.

GUARDIANSHIP OF THE JURISCONSULT (WILAYAT AL-FAQIH)

In Hizbullah's ideology, the fulfillment of the obligation to create an Islamic order is closely tied to the concept of elitism associated with the imams and the mujtahids. In essence Hizbullah subscribes to the doctrine of clerical supremacy, which is based on Ayatollah Khomeini's theory of the guardianship of the jurisconsult, or wilayat al-faqih.

Hizbullah and Shi'ism in general hold that the common man is innately fallible and lacks the intellectual and moral capacity to understand the esoteric meaning of the Qur'an, the Prophet's Sunnah, or the traditions of the imams. They also believe, however, that the imams did have the power of divine investiture and were morally infallible *(ma'sum)*— and accordingly could reveal divine truth. Thus, the imams constituted the divine guides for the community. Following the great occultation *(al-gha'ibah al-kubra)* of the twelfth imam in 941, the mujtahids among the Shi'ites were believed to have been appointed by the twelfth imam as his "general deputies" to guide the believers pending his return.[13] Accordingly, the mujtahids were to assume the role of "functional" imams.

Originally, the traditional Shi'ite theory of authority was pluralist and the mujtahids did not claim infallibility.[14] In other words, Shi'ites were free to choose a leading mujtahid after whom they could pattern their lives; thus the mujtahid would become known as the source of imitation (marja' al-taqlid). The Shi'ites also traditionally regarded any public assumption of political authority by the marja' al-taqlid as theologically problematic, because the establishment of the Islamic order is impossible without divine intervention through the return of the twelfth imam.[15] Ayatollah Khomeini, however, took the radical step of claiming that the imams' right to rule devolved upon the religious jurists and, further, that if one of them succeeded in setting up a government, it was the duty of the other jurists to follow him.[16] This last step was a sharp departure from the traditional Shi'ite principle that no religious jurist has any authority over other religious jurists. As such, Khomeini's theory of wilayat al-faqih radically undermined the position of other preeminent religious jurists, the sources of imitation (maragi' al-taqlid) who had been traditionally and categorically independent.[17]

The essence of Khomeini's theory of wilayat al-faqih, which Hizbullah abides by, had its original exposition in Ayatollah Muhammad Baqir al-Sadr's theory of the marji'yyah. In fact, Dekmejian argues that "in theoretical and practical terms Khomeini's theory of *wilayat al-faqih* and al-Sadr's rule of the leading *marj'a* are synonymous."[18]

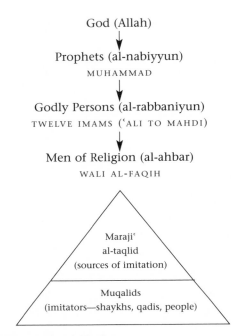

God (Allah)
↓
Prophets (al-nabiyyun)
MUHAMMAD
↓
Godly Persons (al-rabbaniyun)
TWELVE IMAMS ('ALI TO MAHDI)
↓
Men of Religion (al-ahbar)
WALI AL-FAQIH

Maraji'
al-taqlid
(sources of imitation)

Muqalids
(imitators—shaykhs, qadis, people)

Figure 3.1. Hizbullah's Levels of Obedience
Based on Khomeini's Theory of *Wilayat al-Faqih*

However, following Khomeini's theory of wilayat al-faqih, which is derived from verse 44 of *Surat al-Ma'ida* (Qur'an 5:44), Hizbullah identifies three levels of obedience, which bear testimony to God's word (see figure 3.1).

In Khomeini's interpretation of the Qur'anic verse, as well as the traditions of the Prophet and the imams, wilayat al-faqih represents God's testimony during the age of occultation. The word of God was revealed to the prophets, who are represented by Muhammad. Then come the imams, who are equated with *al-rabbaniyun* as godly extensions of the Prophet, followed by *al-ahbar,* that is, men of religion, who are represented by the wali al-faqih.[19] As the rightly guided successor to Muhammad and the imams, the wali al-faqih represents the third level of Allah's testimony in the age of occultation. As such the wilayat al-faqih is the extension of the Prophet's and the imams' wilayat over the ummah.[20] It follows that the Prophet and the imams are God's appointed authority over the people. Therefore, what

God delegated to the Prophet and the imams is delegated to the wali al-faqih, and "anybody who disobeys him or the jurists disobeys God."[21]

Khomeini was careful to point out that the wali al-faqih does not possess Muhammad's and the imams' attributes of a personal covenant with Allah *(al-wilayat al-takwinniyyah),* nor is the wali al-faqih infallible like the Prophet and the imams. However, Khomeini granted the jurisconsult functional wilayat *(al-wilayat al-i'tibariyyah).* It means that the wali al-faqih has sacred knowledge to divine the hidden meaning of the Qur'an to make him participate in the final revelation of the word of God.[22] As such, the wali al-faqih is like the Prophet or the imams because he is but an executor of God's rule and commands.

Khomeini's theory of wilayat al-faqih provided powerful reinforcement of the dominant role of the jurisconsult in Hizbullah's ideology and practices. Seizing upon Khomeini's themes of obedience, Hizbullah's leaders have always pledged loyalty to Khomeini's wilayat and to that of his successor, Ayatollah Ali Khamenei. Sayyid Nasrallah, who received the title of "Proof of Islam" *(Hujjat al-Islam)* from Khamenei, articulates the concept of the power of obedience *(quwat al-ta'ah)* in support of Khamenei's wilayat in particular.[23] Nasrallah argues that the problem of the imamate historically was not the wilayat but the obedience of the people to the wilayat. In his words, "If the ummah had obeyed the Prophet as to 'Ali's wilayat, the history of Islam would have changed."[24] Nasrallah attributes the success of Khomeini's wilayat to the power of obedience of the people. Following Khomeini's formula of prophets-imams-wali (see figure 3.1), Nasrallah asserts that "Imam Khomeini was the hujjat of the Imam Mahdi in this ummah. Today I can say that hujjat al-Mahdi is Imam al-Qa'id (leader) Ali Khamenei, and hujjat al-Imam al-Mahdi is a proof on us, which forces obedience to this imam [Khamenei] who was appointed by Khomeini."[25]

Moreover, Nasrallah states clearly that "the decision of peace and war is in the hands of the jurisconsult, not in the hands of the intellectuals, researchers, scientists, and regular politicians, depending on the circumstances."[26] It follows that the wali al-faqih has the absolute right to elaborate, mold, or alter the ideology and its application, including the decisions of war and peace, to fit changing circumstances. Then Nasrallah asks: "Where is the force in us? What is Hizbullah's secret? The power is in the obedience to Khamenei's wilayat. The secret of our strength, growth, unity, struggle, and martyrdom is wilayat al-faqih, the spinal cord of Hizbullah."[27]

Clearly wilayat al-faqih is binding not only on Hizbullah's leaders and members; the party itself is an extension of wilayat al-faqih, presently under Khamenei's leadership. In Shaykh Na'im Qasim's words, "Not only the party is licensed by al-wali al-faqih but also its activities and decisions, especially those that involve a war of blood *(harb al-dam)* that cannot take place without seeking the approval of al-wali al-faqih."[28] However, in trying to differentiate between the Shari'ah rule that is dictated by the wali al-faqih and details of the party's activities, Shaykh Qasim states that "al-wali al-faqih, for example, decrees a legitimate enforcement in accordance with Islamic law *(amr shar'i)*, that fighting Zionism is a duty *(waja'ib)*, and that the blood sacrificed is a martyr's blood." However, he adds, "the wali does not interfere in the mechanics of the fighting, which is left to the party's leadership to decide upon."[29] Furthermore, amr shar'i implies *taklif shari'* (legitimate religious empowerment) for both the party's leadership and its members. In other words, Hizbullah under wilayat al-faqih not only is legally bound by the commands of the jurisconsult but also bears the politico-religious responsibility for executing the legitimate commands of the wali al-faqih.[30]

The allegiance of Hizbullah to Khamenei's wilayat and marji'yyah explains a number of important aspects of the party's practices. First, Hizbullah's practices can be flexible or rigid, depending on the role of the wali al-faqih, who has the right to alter ideology or guiding principles to fit historical circumstances. Accordingly, Hizbullah's actions or practices are not bound by one rigid rule but by many rules according to the circumstances decided upon by the wali al-faqih, whose authority cannot be challenged.

Second, a legitimate Islamic order and the unity of the ummah can only be established under the wali al-faqih, who is indispensable to the life of the Muslims. Even if conditions militate against the establishment of an Islamic order, Muslims must abide by the guidance of the wali al-faqih in their daily affairs.

Third, Hizbullah's allegiance to the wilayat and marji'yyah of Kha-menei has effectively undermined the position of other preeminent *maraji' al-taqlid,* in particular Sayyid Muhammad Husayn Fadlallah, who erroneously has been called *al-murshid al-ruhi* (spiritual guide) of Hizbul-lah. Interestingly, Fadlallah neither challenged Khomeini's marji'yyah or wilayat publicly, nor accepted Khamenei's wilayat. Nor did he mention his doubts about Khamenei's credentials as marja' al-taqlid.[31]

Fadlallah, however, sees his mission as a leading marja', transcending specific groups to embrace the stewardship of his followers *(muqallid)* in the larger Shi'ite community as well as among other Muslims. In fact, Fadlallah's plans to take over the position of supreme Shi'ite marja', after the death of the supreme marja', Abu al-Qasim al-Khui, in Iraq in 1993, clashed with those of Khamenei, who, besides being wali al-faqih, claimed the position of the supreme marja'.[32] The clash between Khamenei and Fadlallah was reflected in the party's position toward Fadlallah. Although some party members follow the ijtihad of Fadlallah, Hizbullah leaders have succeeded in tilting the majority of the party's rank and file toward the marji'yyah of Khamenei. While the party's leadership considers Fadlal-lah one of the few leading maraji' al-taqlid, they think it is binding on him to follow the wilayat of Khamenei as conditioned by Khomeini—that is, should one of the maraji' succeed in setting up a government, it is the duty of other maraji' al-taqlid to follow him.

Fourth, Hizbullah claims that wilayat al-faqih unites the ummah, Shi'ite and Sunni alike. However, Sunnis reject the claim of divinity or in-fallibility of the Prophet and imams. Moreover, the role of the mujtahid or wali al-faqih as a divinely guided leader participating in the final revela-tion of the word of God is also rejected. The theory of wilayat al-faqih is inimical to Sunni Islam, with the exception of a very few Sunni Islamist movements, such as the Islamic Jihad of Palestine, that more or less oper-ate under the banner of wilayat al-faqih. The closest point of argument between the concept of wilayat al-faqih and Sunni Islam is that the latter believes in the role of the guardian *(wali al-amr),* but it is a belief based on consensus (ijma') rather than divine covenant *('ahd).*

In conclusion, wilayat al-faqih is the nerve center of Hizbullah's combined political and religious functions. The words of Sayyid Nasrallah best summarize the politico-religious relationship between Hizbullah and wilayat al-faqih. Going straight to the point, Nasrallah states, "The spinal cord of Hizbullah is wilayat al-faqih. Take out wilayat al-faqih and Hizbullah becomes a dead body, even a divided one. An ummah without ʿAli is an ummah without spirit, an ummah without Husayn is an ummah without soul, and an ummah without al-wali al-faqih, who must be obeyed, is a dead, torn ummah."[33]

THE HOLY STRUGGLE (JIHAD)

The establishment of the Islamic order and the obedience to the wali al-faqih are reinforced by a third pillar, the holy struggle, jihad. Contrary to the belief that Hizbullah's doctrine of the jihad centers only on armed struggle with the connotation of fighting *(qital)* and martyrdom (shahadah),[34] the party subscribes to the broader meaning of jihad. Seizing upon a number of Qurʾanic verses, the Prophet's traditions, and Khomeini's book *al-Jihad,* Nasrallah, Qasim, and Yazbak stress that "jihad is demonstrated labor and energy in confronting or standing up to the enemy, for the purpose of defeating him and achieving the goals set by God."[35]

As such, Hizbullah's broader meaning of jihad permits two major modes of action, along with two submodes (see figure 3.2).

Each mode or submode is connected to the others and provides

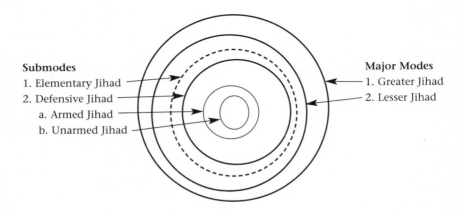

Submodes
1. Elementary Jihad
2. Defensive Jihad
   a. Armed Jihad
   b. Unarmed Jihad

Major Modes
1. Greater Jihad
2. Lesser Jihad

Figure 3.2. Hizbullah's Circles of Jihad

Hizbullah with a justifiable course of action in a specific circumstance. In other words, the party could move from one mode of action to the other, depending on the circumstances.

The Greater Jihad *(al-Jihad al-Akbar)*

The greater jihad involves struggle against oneself *(jihad al-nafs)*, in other words, according to Shaykh Qasim, "placing one's powers and faculties under the yoke of Allah's commands and purging the domain of one's body of satanic elements and their forces."[36] On this particular kind of struggle, Nasrallah stresses that "the battle with oneself is more dangerous than the battle with the external enemy. Thus our struggle against ourselves must be stronger than our struggle with our enemy."[37] By confronting the inner before the external satanic elements, Hizbullah prepares its members and constituency to act with conviction and without fear. Shaykh Qasim states, "The fruits of the greater jihad are the conviction that the individual sacrifices himself and his material well-being and must bear martyrdom for the purpose of confronting the enemy, in the way of God. For without the greater jihad there is no lesser or any other kind of jihad."[38]

Equally important, the greater jihad is a lifetime struggle—that is, it is the beginning and the end of every mode or submode of jihad. On this particular point, Shaykh Qasim and Hizbullah leaders and members always recount the sayings of Prophet Muhammad: "Welcome to the people who finished the lesser jihad and what remains for them is the greater jihad— that is, jihad al-nafs."[39]

Clearly, the centrality of the jihad and its modes are rooted in the greater jihad—an unarmed mode of action that prepares the individual for both armed and unarmed struggle.

The Lesser Jihad *(al-Jihad al-Asghar)*

The lesser jihad subsumes two submodes of jihad.

The Elementary Jihad *(al-Jihad al-Ibtida'i)*. The elementary jihad is also known as the "holy war" or the "offensive war." The ultimate aim of the elementary jihad is hegemonic on a global scale as expressed in at least two well-known Qur'anic verses. Verse 193 of *Baqara* (Qur'an 2:193) states, "Fight them [the unbelievers] until there is no dissension and the religion is entirely Allah's." [40] As for verse 33 of al Tawba (Qura'n 9:33), it renders the legitimacy of jihad: "He hath sent His messenger [Muhammad] with the guidance and the religion of truth, in order that he may set in above all [other] religions, though averse is the polytheists." [41]

Clearly, the elementary jihad is justified in terms of Islam's intrinsic superiority and its obligation to spread its sway over the earth. However, this type of jihad, according to Hizbullah's ideologues, can only be authorized by the Prophet or the infallible imam. On this point, Shaykh Qasim stresses that "in the absence of the Hidden Imam, the jurists *(fuqaha)* cannot authorize the elementary jihad, and accordingly its conditions are not present." [42]

As a result, since the jihad is bound to remain a major weighted factor in Hizbullah's ideology, a large part of the party's efforts must be channeled into the second submode of the lesser jihad.

The Defensive Jihad *(al-Jihad al-Difaʿi).* This mode of struggle consists of repelling aggression upon one's life, the country, and the Islamic ummah, thus preventing oppression and persecution by the enemy or an unjust authority. The defensive mode of struggle does not require the authorization of the Hidden Imam but only that of the wali al-faqih. As such, it is binding on every adult male and female, even the elderly and the sick, to confront and fight the enemy. [43]

In their interpretation of the defensive jihad, Hizbullah leaders stress both armed and unarmed means of achieving their goals, including the establishment of an Islamic order. As stated by Sayyid Nasrallah: "The defensive jihad constitutes armed and unarmed struggle. An armed struggle means fighting the enemy with blood and involves martyrdom. An unarmed struggle involves political, economic, and cultural means. Our defensive jihad in Lebanon involves both forms." [44]

However, the choice between armed and unarmed struggle depends on the circumstances, as sanctioned by the Qur'an. Both Sayyid Nasrallah and Shaykh Qasim derive their views from a number of Qur'anic verses, the most well known being verse 41 of *al-Tawba* (Qur'an 9:41): "wa jahiduw bi amwalikum wa anfousikum" (struggle with your selves and your money). From such verses they read that the struggle in the way of Allah requires armed jihad. In other circumstances, however, the Qur'an has sanctioned unarmed jihad. The Prophet, according to Nasrallah, clearly stated in verse 52 of *al-Furqan* (Qur'an 25:52): "It was not authorized in Mecca to use arms and enter into fighting with Qurayish, but he was asked to struggle politically, economically and culturally." [45]

Furthermore, Hizbullah's leaders and members have frequently made reference to a well-known saying of the Prophet that sanctions both armed and unarmed means of jihad: "Struggle in the way of God with your hands: if you can't, struggle with your tongues; if not struggle with your hearts." [46]

The call for combating the danger to the faith or the enemy by "hand" or by "tongue" (by arms or by persuasion) depends on the circumstances. It follows that, in the case of unarmed means, Hizbullah's members should struggle politically, economically, and spiritually. Such struggle necessitates organization or autonomous associations. Such enclaves should conquer the state from the bottom up by spreading the realm of the enclave, person by person and family by family, by lobbying, by parliamentary participation, and by involvement in other elected professional bodies.

Clearly, Hizbullah's ideology of jihad leaves the precise dosage of the means to pragmatic consideration, but it should invariably be preceded by the greater jihad. It is no longer a matter of fighting a foreign enemy only, but the state itself has become a target of both armed and unarmed jihad. In the final analysis, whatever the exact modus operandi, the aim—seizing political power and establishing an Islamic order—is the same.

UNITY OF THE ISLAMIC UMMAH

The centrality of Hizbullah's belief in the unity of the Islamic ummah is rooted in the liberation of Jerusalem or what is known among the party's rank and file as "the Jerusalem Liberation culture." By focusing on Palestine in general and Jerusalem in particular, Hizbullah has succeeded in undermining to some extent the ideological differences between Shi'ism and Sunnism. Biding to become a bridge between the two, Iran and the Arabs, Hizbullah has always defined itself as a struggle movement against Zionism and its objectives.[47]

In fact, it was Imam Khomeini who focused Hizbullah's attention on the issue of Palestine as a core factor in uniting the Islamic ummah. He repeatedly stressed that "Israel is a cancerous goiter that occupies the liver of the ummah: Palestine."[48] Furthermore, Khomeini called on the Muslims "to rise up and defend Islam and the center of revelation *(wahi)* by armed struggle."[49]

Such doctrine has been upheld by all of Hizbullah's leaders and members. In the words of Nasrallah, "Jerusalem is the land of Allah; it constitutes an Islamic cultural dimension not subject to negotiation or compromise."[50] As such, Hizbullah not only condemns all mediation, peace talks, and agreements between Israel and the Palestinian Authority and Arab regimes, but considers them "a treason against Islam, Muslims, and the Arabs."[51]

The call for a united Islamic ummah against "Zionism" was reinforced by another call of unity and action against "American plans" in support of Israel's objectives in Jerusalem in particular. In pursuing this call by Hizbullah, Nasrallah states unequivocally: "Turn to the resistance and the logic of the jihad. Every Palestinian and every honest man in the ummah has to tell the Americans: you may move your embassy and send your diplomats to Jerusalem. However, honest people might turn your embassy into rubble and send your diplomats home in coffins. This is the answer; this is the only logic that the Americans and Israel understand. I tell the Americans that your embassy, like your Zionist usurped entity, does not have a future in the region in the face of the will, jihad, and shahadah."[52]

In line with such statements, Hizbullah believes that an Islamic unity driven by jihad is the only answer for "Israel, the United States, and arrogant powers who are leading their war against Islam."[53]

Clearly linked to the above doctrine of Islamic unity is the call for a united Islamic front to resist normalization of ties with Israel. If peace is imposed, however, Hizbullah calls on Muslims to stay alert and resist normalization politically, economically, and culturally. "We are present in the parliament, the streets, and other places. We and other Muslims will make sure to prevent normalization with Israel, starting from Lebanon," said Sayyid Nasrallah.[54] To motivate the Muslims to take the necessary steps to fight Zionism and bring about unity, Hizbullah appeals emotionally and practically to the masses across the Arab-Muslim world.

Emotionally, Hizbullah has called on Muslims as well as Christian Arabs to commemorate "the International Day of Jerusalem" with fierce determination. Hizbullah has urged them to take to the streets of their respective countries to express their unity and actively show the world their anger and readiness to give their life in the cause of Jerusalem.

Following Khomeini's fatwa (juridical opinion) of 1979, decreeing that the last Friday of the month of Ramadan is the International Day of Jerusalem, since its inception Hizbullah has constantly celebrated that day. Military marches by Hizbullah fighters were performed in the shape of al-Aqsa Mosque to express the determination of Hizbullah's Islamic resistance in liberating Jerusalem and to show, according to Nasrallah, that "this cancerous [Israel], corrupted bacteria, and the mother of cunning, does not have any choice but death."[55]

Hizbullah's religio-emotional appeal for Jerusalem, which resembles that of Sunni Islamist movements that are otherwise uninterested in Shi'ism, has created a common bond between Hizbullah and the Sunnis over Jerusalem. Sunni Islamist movements such as the Islamic Association of Lebanon and its counterparts in Syria, Jordan, Egypt, and Algeria as well as the Palestinian Islamist groups Hamas and the Islamic Jihad have been involved in their own respective countries and with Hizbullah in Lebanon in the processions of the International Day of Jerusalem.[56]

The religio-emotional appeal for Islamic unity was reinforced at a practical level by providing a coordination network, known as the Islamic Current (al-Tayyar al-Islami). In the words of Nasrallah: "The Islamic Current is the sum of Islamist organizations, supporters, and sympathizers who share with us common ground on the framework of the resistance, liberation of the land, and the defense of the ummah against Zionist projects."[57]

In this context, the Islamist organization supporter might be a member or part of al-Tayyar al-Islami, yet remain ideologically and organizationally independent from Hizbullah. Thus, without meddling in the ideological and organizational details of other Islamist movements and groups, Hizbullah has provided them with a decentralized framework of unity that keeps the ideological particularity of each movement independent. Such a decentralized framework is more appealing to Sunni Islamists than the doctrine of wilayat al-faqih, which is most likely to be rejected by them. It is in this context that one has to understand the coordination and the operational links between Hizbullah and Islamist groups, in particular the Islamic Jihad and Hamas. Such coordination will receive further details in chapter 4.

SOCIAL JUSTICE

Finally, Hizbullah's ideology promises that the Islamic order will provide social justice *(al-'adalah al-ijtima'iyyah)* that cannot be attained under Western-inspired developmental plans or socialist Marxism. Accordingly, Hizbullah leaders such as Nasrallah, Qasim, Yazbak, and others tell Muslims, "Only God's just society aims at social justice." [58]

It should be emphasized, however, that this notion of social justice does not entail social equality, extravagance, material well-being, or other values that Hizbullah clerics claim are Western ideas that corrupt and fragment the Islamic world.

Furthermore, social justice does not condone class conflict; when Hizbullah's ideology speaks of the downtrodden (mustad'afin) versus the arrogant *(mustakbirin)*,, the party does not call for one segment of the Shi'ite or Muslim community to engage in a class conflict with another.[59] Rather, the party calls for transcendence of all class differences to be achieved by the Islamic just order.[60]

Instead, social justice is determined by moral behavior because Islam considers that the life of a man is spiritual and material unity. Thus, social justice means spiritual unity, self-sufficiency, and independence. It means the welfare of the community above and beyond the welfare of the individual. In other words, the provision of social services to the community is a fundamental tenet of faith and not the result of Marxist historical dialectical forces that bring about a socialist state.

The principles of *zakat* (alms giving) and *khums* (a tithe of one-fifth), Islamic duties and taxes paid by the believers, coupled with state policy, will prevent the division of society into classes. Such practices are sometimes labeled "Islamic socialism." However, Islam recognizes private property, in contradiction of the principle of social property. This major difference makes Hizbullah's social justice different from the economic equality sought by socialism. However, the accumulation of wealth through monopoly, usury, and dishonesty is prohibited.[61]

In a society occupied by the apparently unrestricted pursuit by individuals for satisfaction and controlled by authoritarian regimes, Hizbullah's provision of social welfare services—that is, education, health care, and housing—has served the deepest needs of the most deprived of Lebanon's Shi'ites and other Muslims. Through Hizbullah's social welfare services, the downtrodden can escape for the time being injustice caused by people or the system and embrace Hizbullah's social justice that strives to prevent the division of society into classes.

In conclusion, Hizbullah's Islamic ideology is essentially juristical, where the mujtahid, particularly the wali al-faqih, participates in the final revelation of the word of God. Thus, the clerical elite can legitimately elaborate, mold, or alter the party's ideological components—that is, the establishment of the Islamic order, the jihad, the unity of the Islamic ummah, and social justice—to fit changing circumstances. The legitimacy of ijtihad (authoritative interpretation of Islamic law) provides not only a potential source for Islamic legislation but flexibility in the face of changing political circumstances. Neither Sunni fundamentalism, with its stress on the Prophet's ummah and on consensus as the perfect model of the Islamic community, nor Marxism, with its dialectical historical change not subject to human intervention, can provide a similar flexibility for the changing political circumstances provided by Hizbullah's divine jurist. In short, Hizbullah has elaborated an ideology in which the role of the jurist is determinant to the party's future survivability or decay.

4

Clerical Leadership and Hierarchical Structure

Most observers and analysts tend to regard Hizbullah as a conventional political party or a group turned from a terrorist movement into a political party.[1] However, Hizbullah defines itself both as a "struggle movement of faithful Lebanese who believe in Islam, resistance, and liberation of the land" and as "one of the most prominent Lebanese political parties."[2] As such, Hizbullah is first and foremost a *jihadi* movement that engages in politics, and not a political party that conducts jihad. Hizbullah is indeed an Islamic political party, but neither its leadership nor its organizational structure is equivalent to conventional secular parties such as those in the Western democratic or socialist systems.

This chapter examines Hizbullah's leadership and organization as impacted by the party's ideology. The focus here is on the political and military organs of Hizbullah's organization. The analysis will shed light on the controversy over Hizbullah as a conventional political party.

Until recently Hizbullah relied on an organizational structure much of which was underground. In fact, the author was the first to reveal and analyze Hizbullah's organizational structure as it started to shape up and expand since the party's inception.[3] Believing that an imported party structure of the Western or Leninist type was inconvenient and alien to Islam, Hizbullah developed a structure that revolved mainly around the clerical leadership, whose members are considered by the party's ideology to be more knowledgeable about Shar' Allah (God's Law) and closer to the mood of Islam than average Muslims.

The organizational structure of Hizbullah assumes the shape of a hierarchical pyramid coinciding with the territorial division of Lebanon's governorates, in particular the ones that have a majority of Shiʿites—that is, Beirut, Biqʿa, and South Lebanon. Structurally, the party consists of leadership, political and administrative, and military and security organs, along with a number of service subunits within each apparatus (see figure 4.1).

THE LEADERSHIP APPARATUS

Structurally, the party is headed by a collective leadership, rather than by a charismatic personality such as Amal was under Musa al-Sadr. The seven-member Shura Council (Majlis al-Shura or Consultative Council) is elected by the Majlis al-Markazi (Central Council)—an assembly of almost two hundred party founders and cadres—for a period of three years.[4] The leadership apparatus consists mostly of clergy, along with a few lay members. The lay members or the "non-ʿulamaʾ" have, according to Shaykh Qasim, "to demonstrate faith in Islam and a sound belief in wilayat al-faqih and have certain skills in the fields of health, social affairs, and finance and information services."[5] Until 1989, the ratio of clerics to laity in the Shura Council's makeup was six to one. When the party opened up to increased representation of the laity's rank and file after the 1989 Taʾif Agreement, the ratio became four clerics to three laity. However, the 2001 elections of the Shura Council represented a shift back to a six-to-one ratio in favor of the clerics. One major reason was to suppress potential lay elements such as Hajj Muhammad Fnyish and Hajj Muhammad Raʾad and others who sought to relax religious orientation without giving up on the party's ideology. Such a move was not favored by the party's clerics, who pushed for their own dominance. At present the Shura Council is made up of six clerics and one lay member. Among the clerics are Sayyid Hasan Nasrallah, secretary-general; Shaykh Naʿim Qasim, deputy secretary; Shaykh Muhammad Yazbak; Sayyid Hashem Safi al-Din; Sayyid Ibrahim Amin al-Sayyid; and Sayyid Jawad Nour al-Din. Hajj Husayn Khalil is the only lay member. Although the lay members are not required to have studied religion, the title Hajj (one who has made a pilgrimage to Mecca) means faithfulness to and observance of Sharʿ Allah—a requirement for them to qualify to sit on the Shura Council. The number of laity on the Shura Council, whether

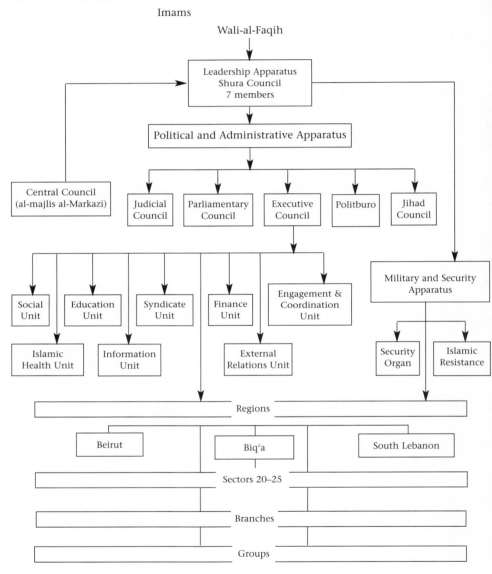

Source: Author's composite figure based on various activities reported by *Al-Ahd* between 1988 and 2002, and on interviews.

Figure 4.1. Hizbullah's Organizational Structure

one or a maximum of three, depends on the need as dictated by the party's clerics.

The election of Shura Council members involves three stages. The first stage is screening of the nominees, clerics and lay, who must meet the leadership qualifications. Those who are found qualified are then eligible for the second stage—that is, they become candidates for election to the seven-member Shura Council. According to Shaykh Qasim, "Although seventy or eighty members might qualify for election, only ten members are nominated, those who are most seconded by their colleagues in the Central Council."[6] The final stage is the election of the seven-member Shura Council out of the actual nominees.

The election process of the Shura Council is reflective of Hizbullah's organizational dynamics. First, the election of the Shura Council members by the Central Council does not necessarily represent the party's rank and file. It is only the few, the party's founders and cadre, who have the right to elect its leadership. Second, the three-stage process—screening, nominations, and elections—requires that the candidate demonstrate his religious qualifications before being recommended to the party's leadership. Such qualifications of selection are essentially alien to conventional or secular political parties. Indeed, the election process of Hizbullah's Shura Council seems similar to that of the election of Iran's Guardian Council, which is elected by the Assembly of Experts that also has jurisdiction over the screening of those nominated.[7]

Once the seven members of Hizbullah's Shura Council are elected, they in turn elect a secretary-general and his deputy and chairs of the five councils of the party's executive administrative apparatus. As it stands, the whole process of election within the Shura Council seems more an appointment process or distribution of responsibilities than an actual election. The Shura Council is too small to allow for a formal election. Equally important, this elitist group is homogeneous; there is consensus over who gets what. As an anonymous source put it to me, "I elect you so you can elect me and there is no problem."

The Shura Council is charged with overall administration, planning, and policy making. Its decisions are final and religiously binding on party members. Decisions taken are reached either unanimously or by majority vote. In case of deadlock or a split among members of the Shura Council, matters are referred to the wali al-faqih, the highest religio-legal authority of the party. "The decisions of al-wali al-faqih are final, binding, and can't be challenged," according to Shaykh Qasim.[8] Thus, the wali al-faqih's decisions and approval not only legitimate the party's actions but also provide a safety mechanism or valve to prevent dissension among the clerical elite.

Despite the fact that Hizbullah's leadership is collective rather than individualistic, the secretary-general's post has lately become the party's center of gravity, the "imperial secretariat." Longer than any other secretary-general, Sayyid Hasan Nasrallah has served four consecutive terms, since the assassination of Sayyid Abbas al-Musawi in February 1992. Although Sayyid Nasrallah may function within the bureaucratic culture of Hizbullah's collective leadership, he has demonstrated significant religious, political, and military skills that have made him a charismatic leader indispensable as secretary-general and propagator of the wilayat al-faqih. Such skills prompted Sayyid Nasrallah's election as secretary-general for the first term in 1992 and again for a second term in 1995. Because the party's electoral rules do not allow for a third term, the election of Sayyid Nasrallah would not have happened had the supreme leader, Ali Khamenei, not bent the rule as wali al-faqih and allowed Sayyid Nasrallah to be elected for a third term in 1998 and a fourth term in 2001. There is no doubt that Nasrallah's combined leadership skills and unquestionable loyalty to Ali Khamenei have made him the central actor in almost all of Hizbullah's political and military decision making. After all, Nasrallah set an example for the party's rank and file in sacrifice and martyrdom when his elder son Hadi became a martyr in April 2000 during an attack against the Israeli troops in South Lebanon.

THE EXECUTIVE ADMINISTRATIVE APPARATUS

The actual operation of the party is entrusted to the executive administrative apparatus, known as the Shura Tanfiz. This apparatus consists of five councils: the Executive Council, the Politburo, the Parliamentary Council, the Judicial Council, and the Jihad Council. Each council is usually headed by a member of the Shura Council and varies in membership size. There is no actual separation between legislative and executive powers, and accordingly, authority and power are concentrated in the seven-member Shura Council. Of the five councils, the Executive Council and the Politburo are the oldest and the most powerful in having a direct impact on the party's social and political activities.

The Executive Council

The main function of the Executive Council (Majlis al-Tanfizi; also known as Shura Tanfiz) is to follow up on the day-to-day activities of the party's various units in the regions, sectors, and branches. The council is headed by Sayyid Hashem Safi al-Din, who is assisted by the head of each eight-member unit *(wahda),* as shown in figure 4.1. The following is an analysis of the various units that the Executive Council supervises.

The Social Unit. The Social Unit provides social welfare services as well as technical help to thousands of Hizbullah members and supporters and to the martyrs' families. The unit is headed at present by Shaykh Husayn Zu'aiter and supervises the work of four semi-autonomous social foundations, which are financed by Iran:

Holy Struggle Construction Foundation (Mu'assasat Jihad al-Bina'). Hizbullah established this foundation in 1988. It has quickly evolved into one of the most prominent nongovernmental organizations of Lebanon's civil society. Although it has an autonomous organizational structure, its overall policies are very much controlled by the party's Social Unit.[9] At present Jihad al-Bina' is headed by Shaykh Ibrahim Ism'ail.

The primary objective of this foundation is "to alleviate the hardships that the disadvantaged population and deprived families face, drawing on the support of Allah in carrying out moral and Islamic duties."[10] The foundation operates in Beirut's southern suburbs, the Biq'a, and South Lebanon (see table 4.1).

Table 4.1 shows that the total number of projects constructed or rehabilitated between 1988 and 2002 are impressive both in size and type. According to the report of the United Nations Economic and Social Commission for Western Asia, Jihad al-Bina' is by far one of the best-equipped

Table 4.1

Projects Implemented by Jihad al-Bina᾽, 1988–2002

Type/Region	Construction	Rehabilitation
Schools		
South Lebanon	6	20
Biqʿa	2	4
Beirut	3	0
Total	(11)	(24)
Homes		
South Lebanon	2	9,229
Biqʿa	1	255
Beirut	0	156
Total	(3)	(9,640)
Shops		
South Lebanon	0	750
Biqʿa	0	30
Beirut	0	20
Total	(0)	(800)
Hospitals		
South Lebanon	1	1
Biqʿa	1	1
Beirut	1	0
Total	(3)	(2)
Infirmaries		
South Lebanon	1	3
Biqʿa	3	0
Beirut	1	0
Total	(5)	(3)
Mosques		
South Lebanon	15	17
Biqʿa	19	35
Beirut	4	3
Jbeil	6	1
Total	(44)	(56)
Cultural Centers		
South Lebanon	1	1
Biqʿa	1	2
Beirut	3	0
Total	(5)	(3)

(Continued on page 51)

Type/Region	Construction	Rehabilitation
Agricultural Center Cooperatives		
South Lebanon	3	0
Biqʿa	4	0
Total	(7)	(0)
Grand Total	78	10,528

Source: Figures compiled by author from Muʾassasat Jihad al-Binaʾ (Holy struggle construction foundation), *Jihad al-Bina: Its Twelfth Spring: 1988–2000* (Beirut: Jihad al-Binaʾ, 2000) and from unpublished 2002 reports provided by Muʾassasat Jihad al-Binaʾ.

organizations.[11] Naturally, the bulk of the various projects were implemented in South Lebanon first, followed by the Biqʿa, because these areas suffered most from underdevelopment and the Israeli occupation. Jihad al-Binaʾʾs development projects not only provided a response to emergency needs, but they also were very much needed by Hizbullah as infrastructure for the flow of its social welfare services. In addition, Jihad al-Binaʾ has provided a supply of potable water and electricity. For example, the foundation built four hundred reservoirs of potable water for the eight hundred thousand residents of Beirut's southern suburbs. It is to be noted that Jihad al-Binaʾ satisfies around 45 percent of the southern suburbs' water needs. This is a considerable achievement for the area that suffers the most from the government's shortfall in creating a sufficient potable water supply. Also, the foundation dug more than fifty-eight artesian wells, divided evenly between the Biqʿa, South Lebanon, and Beirut.[12] Furthermore, the electricity department has manufactured and installed more than twenty big power generators in South Lebanon and the Biqʿa. It has even provided maintenance for the government's power network in these two regions.[13]

In agriculture and rural development, the activities of Jihad al-Binaʾ are as impressive as in the field of engineering. Briefly, the foundation provides technical assistance to farmers in land reclamation and cultivation, opening agricultural roads and installing irrigation networks. Moreover, it supports agricultural production by providing farmers with credit facilities. It has also established a tomato processing and canning industry and a number of dairy farms in the Biq'a region.[14]

The Martyrs Foundation (Mu'assasat al-Shahid). This foundation was established in 1982 under the guidance of Iran's Ayatollah Khomeini. The present head of the foundation is Hajj Husayn Shami. The primary objective of the Martyrs Foundation is to support the families of martyrs, detainees, and resistance fighters as well as civilians.[15] For this purpose the Martyrs Foundation provides children of those families with education and health care. More than two thousand families of martyrs and detainees, and fourteen hundred children, have benefited from the general welfare services of the Martyrs Foundation.[16] It also provides housing, work opportunities, and support to widowed women and runs an employment office for the youth. The activities of the foundation are funded by the Iranian Martyrs Foundation, in addition to funds acquired from individual donors and from Islamic alms (khums) paid by believers. Reportedly, the Martyrs Foundation operates with an annual budget of around US $3 million.[17]

Foundation for the Wounded (Mu'assasat al-Jarha). This foundation was established in 1990 to serve the needs of those who had been wounded and disabled by Israeli attacks. The foundation is headed by Hajj Abu al-Fadl, who guides the activities of a staff of forty divided into seven committees dealing with health, social, educational, information, cultural, and entertainment activities and developmental projects.[18]

The foundation provides beneficiaries with financial support including monthly payments, housing, health services, education, counseling, and support groups using reintegration approaches within the family and society. The foundation has served more than eleven thousand resistance fighters and civilians over a period of eleven years (see table 4.2).

In addition to the above war-related medical emergencies, and health, social, and educational services, the foundation runs two physiotherapy and rehabilitation centers: one called Abu al-Abbas, located in Beirut's southern suburbs, and another in the city of Nabatiyyah.[19]

Khomeini Support Committee (Lujnat Imdad al-Khomeini). This committee was established immediately after the 1982 Israeli invasion. It provides general welfare services to poor needy families, in particular those who suf-

Table 4.2

Services Provided by the Foundation for the Wounded, 1990–2001

Type of Services	Number of Beneficiaries
War Medical Emergencies	
Wounded	120
Disabled	587
Health Services	
Artificial organs	458
Wheelchairs	678
Crutches	2,379
Social Services	
Monthly payments	6,680
Educational Services	
Scholarships	210
Total	11,062

Source: Figures compiled from Mu'assasat al-Jarha (The foundation for the wounded), *Nashat al-mu'assasah li 'aam 2000–2001* (2000–2001 annual activities), 1–3.

fered from the Israeli occupation and attacks. The services of the committee include monthly payments, food portions and coupons, household necessities, clothes, health care, and education.[20]

The committee, headed by Hajj Ali Zriek, operates through a number of specialized teams to determine cases of needy families. Reportedly, the committee provides health services to around 112,500 individuals per year. These services include medications, transfer of patients, medical check-ups, and surgery. Also, around 3,500 orphans benefit from the committee's social welfare services. In addition, the committee provides all types of welfare assistance to around 8,400 families and more than 2,000 students.[21]

The activities of Hizbullah's Social Unit emanate from a strong ideological commitment because social service is a fundamental tenet of the faith. This committee has contributed to the success of Hizbullah in boosting the size of its constituency and its skillful penetration of Lebanon's society, in particular the Shi'ite community. While the Lebanese government has almost ceased to offer social welfare services, Hizbullah has been delivering such services, thus increasing its popularity at the expense of both the Lebanese government and the Amal movement.

The Islamic Health Unit. Known also as al-Haya' al-Suhhiyyah al-Islamiyyah (the Islamic Health Society), the unit provides health care services and preventive care to Hizbullah's regional constituency and to people in deprived areas (see table 4.3). It is currently headed by Hajj Abbas Huballah.

Table 4.3 shows that the Islamic Health Unit provides health care services to over four hundred thousand persons living in Beirut's southern suburbs, Biq'a, and South Lebanon. The cost of such services is estimated

Table 4.3
Institutions of the Islamic Health Unit

Name/Number	Region	Beneficiaries per Year
Hospitals (6)		
The Great Prophet	Southern suburbs	100,000
Dar al-Hawra (for women and children)	Southern suburbs	59,203
Khomeini Hospital	Biq'a–Ba'albek	50,000
Medical Batoul Center	Biq'a–Hermil	Not yet in operation
Hospital of the South	South Lebanon–Nabatiyyah	48,725
Shaykh Raghib Harb Hospital	South Lebanon–Toul	Not in full operation
Dispensaries (21)	Southern suburbs (9)	
	South Lebanon (7)	92,692
	Biq'a (3)	
	Beirut (2)	
Mobile Dispensaries (12)	South Lebanon and Biq'a	30,236
Dental Clinics (10)	Southern suburbs, Biq'a, and South Lebanon	20,736
Civil Defense Centers (7)	Southern suburbs, Biq'a, and South Lebanon	7,536
Total		409,281

Source: Figures compiled from Al-Hay'a al-Suhiyyah al-Islamiyyah (Islamic health society), *Al-Takrir al-thanawi li 'aam 2000* (The 2000 annual report) (Beirut: Hizbullah, 2000), and from Mu'assasat al-Shahid (Martyrs foundation), *Nashat al-mu'assasah li 'aam 1999* (1999 annual activities).

at around US $5 million.[22] These services, by all standards, have become an embarrassment when compared with the Lebanese government's weak or nonexisting health care services in the poor areas served by the Islamic Health Unit as well as in the North. The financial and technical inability of the Lebanese government, in particular the Ministry of Health, to run its state hospitals has caused Hizbullah to take over the hospitals of South Lebanon and Bint Jbeil and operate them under its Islamic Health Unit.[23] While the government has made rhetorical promises to provide basic health care services, Hizbullah's Islamic Health Unit has filled the vacuum and responded to health emergencies and the needs of people before and after the Israeli withdrawal from South Lebanon. By successfully providing health care services through its own hospitals, dispensaries, mobile dispensaries, dental clinics, and a number of civil defense centers, Hizbullah has increased its popularity, thus exposing the ineffectiveness and illegitimacy of the Lebanese government.

The Education Unit. The Education Unit is led by a central office called al-Ta'bia' al-Tarbawiyya (Educational Enforcement Office). At present the unit is headed by Hajj Yusuf Meri', who replaced Hajj Hashem Salhab.[24] The unit provides financial aid and scholarships to needy students of Hizbullah (see tables 4.4 and 4.5).[25]

As shown in table 4.4, Hizbullah's Education Unit spent over 21 billion Lebanese liras (US $14,215,000) between 1996 and 2001 on financial aid and scholarships. This amount reflects the serious commitment that

Table 4.4
Education Unit Financial Aid and Scholarships, 1996–2001

Year	Amount (in Lebanese Lira)
1996–97	3,854,198,030
1997–98	5,791,069,004
1999–2000	6,377,899,500
2000–2001	5,304,112,500
Total	21,327,279,034

Source: Al-T'abi'a al-Tarbawiyyah (Education enforcement office), "Al-Takrir al-thanawi li 'aam 2000" (The 2000 annual report), in *Al-Ahd,* November 24, 2000, 9.

Table 4.5

Types of Education Unit Aid by Amount (in Lebanese Lira) and by Region, 2000–2001

Type of Aid	South		Biq'a		Beirut	
	Amount	No. of Students	Amount	No. of Students	Amount	No. of Students
Token	67,000,000	3,800	30,000,000	611	16,722	1,120
Financial	109,000,000	2,180	144,337,000	2,532	40,999,500	819
Scholarship	290,000,000	580	249,000,000	1,207	4,407,045,000	8,643
Total	475,000,000	6,560	423,337,000	5,489	4,464,775,500	10,582

Source: Educational Enforcement Office, 2000–2001 Annual Report, *Al-Ahd,* November 24, 2000, 9.

Hizbullah has to the needy students of its constituency. More important, Hizbullah's spending in this area has been extremely effective in expanding the party's base in a country where the public school system suffers from lack of funds, building facilities, and advanced learning technology.

The aid program of Hizbullah's Education Unit takes many forms. For example, the amount spent by the unit for the year 2000–2001 totaled almost 5.5 billion Lebanese liras ($3,569,408) and benefited around twenty-three thousand students, as shown in table 4.5. Other types of aid in kind involve paying for school textbooks and instructional material, and paying part of the registration fee of students in public schools or in private schools with reasonable tuition.

The bulk of the unit's aid, however, seems to go for scholarships that cover full tuition of students plus living expenses. As table 4.5 shows, the number of needy students who have benefited from Hizbullah's scholarships are by far greater in Beirut than in Biq'a and South Lebanon. This is natural because the cost of education and living in urban dwellings is much higher than in the rural areas of the Biq'a and South Lebanon. Overall, Hizbullah's Education Unit spent a total of 4,464,775,500 Lebanese lira ($309,850,000) on the three types of aid in the Beirut area compared with 475,000,000 Lebanese lira ($3,166,666) and 423,337,000 Lebanese lira ($2,822,225) in South Lebanon and Biq'a respectively.

In addition, the Education Unit supervises and coordinates the work of a network of Imam al-Mahdi schools and al-Mustafa schools that are administratively placed under Hizbullah's Islamic Institution for Education and Culture. The network of Imam al-Mahdi schools is geographically widespread, in comparison to al-Mustafa schools, which operate in Beirut's southern suburbs. At least ten al-Mahdi schools serve the needs of students in Hizbullah's ten regions (see table 4.6).

Furthermore, the Education Unit provides needy students with specialized higher education in applied sciences as well as religious studies through a number of institutes such as the Technical Institute of the Great Prophet, the Technical Institutes of Sayyid Abbas al-Musawi, the Institute of Sayydat al-Zahra', the Institute of Shaykh Raghib Harb, and the Islamic Shari'ah Institute.[26]

Clearly, the Education Unit of Hizbullah has made a difference in the lives of poor and needy students who have benefited from its financial aid and scholarships, and the almost cost-free education in Hizbullah's schools and institutes. It thereby has made Lebanon's Ministry of Education look mute or muzzled with regard to providing public educational services to the poor. The total expenditure on education by the Lebanese government has not exceeded 812,608 Lebanese lira ($541,739) per year

Table 4.6
Distribution of al-Mahdi Schools by Region

Region	Locality	Area m^2
South Lebanon	Sharqiyyah	4,500
South Lebanon	Majdel	3,500
South Lebanon	Sour	10,991
South Lebanon	'Ain Kana	3,400
South Lebanon	Ghazieh	3,500
South Lebanon	'Ain Mezrab	3,400
Beirut	Beir Hasan	3,684
Beirut	Ouzai '	2212
Biq'a	Bezzaleyah	2300
Biq'a	Chmestar	3300

Source: Mu'assasat Jihad al-Bina' (Holy struggle construction foundation), *Jihad al-Bina: Its Twelfth Spring: 1988–2000* (Beirut: Jihad al-Bina', 2000), 10.

and remains far behind in comparison with Hizbullah. In this endeavor, the party has accumulated considerable support among needy Muslim students, in particular the Shi'ites.

The Information Unit. The Information Unit is in charge of Hizbullah's propaganda policies and is headed by Hajj Hasan Ezz al-Din. The unit oversees and controls the functions of Hizbullah's media outlets (see table 4.7).

Hizbullah's media outlets are well established in the field of information, as shown in table 4.7, despite the fact that the Lebanese government has not granted licenses to some of the party's outlets.[27] By all standards, the size of Hizbullah's media outlets—one television station, four radio stations, and five newspapers and journals—is far greater than that of any other political party in Lebanon or the region.

Through its media outlets, the Information Unit has played a vital role in reinforcing Hizbullah's ideology and policies:

1. *The television station of the Resistance.* The true propaganda medium of Hizbullah is al-Manar (lighthouse or beacon) satellite television station.

Table 4.7
Hizbullah's Media Outlets

Outlet	Location	Legal Status
TV Broadcasting Station		
Al-Manar (The beacon)	Southern suburbs–Haret Hurick	Licensed
Radio Stations		
Al-Nour (The light)	Southern suburbs–Haret Hurick	Licensed
Al-Iman (The faith)	Southern suburbs	Licensed
Al-Islam (Voice of Islam)	South Lebanon	Licensed
Sawt al-Mustad'afin		
(Voice of the oppressed)	Biq'a	Not licensed
Newspapers/Journals		
Al-Ahd	Haret Huriek	Licensed
Al-Bilad	Beir al-Abd	Licensed
Al-Muntalaq	Beir al-Abd	Licensed
Al-Sabil	Beirut	Not licensed
Baqiatou Allah	Haret Huriek	Licensed

Source: Author's data.

Although Resistance fighters guard the station's five-story building in the southern suburb of Beirut, al-Manar has a corporate atmosphere with several hundred employees, a prayer room, a cafeteria, and several studios fitted with state-of-the-art editing and production suites.[28]

Al-Manar has come a long way since it first began broadcasting in 1991. At the time, the station's message was just one of the many differing opinions populating the pre-1997 broadcast. Aimed solidly at a Shi'ite audience, it offered a muscular mixture of revolution and religion. However, with news bulletins, political commentaries, and announcements of martyrdoms and casualties, including those of the Israeli army and the SLA, supplemented by clips of resistance activities shot on site by al-Manar's intrepid flak-jacketed, camouflaged cameramen, Hizbullah has brought the battle against Israel home in uncompromising fashion. For the first time in the history of the Arab-Israeli conflict since 1948, Arabs and Muslims have seen Israeli soldiers inflicted with death and injuries at the hands of Hizbullah's Islamic Resistance. Hizbullah's success in turning the picture in the Arab-Muslim society upside down from a widespread feeling of defeat into a victory against Israel has earned al-Manar an enthusiastic following in countries across the region.

During the Israeli occupation, al-Manar broadcast repeated messages in Hebrew aimed at demoralizing Israeli soldiers in the occupied zone and explaining that bombs dropped on their Lebanese counterparts would lead directly to Katyusha rockets on settlements over the border. As the death and injured toll of Israeli soldiers grew inexorably, al-Manar stepped up its psychological warfare campaign by launching its famous "Who's next?" campaign, a constantly updated photo gallery of the latest Israeli casualties that ended with a blank space and a large question mark over the silhouette of the next casualty to be. Screened in both Hebrew and Arabic, "Who's next?" was clearly designed to increase pressure within Israel to end the occupation. Over the years, more anti-Israeli programs and psychological warfare programs were added, such as "The Spider House," "In Spite of Wounds," "The Viewer Is the Witness," "Terrorist-Zionist Crimes," and "The Upside-Down Picture." The aim of these programs has been to reinforce the anti-Israeli socialization process and to portray the resistance fighters as individuals who have no fear of death.

Backed by Iranian funds, expatriate Muslim donors, in particular Shi'ites, and increasing commercial receipts from the sale of advertisements, al-Manar has blossomed into a multimillion-dollar operation with more than ten million viewers. Aiming at winning the hearts and minds of the world, al-Manar has extended coverage to Africa, Europe, North America, and Latin America, with news bulletin services in English and French languages. These services, of course, aim at addressing Western opinion directly by explaining the party's point of view on issues happening in the region.

With the Israeli withdrawal from Lebanon in May 1999 and the inception of the second Palestinian intifada in December 2000, al-Manar found a new purpose. It changed its narrow image from being the channel of the resistance into a wider image of being the channel of Arabs and Muslims. Within a matter of weeks of the onset of the Intifada, the station's exhaustive coverage and proudly pro-Palestinian stance made it the most popular station among Palestinians in the West Bank and Gaza, and with Palestinians everywhere. While most Arab and Muslim stations confined their coverage of the conflict to news bulletins and crying over Jerusalem, al-Manar opted for substance over tears. In addition to its own messages of support and regular raw footage of Palestinian Resistance "martyrdom" operations and attacks against the Israelis, the station offered endlessly looped footage of Hizbullah's Resistance ousting Israel, a kind of "how to" campaign that was intended to instruct as much as to inspire. Furthermore, hundreds of Sunni Islamists and Palestinian leaders were given free time and a political platform to voice their ideological doctrine, resistance plans, and anger against Israel. Many Israelis watched in astonishment as Arab and Muslim attitudes were transformed from passivity into militancy, while al-Manar television reinforced the image of the Islamic Resistance as the role model for the Islamists and Palestinians to follow in the war against Israel.

To this end, al-Manar television and Hizbullah together moved to mobilize Arab and Islamic media by organizing a second Arab and Islamic International Media Conference to Support the Palestinian People, which took place in Beirut September 18, 2003. It was a bid to breed a unified media strategy, similar to al-Manar's, in supporting the ongoing struggle in the Palestinian territories and targeting Western audiences to let them re-alize the legitimacy of the Palestinian struggle and resistance. The latest example of al-Manar's psychological warfare against Israel has been the air-ing of the Syrian-produced drama series *al-Shatat* (The diaspora) on the history of Zionism over a period of 136 years. It starts in 1812 and out-lines what has been described as a Jewish plan to dominate the world. The Lebanese and Syrian governments came under pressure for allowing the series to be aired, as the United States and Israel fumed over al-Manar programming. The United States and Israel described the series as anti-Semitic. However, the Lebanese government turned down the request of the United States to stop the series from airing, arguing that al-Manar is a licensed private enterprise that enjoys press freedom.[29]

2. *Lesser outlets.* As for other outlets, Hizbullah's radio stations, news-papers, and journals play a role equal to that of al-Manar in serving the party's cause. The al-Nour radio station and *al-Ahd,* a weekly paper whose name changed to *al-Intiqad* after being licensed, are the two main media outlets that inform and educate Hizbullah's constituency religiously, ideo-logically, and politically. In a nutshell, Hizbullah's Information Unit does not require its media outlets to explain matters and issues rationally but to enter into the hearts and minds of the party's members, supporters, and friends and to ideologically indoctrinate them.

The Syndicate Unit. This is a fairly new unit. It was added to the Ex-ecutive Council's units in 1996.[30] While Hajj Ahmad Malli heads the Free Professions in the Syndicate, Hajj Hashem Salhab heads the Syndicate Unit. The primary function of this unit is to guide Hizbullah's representa-tives in the various syndicates and associations of lawyers, doctors, engineers, workers, businessmen, faculty, and students. The Syndicate Unit thus hopes to penetrate and create autonomous enclaves in the civil society that work to serve the party's cause.

As for accurate figures of Hizbullah's representation in Lebanon's various syndicates and associations, these are not publicly available. Re-portedly, however, Hizbullah's Syndicate Unit has representatives in the Lebanese Labor Federation, the Lebanese Trade Union, the Lebanese Farm-ers Union, the Lebanese University Faculty Association, the Engineers Syndicate Association, and the Lebanese University Student Association.[31]

As for other syndicates, such as the Lebanese Lawyers Association and the Medical Doctors Association, Hizbullah has played a significant role in supporting friends to win the elections but the party never nominated a Hizbullah member to the committees of these associations.[32]

It is beyond any doubt that Hizbullah's Syndicate Unit has benefited from free space created in the civil society. Such free space has provided Hizbullah in particular and Islamists in general with an ever-flowing reservoir of new recruits and opportunities to propagate their message.

The External Relations Unit. The External Relations Unit is another new addition to Hizbullah's Executive Council. The unit was first headed by Hajj Yusuf Meriʿ in 1996. Now Shaykh ʿAli Daʿoun heads it. The primary function of the unit is to follow up on the party's day-to-day external relations.[33] Consequently, this unit may liaise directly with government agencies, political parties, and nongovernmental organizations. For example, the unit may send a representative to attend a meeting, sessions, or talks that may have a direct bearing on the party's projects or political activities. On the other hand, the unit receives representatives from parties, governmental institutions, and nongovernmental organizations who are interested in holding talks with Hizbullah on issues of mutual concern.[34] The record of this unit has remained somehow invisible and unknown in comparison with other units of the party's Executive Council. Perhaps this invisibility can be attributed to the fact that it is primarily the party's secretary-general or his deputy who handles political matters, internal or external. It is also the case that the final say on external matters within the unit belongs to the chair of the Executive Council. In short, the External Relations Unit seems to be a public relations office that assists the chair of the Executive Council.

The Finance Unit. The Finance Unit evolved from a committee known as Hizbullah's Finance Committee, which previously handled the party's financial matters. However, due to the expansion of the party's organizational structure, as early as 1990 the committee was transformed into a unit. At present, the unit is headed by Hajj Sultan al-Asʿad. Its main functions are bookkeeping, auditing, and spending, upon the approval of the Shura Council or the chair of the Executive Council.[35] Effectively, the Finance Unit, when authorized, covers the party's expenditures that range from members' salaries to all kinds of spending on its activities. It is not clear, however, whether the Finance Unit collects the party's revenues or funds directly or handles paperwork related to budgeting. Theoretically, the Finance Unit is in charge of direct collection of the party's revenues. Practically, on the other hand, the unit seems to have limited jurisdiction in this area. It appears that the party's leadership apparatus is in charge of collecting and receiving funds, in particular if they come from Iran or from Islamic duties (khums), paid by the believers.

Whatever is the case, the revenues or funding cycle of Hizbullah's activities come from at least four sources.[36] The first source of Hizbullah's funding is Iran, a fact that Hizbullah's leaders are not afraid of admitting publicly. "Iran's financial involvement in the bulk of our development and social service services is not a secret," said Sayyid Hasan Nasrallah.[37] While no specific figures are made available by the party on Iran's funding of Hizbullah's projects, it is estimated that the annual fund stands at one billion dollars. Reportedly, this amount does not include Iran's spending on Hizbullah's military apparatus and the Islamic Resistance activities. Such spending is believed to be higher than spending on developmental and social programs. Although it was said that under Rafsanjani's and Khatami's presidencies Iran cut its financial support to Hizbullah by almost 70 percent, Iran's funds and support have never been effectively cut off.[38] It is to be noted that Iran's funding of Hizbullah's social and military activities need not be approved by Iran's president or government. Most of the funds come from foundations and charitable organizations under the direct control of the wali al-faqih, Ali Khamenei, and those funds fall outside the books of Iran's Ministry of Finance and the power of Iran's president. Additional funds come from Iran's Islamic Revolutionary Guards and Iran's intelligence services, which are under the authority of Ali Khamenei, not President Muhammad Khatami.[39] Thus, an effective cut of Iran's support to Hizbullah has never taken place.

The second source of Hizbullah's funding involves what Sayyid Nasrallah calls *"huquq al-Shar'iyyah"* (legitimate Islamic rights) and the khums (one-fifth of one's annual income).[40] In Shi'ite jurisprudence, this means that it is legally binding on the believers to pay one-fifth of their annual income to the 'ulama', who are authorized by the supreme authority or marja' al-taqlid to collect the khums.[41] This practice, however, is not up-held in Sunni jurisprudence. The Sunni 'ulama' consider the khums to be a payment of the spoils of war, which existed only during the early days of the ummah, not at the present time. Regardless of differences between Shi'i and Sunni jurisprudence, according to Sayyid Nasrallah, "there are many Shi'ite believers who pay to the party the one-fifth," and "we have license from the Shi'ite supreme authority [Ali Khamenei] to collect and benefit from such khums."[42] In fact, Sayyid Nasrallah and Shaykh Yazbak are each a *wakil* (representative) of Khamenei over the legitimate rights in Islam. Ac-cordingly, followers of Khamenei's marji'yyah, wherever they are found, are bound to pay khums to the marja', Khamenei, through his wakil. The wakil in turn, upon authorization from the marja', benefits from the accu-mulation of khums. Although Hizbullah does not disclose figures about the khums, Sayyid Nasrallah states that "the funds are big, important, and they are spent on jihad, educational, social, and cultural affairs."[43]

The third source of Hizbullah finances is donations from individuals, groups, shops, companies, and banks, as well as their counterparts in countries such as the United States, Canada, Latin America, Europe, and Australia.[44] The donations are mainly solicited by members of the Associa-tion for the Support of the Islamic Resistance (Haya't Da'm al-Muqawamah al-Islamiyyah), which Hizbullah established in 1990.[45]

The fourth source of funds is Hizbullah's business investments, taking advantage of Lebanon's free market economy. While figures are not avail-able about Hizbullah's investments, reportedly the party has established a commercial network that includes dozens of supermarkets, gas stations, department stores, restaurants, construction companies, and travel agen-cies, in particular those that deal with trips to the holy places of Mecca, Medina, Najaf, Qum, and Mashhad; funds also are derived from offshore companies, banks, and currency exchange.[46]

It is to be noted that long before the "war against terrorism" that the United States launched after September 11, 2001, the party had been aware that its bank accounts might be frozen by the United States. As a result, Hizbullah does not keep its major funds in Lebanese or foreign banking ac-counts other than in Iran. Since, in accordance with the Shari'ah, the party does not accept interest from its money, most of its funds are kept in accounts in Iran's Saderat Bank in Tehran. This bank then transfers money to Hizbullah, according to its need, through its branches in Lebanon and the region. For practical reasons, small accounts that do not necessarily reflect the real assets of the party may have been kept in local banks under disguised names known only to the supreme leaders of the party. These disguised financial transactions make it extremely difficult to freeze the party's assets, unless the assets of the Saderat Bank of Iran or the assets of Iran itself are frozen. At present, the party does not seem troubled by the issue of the freezing of its accounts; as Shaykh Qasim said, "Let them [the Americans] search, they will find nothing."

The Engagement and Coordination Unit. Known among the party's rank and file as Wahdat al-Irtibat wal-Tansiq, this unit is headed by Hajj Wafiq Safa'. It investigates and handles normal security matters that have a direct bearing on the party and its constituency.[47] Complex security matters, operations, and intelligence, on the other hand, are handled by the party's security organ, which will be discussed in the section on the party's military and security apparatus.

The Engagement Unit collects information about acts that constitute threats to the party's interest, members, or property. Based on information received, the unit has arrested a number of individuals whose acts ranged from murder, robbing, and theft to political offenses such as spying, espionage, and surveillance. Those who are accused of ordinary crimes are arrested and eventually transferred to the Lebanese authorities. Those who are accused of criminal political acts are arrested and transferred to the party's security organ and most likely will be incarcerated.[48] However, it is to be noted that this practice, in cases where the offenders are Lebanese nationals, has been abandoned lately. Since Israel's withdrawal, the party's security organ has released Lebanese offenders to the Lebanese authorities but not foreign offenders, who might be kept locked up behind bars.

The Engagement Unit, furthermore, is charged with settling problems that arise between Hizbullah's members and the Lebanese authorities and others in society. In such a case the unit tries to resolve the conflict through mediation. Sometimes, however, mediation fails and tension prevails, thus leading to confrontation, as in the case of September 1993 when the Lebanese army shot and killed thirteen members of Hizbullah who had demonstrated with thousands of others against the Oslo Peace Accord.[49] Moreover, confrontation between members of the Engagement Unit and Amal over power, domination, and security matters was frequent during the late 1980s and early 1990s.

Finally, the Engagement Unit is involved in watching over the public activities of the party and its leaders. It provides protection for party members through hundreds of its members who act both overtly and covertly. By providing information, coordination, and protection, the unit acts as an early warning agency for the party's leadership and the security apparatus on potential threats and dangers against the party.

Politburo

Hizbullah's Politburo is not a decision-making apparatus but rather an advisory one that assists the work of the party's secretary-general and the Shura Council. The chairman of the Politburo is usually a member of the Shura Council or a party cadre appointed by the council. The size of the Politburo ranges from eleven to fourteen, as has been the practice since 1980s. At present the Politburo is composed of eleven members and is headed by Sayyid Ibrahim Amin al-Sayyid. He is assisted by a vice chairman, Hajj Mahmoud Quamati. The other nine members are drawn from the party's clerical and lay cadre. They are Shaykh Muhammad Kawtharani, Sayyid Nawaf al-Musawi, Sayyid Hasan Fadlallah, Hajj Hasan Hodrouj, Hajj Muhammad Fnyish, Hajj Hasan Ezz al-Din, Hajj Abdul Majid Ammar, Hajj Muhammad Afif, and Hajj Ghalib Abu Zaynab.

Functionally, the Politburo follows up on day-to-day political activities of the party. It plays a vital role in putting together the party's election programs, campaign committees, and alliances. In other words, the Politburo promotes the party's political interests and seeks support for its policies and programs.

The Politburo has a number of committees, created according to need. The most important are the Cultural Committee, the Palestinian Affairs Committee, and the Security Zone Committee.

The Cultural Committee, which was headed by Shaykh Muhammad Kawtharani (who now heads the Islamic Affairs file), deals with a number of activities that uphold the party's political outlook. For example, resisting normalization with Israel is the most focal concern and issue of the committee.[50] Teachers, professors, journalists, and businessmen are contacted and mobilized to be part of an association that represents different segments of Lebanon's society, to resist normalization with Israel and American cultural and educational influences.[51] Although the Politburo has not announced formally the existence of "the commission for resisting normalization with Israel,"[52] Sayyid Hasan Nasrallah has alluded to the presence of such a commission not only in Lebanon but also in Egypt, Kuwait, Yemen, and Jordan.[53] It is important, however, to note here that Hizbullah's Commission for Resisting Normalization with Israel does not mean dropping the option of armed jihad. Rather, armed resistance and unarmed means, such as resisting normalization, go hand in hand and the preference of one option over the other is determined by the circumstances.

Another important Politburo committee is the Palestinian Affairs Committee. Hajj Hasan Hodrouj heads this committee. It follows up on strengthening ties with Palestinian groups, in particular the Islamic Jihad, Hamas, and other Palestinian rejectionist groups. The committee is also involved in coordinating many of the political activities in the Palestinian refugee camps, in particular in Borj al-Barajneh, Sabra, and Chatilla and al-Bus in Tyre.

Hajj Abdul Majid Ammar headed the Security Zone Committee until it was disbanded after the withdrawal of Israel from Lebanon. The committee was created in response to the Israeli occupation of southern Lebanon. It has followed up on the conditions and needs of the displaced southerners and transmitted their concerns to the party's leadership. By the time Israel withdrew from South Lebanon on May 25, 2000, the committee supervised the return of the party's members to their villages and homes. The committee has been very active in coordinating the work of the party members in the "liberated" towns and villages. Many studies and plans were pushed ahead of time by the committee to respond to the needs of the party's constituency in the liberated areas. After the withdrawal of Israel, this committee ceased to exist.

Other members of the Politburo serve as consultants to party leaders, such as Hajj Muhammad Afif, who serves as information consultant to the secretary-general. In short, the Politburo acts under the instructions of the party's Shura Council and advises on important political matters.

The Parliamentary Council

The Parliamentary Council was established immediately after the 2000 parliamentary elections, to tighten party discipline and strengthen effectiveness among Hizbullah's representatives in the Lebanese parliament. In fact, Sayyid Nasrallah stressed that "being a Member of Parliament does not mean that Hizbullah's elected representatives are above the Shura Council's authority." [54] As such, the Shura Council is the sole authority on choosing Hizbullah's nominees to the parliamentary elections. Accordingly, Hizbullah's elected representatives to the Lebanese parliament are bound by the decisions and wishes of the Shura Council. Thus, they owe their position to the party's leadership and not to their personal stature. As such, their political views must reflect the party's views and not their own.

The size of the Parliamentary Council is determined by the results of the parliamentary elections. Hizbullah's representation in the Lebanese parliament was seven seats in the 1992 Parliament, eight seats in 1996, and nine seats in 2000.[55] At present the council is made up of nine members: Hajj Muhammad Ra'ad (chair), Hajj Muhammad Fneish, Hajj Abdullah Qasir, Hajj Nazih Mansour, Sayyid Ammar al-Musawi, Hajj Husayn al-Hajj Hasan, Hajj Muhammad Yaghi, Hajj 'Ali 'Ammar, and Hajj Muhammad Berjawi.

By having a parliamentary council, the party's leadership has made it clear that its members in Parliament act collectively under the instructions of the Shura Council. Their main function is to follow up, inside and outside the Parliament, on decisions and policies made by the Shura Council. They are not to make individual decisions or to take a stance that is independent from the party leadership's decision.

The Judicial Council

Shaykh Muhammad Yazbak heads this council. It consists of Hizbullah's judges and judicial officials.[56] The primary function of the council is conflict management and resolution within the Shi'ite community. In other words, members of the council resolve conflicts arising in Hizbullah's areas of control. The council rules on the people's violations of the Shari'ah. It also rules on disputes of a civil nature.[57] Hizbullah's judicial system will be addressed further in chapter 5.

The Jihad Council

Reflecting its ideological commitment to jihad, Hizbullah established the Jihad Council in the mid-1990s. Because of its importance, the council is said to be headed by Sayyid Hasan Nasrallah himself. It consists of a number of former and present ground commanders of the Islamic Resistance.[58] Reportedly, the council also includes a senior officer from Iran's Islamic Revolutionary Guards.[59]

The Jihad Council assesses the circumstances and decides on strategies and tactics of jihad. However, it is to be noted that the actual implementation, in the case of armed jihad, is left to the party's military apparatus. As such, the main function of the Jihad Council can be encapsulated as diagnosis of the enemy and the means to be used against it.

Diagnosis by the Jihad Council members involves identifying the danger facing the party or the ummah, the actors behind the danger, whether local, regional, or international, and the imminence of the danger and its immediate impact on the party. For example, the Jihad Council has identified the United States as a danger to Islam because of its support for Israel. The danger posed by Israel and its supporters is a prolonged one that, according to the council, aims at destroying the resistance in the region as well as the aspirations of the Islamic ummah. Another danger would be, for example, the peace process and normalization with Israel, which Hizbullah is determined to resist on all fronts. A third danger would be what is termed as "Westoxication"—intoxication by Western ideas such as nationalism, socialism, liberalism, women's rights, and Western democracy, which are seen as being totally alien to Islam.

As for the means of combating the danger, they range from the use of arms including martyrdom and fighting to unarmed political means that aim at conquering the state and society from the bottom. However, when armed jihad and martyrdom are recommended by the Jihad Council, the Shura Council has to obtain clearance from the wali al-faqih, who has the final say on such means of jihad. In a situation in which the ground rules preclude armed jihad, the Jihad Council members understand that their aim of jihad is not a zero-sum game. Rather, jihad, armed or un-armed, is a means to sustain a formidable challenge to danger whether it comes from outside, such as Israel and the United States, or from within the Lebanese state or other anti-Hizbullah groups. In Hizbullah's terms, the precise "dosage" of the jihad is to be left to pragmatic consideration, but it should invariably be preceded by mobilizing all resources so as to act accordingly.

THE MILITARY AND SECURITY APPARATUS

The military and security apparatus of Hizbullah relies on a largely in-visible organizational structure that makes it extremely difficult for its enemies to penetrate the party. Despite its inscrutability, some of the or-ganizational structure of the party's military and security apparatus is known.

Based on scattered indicators of the activities of the party's military and security apparatus, as reported in *al-Ahd,* Islamic Resistance commu-niqués or publications, and some interviews by Hizbullah's leaders, the apparatus is composed of two main organs: the Islamic Resistance (al-Muqawamah al-Islamiyyah) and the Party Security (Amn al-Hizb). Unlike the other organs of the party's organizational structure, the military and security apparatus is under the direct control of the party's Shura Council, in particular the secretary-general (see figure 4.1).[60]

The Islamic Resistance

The Islamic Resistance consists of at least two main sections: the enforce-ment and recruitment section and the combat section.

The enforcement and recruitment section provides the recruited fight-ers with ideological indoctrination that reinforces the party's beliefs in wilayat al-faqih and the religious command (taklif shariʿ) to fight the enemies.[61] Indeed, the most powerful symbol of Hizbullah's fighters is the martyrdom of Imam Husayn and all those who have followed such a path in Shi'i history. Such a belief in martyrdom has made Hizbullah's fighters willing to die for the party's cause.[62]

The combat section, on the other hand, provides training in martial arts, marksmanship, medical support, and weaponry. The outcome of training determines one's position in one of the four organs of Hizbullah's combat section. The first organ consists of what are known as the martyrs *(istishadiyyun)*, individuals who are willing to lead a suicide operation even when they are convinced that chances of escaping death are zero percent. The second organ includes the commandos or the special forces. This organ consists of Hizbullah's elite fighters who have distinguished themselves in guerrilla warfare. The third organ consists of the rocket launchers and fighters with experience in operating all kinds of weapons, in particular, surface-to-surface or surface-to-air rockets and mortars. The fourth organ is composed of regular fighters who also have sufficient skills to lead attacks but who are mainly in charge of surveillance, logistics, and medical support.

The basic element of Hizbullah's Islamic Resistance organization hinges around the collective *majmu'ah* interspersed throughout the Shi'ite region. Each group is self-contained and semiautonomous. Thus, if one is plucked from the main branch, the others cannot be discovered easily. In structural terms, groups communicate through military sector commanders who in turn communicate through a military regional commander who is usually a member of Hizbullah's military operational headquarters. Theoretically, the headquarters is under the control of the Shura Council. Practically, however, the operational headquarters is under the direct control of the party's secretary-general, who has the final say on all military operations.[63] Reportedly, Hizbullah's military operational headquarters includes top-ranking officers of Iran's Islamic Revolutionary Guards. Although the guards withdrew in the early 1990s, Secretary-General Nasrallah has made reference to their continued stay in some parts of Lebanon.[64] Without disclosing the number of the guards, the party's military apparatus seems to rely extensively on the logistics and military training of the guards. In this connection, Hizbullah's training camps do not have fixed locations. For purposes of security, they are usually relocated from time to time. Reportedly, however, sophisticated training of Hizbullah fighters, in particular its elitist commandos, takes place in the Islamic revolutionary training camps in Iran.[65]

Hizbullah's fighters are mainly civilians, which has made it extremely difficult for Israel to strike at them directly. The fighter could be a carpenter, farmer, worker, or student who is instructed at times to join his majmu'ah to participate in fighting the enemy. To keep those operations secret and discrete, the military operational headquarters of Hizbullah does not inform its fighters about the nature of the operations or about their timing. Once the majmu'ah is assembled, the fighters are instructed by one of Hizbullah's military sector commanders about the nature of the operation.[66] Following guerrilla warfare techniques, which will be discussed in chapter 5, Hizbullah has launched thousands of military attacks against Israel since 1982.

The Security Organ

This organ is the most discreet and covert of all of Hizbullah's structural units. A member experienced in security and intelligence matters, whose loyalty to the secretary-general and the Shura Council is beyond any doubt, heads this organ. The head and members of the security organ work covertly and are usually invisible to many of the party's members. Reportedly, the security organ is divided into two sections.

The first section is known as the Party Security (Amn al-Hizb). It is charged with internal security matters within the party and society at large. Its main mission is to prevent Hizbullah's enemies from penetrating the party's organization and to prevent dissension among party members. As such, information, reports, and files are collected on all individuals and groups who approach the party, in particular those who are suspected of conspiring against the party. Also, the party's security section keeps a file on all party members.[67] For example, the party leaders and members are required to inform the party's security section about their meetings, contacts, and relations with all individuals or groups. Reportedly, information has to be in writing, specifying the name of the contact, the place of the meeting, and the time.[68] Failure to make such a report might jeopardize the status of the party member, prompting action by the security section that ranges from expulsion to arrest. It is worth noting, however, that Hizbullah's members normally comply with the directives of the party's security section because of the doctrine of takalif al-shariʿ, and not as a result of fear. According to Sayyid Nasrallah, "Israel and the United States have made great efforts to penetrate our organizational structure through recruiting party members, promising them money, women, glory, and power positions." He adds, "But they [Israel and the United States] were always confronted with rejection because, for Hizbullah's members, there is a self-immunity resulting from faith, religion, and ideological commitment." In Nasrallah's view, "Hizbullah is a group seeking *akhira* (the heavenly world), shahadah (martyrdom) and *mawt* (death), so the members cannot be easily drafted by the enemies."[69] Accordingly, the synthesis of a powerful security organ plus ideological commitment by party members has made it extremely difficult for the party's adversaries to succeed in penetrating the party's iron-gated security system.

The second security section is known as External Security (Amn al-Khariji) or Encounter Security (Amn al-Muddad). The primary function of this section is to counter intelligence attempts by the party's internal and external enemies who aim at penetrating the party's structure.[70] Whether Hizbullah's External Security section has active cells in Cyprus, Belgium, Switzerland, Germany, England, the United States, or Canada has remained a matter of speculation by many reporters.[71]

Furthermore, it is not certain that Hizbullah's External Security section is an extension of Iran's intelligence, the Savaʾma.[72] Reportedly, the Iran-Hizbullah chain of security engagements was revealed during the abduction of an Israeli Mossad colonel, Elhanan Tennenbaum, on October 15, 2000. Tennenbaum contacted a Hizbullah sympathizer in Switzerland who is believed to be a close associate of one of Hizbullah's top leaders. The sympathizer, who turned out to be a member of an Iran-Hizbullah intelligence cell operating in Switzerland, provided Tennenbaum with inside information about the party. After several meetings Tennenbaum agreed to travel to Beirut to meet the Hizbullah leader.[73] Reports, however, are not clear on whether Tennenbaum was abducted in Switzerland and transferred to Beirut by an Iranian aircraft, or was abducted by Hizbullah members who waited for him at Beirut International Airport.[74] In any case Hizbullah denied the Israeli accusation of Iran's involvement, categorizing it as a "myth."[75] However, a German brokered deal succeeded in January 2004 in swapping Tennenbaum and the bodies of three Israeli soldiers kidnapped by Hizbullah for twenty-three Lebanese fighters and more than four hundred Arab detainees held in Israel.

Also, Hizbullah has denied any relationship with the Islamic Jihad (al-Jihad al-Islami), which was the main organ of Hizbullah's security apparatus in the 1980s.[76] Reportedly, Imad Mughniyyah and Abdel Hadi Hamadeh were said to be the masterminds of the Islamic Jihad suicide bombing of the U.S. Embassy and the marine barracks in 1983, and later in the kidnapping of Western hostages. According to Nasrallah, "There was an organization other than Hizbullah called al-Jihad al-Islami. It was made up of honest *mujahiddun* individuals. They executed the operations against the U.S. Marines and the French, and kidnapped the Western hostages." He adds, "Whether it is still in existence or not, to know we have to search."[77]

The Hizbullah military and security apparatus remains a powerful presence in Lebanon and the region, with at least five thousand active fighters and almost three thousand security personnel.[78] Observations of the party's activities and rallies lately suggest that this figure has risen to over twenty thousand fighters and five thousand security personnel.

MEMBERSHIP

Hizbullah is a combination of what Maurice Duverger and Giovanni Sartori call mass party and cadre party.[79] In terms of size, Hizbullah is a mass party; the number of its members is estimated at more than two hundred thousand, of which the absolute majority is Shi'ites. This makes the party the largest in size among all Lebanese political parties and factions including Amal. On the other hand, Hizbullah is a cadre party, with an elite leadership apparatus. Also, the financial dimension, which the party depends on, comes from the khums and donations of some wealthy members who follow the marji'yyah and wilayat of Ali Khamenei, not to

mention from Iran's massive subvention to the party.[80] Although the classification of Hizbullah as a mass/cadre party might make it seem similar to
that of conventional parties, the recruitment and socialization processes of
its members are particularistic rather than universalistic. The major char-
acteristic that sets Hizbullah apart from the conventional or secular parties
is that the latter rely on universalism rather than particularism.

Structurally speaking, the party's political and military apparatus is active in regions that mainly have a Shi'ite majority, that is, Beirut, Biq'a, and
South Lebanon. The Beirut region is headed at present by Hajj Ahmad Safi
al-Din; the Biq'a by Shaykh Ali Da'oun (former commander of South
Lebanon); and South Lebanon by Shaykh Nabil Qawok. Although northern Lebanon has no significant Shi'ite community, the party designated
Hajj Muhammad Saleh as head of the northern region. Each region is divided into twenty to twenty-five sectors, each of which includes tens of
branches. Members are organized into hundreds of groups that constitute
the main entry to the party. There are two ways for an individual to become a member of Hizbullah: vertical and horizontal methods.

The vertical method is the rule where the individual joins the party at
the entry level through the majmu'ah. The party's regional reinforcement
and recruitment section, however, makes sure that the new recruits undergo two stages of transformation before they become fully fledged party
members. The first stage is called the reinforcement *(ta'bia),* which lasts at
least one year. During this period, the new recruits are taught Hizbullah's
ideology and culture.[81] In other words, the ta'bia stage prepares the new recruits to follow the Islamic text as interpreted by Hizbullah's marji'yyah.
They are also taught to accept the legitimate commands of the party's leadership and above all martyrdom as the most important dimension of
faith.[82] Thus, recruits who demonstrate commitment, endurance, and loyalty to the party are accepted into the party's membership. However, it is
worth noting that the final acceptance is very much determined by the
party's security section, for without its clearance the new recruit cannot
hope to become a party member. As discussed earlier, the party's security
section keeps a record on each member, before and after joining the party.

Once the new recruits pass the ta'bia, they undergo the second stage,
ordered discipline *(intizam).*[83] During the one year of intizam, the recruits

are taught the party's discipline, reinforced by various assignments and physical exercise and military training. The end result of this process is determining the role and position of the new member within the majmu'ah at the branch level. Those who excel in military abilities will be fighters. Others will serve in the political and social units of the party.

The horizontal method, on the other hand, is the exception. This method permits individuals with needed specialization to join the party at the intermediate level—that is, the units of the party's Executive Council. In addition to their specialization, individuals should have demonstrated religious faith and support to Hizbullah's cause. Letters of recommendation from Hizbullah's clerics or other 'ulama' whom Hizbullah trusts indicate such demonstration. As such, letters of recommendation are considered as a substitute for the ta'bia that is a must in the case of the vertical method of recruitment. Still, a security clearance from the party's security section is required for this category before an individual becomes a party member. Those who join the party through the horizontal method are very few. Once the party approves their membership, they are tied to the divisions of the Executive Council such as the social, political, financial, or educational divisions. Medical doctors, engineers, university professors, and graduate students with needed specialization, in particular specialties in computers or media, are best reflective of those who join the party through the horizontal method. This does not exclude their later joining the combat organ, pending training.

Although figures are not available on the socioeconomic status of Hizbullah's members, my field observation indicates that Hizbullah's amorphous mass consists of two categories. One category includes the "oppressed" (mustad'afin)—the lowly mass constituency. As the most traditional sector of the society, they nurture a deep and abiding commitment to Shi'ite tradition. This factor, combined with their lowly socioeconomic position, makes them readily receptive to Hizbullah's message. Important examples include poor Shi'ite peasants of South Lebanon and the Biq'a and the urban poor of Beirut.

Another category or social class that Hizbullah members come from is the indigenous traditional Shi'ite elements of the petty bourgeoisie or occupational clusters such as shopkeepers, small and medium-size businessmen, small landowners, professionals, teachers, and clerks who are opposed to the dilution of Islamic ethos under the impact of foreign political, economic, and social penetration. They are devoutly religious people whose shift to Hizbullah is a consequence of their perception that the Lebanese state operating within the framework of the global economy is a threat to their religious identity and their economic interests. Thus, a segment of the Shi'ite middle class in the urban centers shifted to Hizbullah as Lebanese state policies failed to provide equal opportunity and development of a middle class united economically regardless of sectarian divisions.[84]

THE ISLAMIC CURRENT

The Islamic Current (al-Tayyar al-Islami) is connected to Hizbullah's organizational structure. It means the collectivity of supporters and sympathizers who share many of the ideas and activities of Hizbullah, without necessarily being members of the party.[85] In other words, in a multiconfessional society such as Lebanon, a loose structure seems necessary to attract individuals and groups to support specific issues, without imposing on them the party's ideology or structure. As such, inclusion in Hizbullah's Islamic Current leaves the individual or the group free outside the party structure, but within its umbrella to support a common cause as a "fellow traveler."

Within Hizbullah's Islamic Current is Islamic Amal, led by Husayn al-Musawi, a teacher by profession.[86] Another Shi'ite constituent of the Islamic Current is the Faithful Resistance (al-Muqawamah al-Mu'minah), led by Hajj Mustafa al-Dirani, former head of Amal's security who was kidnapped by Israel in May 1994. Reportedly, al-Dirani had captured the Israeli pilot, Ron Arad, whose fighter jet was downed in October 1986 over southern Lebanon. It was believed that al-Dirani held Arad until the early 1990s, after which he handed him over to Iranian intelligence.[87] In May 1994, al-Dirani was kidnapped by Israel from his home town, Qasrnapa in the Biqa'. He was released in January 2004, in a swap of prisoners between Israel and Hizbullah.

Beyond the Shi'ite constituents, the Islamic Current includes a number of Sunni Islamist groups and movements that coordinate some of their activities with Hizbullah. Topping the list of such groups is the Islamic Jihad of Palestine (al-Jihad al-Islami fi Filistin), followed by Hamas, an Arabic acronym for Harakat al-Muqawamah al-Islamiyyah, and last but not least the Islamic Association (al-Jama'h al-Islamiyyah) of Lebanon.[88]

Also, the Islamic Current consists of some umbrella organizations such as the Assembly of Muslim Clergy (Tajamu'a al-'Ulama' al-Muslimin), and the Lebanese Resistance Brigades (Sarayyah al-Muqawamah al-Lubnaniyyah). While the first one is a coalition of Sunni and Shi'ite clerics that works on bridging differences in jurisprudence,[89] the second consists of Lebanese Islamists and non-Islamists. Hizbullah formed the brigades in 1997, in response to those who expressed interest in fighting Israel. However, the party opted to have a separate mechanism and structure for the brigades independent from the party's Islamic Resistance.[90] Operations were coordinated between the two but the status of each one has been maintained as separate. Thus, being a fighter in the brigades does not mean being a fighter in Hizbullah's Islamic Resistance. Indeed, the separation was intended to prevent any penetration of the Islamic Resistance through membership in the brigades.

In conclusion Hizbullah's organizational structure combines religious, political, and militaristic units and mechanisms. The wilayat al-faqih doctrine and practice generate a clerical leadership that has the final say over the party's decision-making process. Despite the presence of lay members in the leadership and the administrative executive apparatus, the final say over the party's operations and policies belongs to the clerical leadership.

The leadership and the executive apparatus cannot be made secure without the military and security apparatus. Under the direct control of the clerics, not the laymen, the military and security apparatus forms Hizbullah's iron gate. Furthermore, such synthesis of religion and military points in the direction of future plans for long-term armed resistance, defying the argument that Hizbullah has shifted ground toward secular politics.

Finally, although Hizbullah's organizational structure is hierarchical and extremely disciplined, elements of flexibility in the party's leadership are discernable. This is reflected clearly in the ability of the party to move between the military and the political apparatus, depending on the circumstances. Put differently, whether a given situation requires a political response, a military response, or both, the party is well structured to handle it. Accordingly, one cannot but conclude that Hizbullah is an Islamist religious, political, and jihadi party, which makes it only vaguely reminiscent of conventional parties.

5

Operational Choices

Between Militancy and Gradualist Pragmatism

Hizbullah's ideology calls for combating the danger to the faith and establishing the Islamic order "by hand or by mouth" (by force or by persuasion), as dictated by circumstances. Put hypothetically, the more favorable the circumstances, the more likely it is that Hizbullah will resort to militancy and armed jihad in achieving its goals. Inversely, the less favorable the circumstances, the more likely it is that the party will resort to gradualist-pragmatic and unarmed means to operate within the confines of legality as defined by the government. To raise the moderate/extremist distinction is to disregard the fact that the choice of mode of action depends pragmatically upon the circumstances, as the application of jihad always depends on the decision of the party's clerical leadership.[1]

This chapter analyzes Hizbullah's operational choices, focusing on the local and regional political circumstances that have led Hizbullah to fluctuate between militancy and gradualist pragmatism, as well as the rationale behind preserving both modes of operations.

THE RESORT TO MILITANCY

The local and regional circumstances of the early 1980s were very favorable to Hizbullah's militant mode of action. In fact, there was no single power or serious obstacle in the way of Hizbullah. The divided government that followed the 1975 civil war in Lebanon did not have much power to prevent Hizbullah's militancy, which aimed at seizing power and establishing an Islamic order. Moreover, Syria, which exercised state-like authority over major parts of Lebanon, was forced out of most Lebanese territory by Israel in 1982. Accordingly, Syria was willing to accept any help from Iran, Hizbullah's mentor, against the hostile foreign forces—Israel and the United States—entrenched in its Lebanese backyard. Prompted by their local interests but equally by complex anti-Israel motives and strategic concerns, Iran and Syria encouraged and supported Hizbullah's armed jihad. Even Israel, which controlled more than half of Lebanon and forged the May 1983 Israeli-Lebanese accord—the second Arab-Israeli peace treaty after the 1978 Camp David agreement—had become an ineffective occupying power, unable to prevent Hizbullah's Islamic Resistance from neutralizing the results of the 1982 invasion.[2] As such, the preconditions for Hizbullah's exercise of its militant mode were all present.

True to its Islamist creed of armed jihad, Hizbullah aggressively adopted a militant mode of action from 1982 to 1990, primarily aimed at liquidating the foreign presence in Lebanon and building an Islamic order in its areas of control. The armed jihad employed by Hizbullah has included a variety of techniques, among them martyrdom operations, guerrilla warfare, hostage taking, and forceful seizure of power.[3]

Martyrdom Operations

The aim of martyrdom operations was to rid Lebanon of all foreign presence. The range of potential targets of foreign presence was wide, but first and foremost were the Israeli occupation forces, followed by the U.S. and French contingents. Initially, facing the Israeli invasion in June 1982, a loose cooperative structure emerged, known as the Lebanese National Resistance (LNR), which included a certain section within Amal, components of the Lebanese National Movement, and remnants of the Palestinian military presence, mainly anti-Arafat.[4] The LNR, which was commanded by Syria, was more of a politically convenient umbrella structure than a truly cohesive military organization. In the wake of the uncertain effectiveness of LNR operations that were unable to stop Israel's advancing forces, the then nascent Hizbullah launched its first martyrdom operation in November 1982, destroying the Israeli military headquarters in Tyre (see table 5.1).

Table 5.1

Martyrdom Operations by Hizbullah and Linked Groups, 1982–1983

Group/Name	Target	Place	Casualties	Month/Year
Hizbullah	Israeli military hdqtrs	Tyre	90 Israeli dead	November 1982
Hizbullah	Israeli military hdqtrs	Tyre	29 dead, 30 injured	October 1983
Islamic Jihad	U.S. Embassy	Ras-Beirut	80 dead	April 1983
Islamic Jihad	U.S. Marine compound	Beirut–Airport Blvd.	241 U.S. dead	October 1983
Islamic Jihad	French air force barracks	Beirut-Cola Roundabout	80 French dead	October 1983

Source: Author's data, compiled from various Lebanese newspapers and magazines, 1982–83.

Ahmad Qasir carried out the first operation, known by the name of Jal al-Bahr. It killed ninety Israeli soldiers and officers, as well as a number of Lebanese and Palestinians who were held prisoner in the complex. As for the second attack, it was carried out by 'Ali Safi al-Din against the new Israeli military headquarters in Tyre. The attack killed twenty-nine Israeli soldiers and officers and injured thirty others.[5] However, Hizbullah neither declared its responsibility for the operation of Jal al-Bahr nor named its executor. The reason was to protect Shaykh Raghib Harb, Hizbullah's leader in the Islamic Resistance who had mobilized the Shi'ite youth in South Lebanon for carrying out martyrdom operations, as well as Muhammad Sa'ad, Amal's resistance leader, who had a close relationship with Shaykh Harb and coordinated with him in the execution of the operation. However, after the assassination of Shaykh Harb in 1984 and Sa'ad in 1985 by Israel, both the responsibility and the names of the individuals engaging in self-martyrdom were made public by the Hizbullah.[6]

Hizbullah's martyrdom operations against the Israeli army not only signaled the birth of a new technique of armed jihad, but also, more importantly, were intended to disorient the psychology of the Israeli soldiers. While Hizbullah's fighters lined up for martyrdom operations under the command of the party's clerical leadership, the Israeli soldiers had to overcome their feelings of isolation and helplessness, despite their tanks and warplanes, in a foreign land.

The Israeli forces were not the only targets of Hizbullah's operations. A number of martyrdom operations were carried out against Western targets by underground groups linked to Hizbullah, if not directly controlled by the party. The first such action was Islamic Jihad's bombing of the U.S. Embassy in Ras-Beirut in April 1983. The operation turned the embassy into rubble, killing eighty embassy personnel and visitors, including U.S. agents in charge of security matters in the region.[7] Six months later, in October 1983, two suicide commanders, each one driving a car loaded with high explosives, attacked simultaneously the compounds of the U.S. Marines and French troops. Two hundred forty-one U.S. Marines and eighty French paratroopers were killed instantly in their barracks. The two attacks were claimed by the Islamic Jihad (al-Jihad al-Islami), which issued a communiqué proclaiming "death to Israel, death to America and the West."[8] Soon the campaign of martyrdom operations spread to Kuwait in an effort to compel Kuwait to abandon its support of Iraq in its war with Iran.[9]

The martyrdom operations were generally supported by the Muslim community, which perceived the American and French contingents not as peacekeeping troops but as supporters of Israel's occupation and the election of Amin Gemayel to the presidency, after the assassination of his brother Bashir, in September 1982. In fact, Lebanon's Muslim majority considered the election of Bashir to be a victory for the Christian Lebanese Forces, headed by Bashir Gemayel and collaborating with Israel's occupation army. To avenge Bashir's death, the Israeli and Lebanese forces entered the Sabra and Chatilla Palestinian refugee camps in Beirut and killed more than one thousand Palestinians and Lebanese citizens.[10] To add to the fuel, in May 1983 former president Amin Gemayel signed the Lebanese-Israeli accord that had been brokered by the United States and would have had the effect of converting Israel's initial military gains into future political and diplomatic advantage. The agreement, however, led to a bloody confrontation between the Lebanese army and the Islamist forces led by Hizbullah during which many people were killed in June 1983. As a result of Hizbullah's martyrdom operations, American and French troops were evacuated from Lebanon in February 1984. Moreover, Hizbullah's attacks contributed to the Israeli withdrawal from Beirut and Mount Lebanon into a self-established security zone in South Lebanon. Despite the fact that Hizbullah inched toward a gradualist-pragmatic mode of action after the Ta'if Agreement of 1989, the campaign of martyrdom operations against Israel continued until the withdrawal of Israel from southern Lebanon on May 25, 2000 (see table 5.2).

It is clear from table 5.2 that Hizbullah's martyrdom operations aimed at producing quick and favorable results. The purpose after all was to defeat Israel by attrition and demoralization rather than by decisive military confrontation. Furthermore, to the Israelis these suicide attacks indicated the arrival of a particularly deadly and implacable form of terrorist action, compared to the old established techniques of Palestinian terrorism that seemed amateurish in comparison. As one of Hizbullah's leaders puts it, "Neither their [Israeli] tanks, nor their jets scared the mujahiddun who loved martyrdom."[11]

Table 5.2
Hizbullah's Martyrdom Operations Against Israeli Forces, 1985–1999

Name of Martyr	Target	Place	Casualties	Month/Year
Abu Zaynab	Military command post	Khiam	12 dead, 14 injured	March 1985
Haytham Dbouq	Military motorcade	Tal-Nhas	25 dead, 11 injured	August 1988
Shaykh Asa'ad Berro	Motorcade	Qliy'a	25 dead and injured	August 1989
Ibrahim Daher	Infantry patrol	al-Jarmaq	9 dead and injured	April 1995
'Ali Ashmar	Command post	Rab-Thalathin	None	March 1996
'Ammar Hammoud	Military camp	Marja'youn	None	December 1999

Source: Author's data, compiled from Ahmad al-Musawi, "Shuhadaa wa-istishhadiyyin" (Martyrs and self-martyrs), *Al-Shir'a,* June 5, 2000, 33–34.

Hostage Taking

The success of the martyrdom operations paved the way for another technique of armed struggle against foreign presence: hostage taking. As in martyrdom operations, this technique is considered a form of terror that ultimately attacks men's minds by convincing the people that the revolutionary or militant movement is powerful and the state is weak.[12] Not knowing where the militants (or "terrorists") will strike can immobilize thousands of troops and disrupt the functions of government.

In fact, it was the very chaos of Lebanese politics during the civil war (1975–91) that provided Hizbullah and its allied groups with an opportunity to assert their dominance. With the collapse of the Lebanese army and the absence of a central government in February 1984, groups reportedly working under Hizbullah launched a series of kidnapping and hijacking operations against Westerners. The Islamic Jihad claimed responsibility for kidnapping dozens of Americans, British, and French in March 1984. Whether Imad Mughniyyah controlled these operations or whether he is still active and in charge of Hizbullah's external security apparatus is still speculative.[13]

Other linked groups, the Revolutionary Justice Organization (Munazzamat al-'Adalah al-Thawriyya) and the Oppressed of the Earth Organization (Munazzamat al-Mustad'afin fil-Ard), were also implicated in hostage taking. Both served as covers for Hizbullah's militant activities and held Western hostages. While the former claimed responsibility for kidnapping four university professors whom it described as spies, the latter claimed responsibility for kidnapping two U.S. citizens and four French television crewmen. Both organizations have been inactive since 1988.[14]

On the other hand, the Islamic Movement (al-Harakat al-Islamiyya), a seemingly independent clandestine group based in the Biq'a and headed by Sayyid Sadiq al-Musawi, targeted Saudi diplomats in revenge for the Saudi execution of Shi'ite activists. Though apparently inactive since 1989, the movement may have gone underground.[15] By 1988, the number of foreigners kidnapped in Lebanon totaled eighty, and some were held hostage for up to eight years.[16]

As for the hijacking of a TWA plane in 1985 and Kuwaiti planes in

1984 and 1988, Hizbullah was deeply implicated in these operations. According to some analysts, Hizbullah's intention in the American TWA hijacking was to secure the freedom of 766 Lebanese prisoners held in Israel, some of whom had participated in resistance operations. The hijacking of the Kuwaiti planes was aimed at winning freedom for Lebanese Shi'ites held by Kuwait for the bombings there. The hijackers killed passengers to demonstrate their power and resolve.[17]

Hizbullah's leaders have continued to deny their involvement in the kidnappings and hijackings. In the words of Sayyid Nasrallah: "The truth of the matter is that there was something other than Hizbullah, called the Islamic Jihad, who kidnapped the hostages. There exist videocassettes, communiqués that bear the signature of the Islamic Jihad. It is independent from the party. It is absolutely incorrect that the Islamic Jihad is a cover name for Hizbullah."[18] The complexity of personal, sectarian, and ideological relations with the external sponsors was reflected in the longevity of the hostage crisis. Syria's embarrassment over its inability to prevent hostages from being taken or to ensure their rapid release was obvious. The line between ensuring outside acknowledgment of Syrian and Iranian influence in Lebanon and being held directly responsible for events occurring there was not always an easy one to tread. Although the Iranian government maintained its distance from the operational elements involved, its influence on the hostage takers was deemed sufficient to prompt the 1990 U.S.-Israeli opening to Iran. Such opening culminated in the Iran-Contra deal in 1986, which proposed to release the Western hostages in return for American arms needed by Iran in its war against Iraq.[19] Despite the importance of Syria's role in Lebanon, the Iranians appeared to hold the decisive key to ending the crisis. Eventually, when Iranian national interest dictated that all hostages be released in 1990–91, neither Hizbullah nor its allied groups were able to prevent the releases from being pushed through.

Guerrilla Warfare

The terror campaign of Hizbullah only served its aim in the initial stage. It drove its enemies into retreat and created a secure area of control as a base for the party's growing guerrilla operations. It has been proposed by writers that where a solid basis for revolutionary organization already exists, "terror" is unnecessary, even unproductive.[20] In addition, terror alone cannot sustain a mass constituency and its support in the long run due to local, regional, and international complications that militancy creates. As such, Hizbullah's techniques of armed struggle have become more focused, guerrilla-type warfare, particularly after the party secured areas of control.

In general, Hizbullah's guerrilla warfare techniques share many similarities with other guerrilla warfare experiences. These similarities include local support, a geographic base, centralized and decentralized military structure, mobility, and military tactics (ambushes, booby traps, and quick military engagements).[21] However, Hizbullah's experience in guerrilla warfare is undoubtedly unique and different from others in at least two ways.

The first major difference is recruitment. Hizbullah's fighters have to undergo the greater jihad, that is, spiritual religious transformation, if they are to master the smaller jihad, that is, armed struggle that requires martyrdom. By overcoming one's self and earthly desires, through acceptance of the virtue of martyrdom, Hizbullah's fighters have been able to evoke alarm and fear among their enemies. The argument that "guerrilla warfare obviously is not for innocent youth motivated primarily by romantic idealism but for seasoned veterans whose living conditions are constantly in flux," does not apply to Hizbullah's guerilla warfare.[22] Hizbullah has made Muslim youth in general love martyrdom. In addition, to assume, as did Che Guevara in Bolivia or Yasser Arafat in Lebanon, that all that is needed for successful guerrilla warfare is the presence of armed men, seeking liberation from "oppression" or "occupation," seems to be an insufficient condition from Hizbullah's perspective. Trusted and experienced veterans and fighters are needed. But what was imperative was youth transformed into fighters and martyrs, who were able to march into the difficult terrain of southern Lebanon and the western Biq'a and launch successful guerrilla warfare against Israel and the SLA. These fighters neither preached liberation nor gave public speeches. They simply launched operations under Hizbullah's banner of the taklif of the wilayat—the religious command of the Guardianship. This is something that is rarely found or is only vaguely reminiscent, in the experiences of the Palestinian organizations, or in other insurrectionary movements of the Middle East, East Asia, and Latin America.

Another important difference when compared with other guerrilla warfare experiences is the strict discipline that Hizbullah's fighters possess. Most important, as Hizbullah religiously and ideologically sanctions military operations, it prohibits plundering and banditry among the population in the party's areas of control. Banditry was one of the major problems that faced some of the Palestinian guerrilla organizations in Lebanon from 1967 until the eviction of the PLO in 1983. Instead of upholding strict party discipline, the Palestinian organizations were accused of turning into bandits as they subjugated the population in their area of control, particularly in South Lebanon.[23]

The Islamic Resistance (al-Muqawamah al-Islamiyyah), formed by Hizbullah in 1984, was a clear indication of the party's determination to pursue a disciplined armed struggle through the use of guerrilla warfare techniques; a task made all the easier by the continued Israeli occupation. By the time the suicide attacks forced the Americans and the French troops into full retreat from Lebanon, and the Israeli forces into the security zone, Hizbullah had moved to expand its geographic base necessary for guerrilla warfare. At first, the Ba'albek-Hirmil district of the Biq'a served as an ideal sanctuary for Hizbullah's resistance. This rugged terrain, which previously impeded the movement of Lebanese government troops, was in fact not occupied by Israel. The area is near the border of friendly Syria, which allowed a supply line of logistical support to run from Iran to Hizbullah's guerrillas. Equally important, the makeup of the local population, totally Shi'ite and organized along kinship networks, was extremely advantageous for recruitment, information, and refuge. As a matter of fact, the vast majority of Hizbullah's leaders came from the towns and cities of Ba'albek-Hirmil. Shaykh Subhi al-Tufayli, Sayyid Abbas al-Musawi, Sayyid Husayn al-Musawi, and Sayyid Ibrahim Amin al-Sayyid came from Brital, Nabi-sheet, and Ba'albek.[24] Through their kinship networks in the various towns and villages of the district, Hizbullah's leaders recruited members and solicited support for the party's cause.

While the Ba'albek-Hirmil district remained a base of Hizbullah's guerrilla resistance, in 1984 Beirut's "liberated" southern suburbs became the political headquarters of the party. It is from these two bases that Hizbullah was able to control and direct its guerrilla warfare against Israel. With the rise of the Islamic Resistance in South Lebanon, Israel unilaterally withdrew its forces to a self-proclaimed security zone that it had occupied in 1978.[25] As Israel went about strengthening its Maronite ally, the SLA, to bear the burden of guarding and protecting the security zone, Hizbullah pursued its smaller jihad under the unequivocal banner of Islam and liberation of the land.

While it is beyond the scope of this book to discuss in detail all guerrilla warfare operations launched by the Islamic Resistance, table 5.3 sheds light on the number of Islamic Resistance operations that eventually led to an almost full Israeli withdrawal from South Lebanon on May 25, 2000.

Up until 1984, Hizbullah, together with Amal and Palestinian guerrillas, took part in the Lebanese National Movement operations against Israeli forces and their allies, the SLA. However, from 1985 onward, attacks were carried out separately by the Islamic Resistance, which Hizbullah created.[26] As table 5.3 shows, the Islamic Resistance operations steadily increased from 100 operations for the period 1985–89 to 1,030 for 1990–95, to a peak of 4,928 operations for 1996–2000. The drastic decrease, to 16 operations in 2001–2, was tied largely to the Israeli withdrawal from South Lebanon and to other reasons that will be explained shortly. However, the fact remains that the highest number of Islamic Resistance operations against the Israeli forces in South Lebanon occurred in the period 1996–2000. Of the 4,928

Table 5.3

Militant Operations by the Islamic Resistance, 1985–2004

Year	Number of Operations
1985–1989	100
1990–1995	1,030
1996–2000	4,928
2001–2004	16
Total	6,074

Source: Author's data compiled from *Al-Ahd,* Al-Intiqad 1988–2004.

operations carried out by the Islamic Resistance in that period, the largest number, 1,528, were carried out in 1999.

Indeed, the Israeli army became increasingly frustrated in its attempts to preempt Hizbullah's operations, which had become efficiently deadly after the mid-1990s. For example, the operation of Insariyyah in September 1998 marked the bloodiest battle ever waged between Hizbullah's Resistance and the Israeli army. Twelve Israeli naval commandos from the elite flotilla *Shayyit* were killed when they stumbled into an ambush set by Hizbullah outside Insariyyah village in South Lebanon.[27] While the destruction of the elite Israeli unit stunned Israel, Hizbullah turned the battlefield victory into a propaganda coup, capitalizing on the mix-up by the Israelis over the remains of their commandos, which were subsequently returned to Israel in exchange for the bodies of the Islamic Resistance fighters and prisoners from the Khiam detention camp. Shaykh Nabil Qawok, Hizbullah's southern commander, said, "It is still too early to tell the secret of Insariyyah. The Israelis knew that Hizbullah was aware of their raid but they did not know how. I say our presence there was not a coincidence."[28]

Whatever the truth was behind Hizbullah's information about the Israeli raid on Insariyyah, Islamic Resistance operations of 1998 like Insariyyah were a major turning point, representing an increase in operations carried out in 1999 (see table 5.4).

Table 5.4 shows without question that Hizbullah has done more to combat Israel than any other force in Lebanon or even in the Arab world. The year 1999–2000 is the most documented in Hizbullah's Islamic Resistance record. The party has referred to 1999–2000 as "the year of the resistance par excellence."[29]

As shown in table 5.4, out of 2,441 operations launched against Israeli forces and the SLA in 1999, Hizbullah's Resistance carried out 1,528 operations (63 percent), followed by Amal with 711 operations (29 percent), and the Lebanese Resistance Brigades with 167 operations (7 percent). As noted earlier, however, the brigades were Hizbullah's creation, launching operations against Israel under the banner of the Islamic Resistance. However, the participation of other forces such as the Lebanese National Resistance, the Syrian Social National Party, and the Islamic Jihad remained symbolic and otherwise ineffectual.

Table 5.4

Militant Operations by Responsible Group, 1999–2000

Responsible Group	Martyrdom Operation	Penetration	Confrontation	Ambush	LandMine	Attack	Shelling	Katyusha	Sniping	Unknown	Total
Islamic Resistance	1	6	10	19	58	1,165	255	10	4	0	1,528
Amal	0	0	0	19	5	586	92	0	9	0	711
Lebanese Resistance Brigades	0	0	0	0	81	158	8	0	0	0	167
Syrian Social National Party	0	0	0	0	0	2	1	0	0	0	3
Lebanese National Resistance	0	0	0	0	0	17	1	0	0	0	18
Harakat al-Jihad Islami	0	0	0	0	0	6	0	0	0	0	6
Unknown	0	0	0	0	0	0	0	0	0	8	8
Total	1	6	10	38	64	1,934	357	10	13	8	2,441

Source: Figures compiled from Hizbullah, *Safahat ʿIzz fi kitab al-ummah* (Glorious pages in the book of the ummah) (Beirut: Hizbullah Central Information Office, 1999), app. 1.

As for the type of operations used by Hizbullah, attacks topped the list with 1,165 operations, followed by 255 shelling operations, 58 land mines or roadside bombs, 19 ambushes, 10 confrontations, at least 10 attacks on Israeli settlements with Katyusha rockets, 6 penetrations, and 1 martyrdom operation.

The two most effective operations launched by the Islamic Resistance in 1999 took place during the months of February and March. The first operation occurred when Hizbullah fighters ambushed 35 Israeli soldiers from the elite paratroop unit that raided Birkat al-Jabour in the western Biqʿa. The military engagement between the two groups led to the killing of the commander of the Israeli unit and three of his lieutenants.[30] Days after the February operation, the squad of Slouqi Valley Martyrs of Hizbullah's Islamic Resistance detonated in March a powerful explosive device as an Israeli command convoy was traveling the road between Marjʿayoun and Hasbaya along the Lebanese-Israeli border. The blast immediately killed Brigadier General Erez Gerstein, head of the Israeli army's liaison unit in South Lebanon, along with two other soldiers and an Israeli radio reporter. The killing of the Israeli general was one of the worst setbacks of the Israeli occupation of South Lebanon and shocked the Israeli public, who were weary of the Lebanon quagmire.[31] Hizbullah secretary-general Sayyid Nasrallah hailed the Islamic Resistance as "victorious" in its killing of the top Israeli commander, saying, "With the killing of the wretched Zionist general falls the great myth."[32]

As the Islamic Resistance continued its guerrilla warfare against the Israeli army, Hizbullah tightened the screws on the SLA. In fact, the twenty-five-hundred-strong militia was in disarray. Its militiamen suffered from low morale after Hizbullah's successful guerrilla warfare against the Israeli army. It also suffered a number of defectors, particularly from its intelligence service. When Israel pulled out from the Jezzini region, a stronghold of the SLA, in January 1999, General Antoine Lahad and his principal field officer were embroiled in a bitter discussion over the fate of the militia.[33] As a result, the SLA withdrew from the region, leaving behind them unanswered questions about their fate. However, in the wake of Israeli prime minister Ehud Barak's expressed intention to withdraw from Lebanon by July 2000, Hizbullah had dealt a severe blow to the SLA deep in the occupied zone. The Resistance fighters, in an operation later described as extremely sophisticated in intelligence gathering and planning, killed Aql Hashim, the SLA's second in command after Lahad. In spite of tight security measures taken by the SLA, Hizbullah's guerrillas reached Hashim's secured farm, planted a very powerful explosive device, and detonated it as Hashim was wandering around his farm. The blast immediately killed Hashim and injured four of his bodyguards.[34] The "execution" of Hashim as read by the Islamic Resistance communiqué led to the crumbling of the SLA and later to the collapse of the militia. Reportedly, Hashim had been prepared by Israel to replace General Lahad, who was angry at the Israeli officials because they were vague about the fate of the SLA.[35]

There is no question that Israel and its ally the SLA tried all destructive powers at their disposal to stop Hizbullah's guerrilla warfare operations. The Grapes of Wrath campaign carried out by Israel in early 1996, killing more than one hundred civilians at the UN monitoring site in Qana, did not prevent Hizbullah's guerrillas from carrying out their attacks. Although the April 1996 Grapes of Wrath understanding between Lebanon, Syria, and Israel succeeded somehow in the early stages in confining Hizbullah and Israeli operatives to the security zone and restricting them from attacking civilians on both sides of the border, the agreement failed to curb Hizbullah's operations.[36] On the contrary, Hizbullah, tacitly party to the written agreement, found by it an instrument to triple its guerrilla operations, particularly after 1996, a move that Israel strived to prevent completely. Both sides accused each other of violating the agreement. While Israel shelled civilian targets, Hizbullah bombarded the Israeli settlements at the border with Katyusha rockets.[37] The commission (consisting of the United States, France, Israel, Syria, and Lebanon) established by the April understanding and based at Naquora, the site for the UNIFIL headquarters in South Lebanon, received hundreds of complaints. The highest number of these was in 1999 during which Hizbullah filed 125 complaints and Israeli filed 85 complaints.[38]

Although Hizbullah has suffered heavy casualties for its guerrilla warfare against Israel, the overall ratio of Hizbullah casualties to those of the Israeli army and SLA, for the period 1982–1999, was almost one to one (see table 5.5).

Table 5.5

Hizbullah, SLA, and Israeli Casualties, 1982–1999

Name	Killed	Wounded
Hizbullah	1,248	1,000
SLA	1,050	639
Israel	200	300

Source: Author's data, compiled from Hizbullah, *Safahat 'Izz fi kitab al-ummah* (Glorious pages in the book of the ummah) (Beirut: Hizbullah Central Information Office, 1999), 530.

Compared with Israel alone, Hizbullah's losses are far greater. Hizbullah lost 1,248 fighters versus the Israeli loss of 200 soldiers, a ratio of more than six to one in favor of Israel. However, when Israel's casualties are added to those of the SLA (1,050), the ratio of Hizbullah casualties to those of Israel and the SLA becomes almost one to one.

As a result, neither the Israeli army nor the SLA was able to force a decisive showdown with Hizbullah. The need to get out of such a lost war was made clear by one of Israel's senior officers: [39]

> Show me a single case in history in which an army managed to occupy territory over time and defeat a guerrilla organization that benefited from a massive support and political backing from the local population. Even if unilateral withdrawal is interpreted as weakness, that does not mean it ought to be ruled out. There are plenty of nations that have already done it: the Americans folded in Vietnam and the Russians ran as fast as they could from Afghanistan. We can also get out. I don't think there is one sane Frenchman who is now sorry about withdrawing from Algeria. The truth is that there isn't a whole lot the IDF can do against Hizbullah.

As the Israeli rhetoric over withdrawal accelerated in 1999, Prime Minister Barak announced that "by July 2000, the army will withdraw to the international border that we will defend the north of the country." He added, "I don't advise anyone to tell us when we draw back and are sitting on the border." [40] However, the Israeli cabinet did not wait until July; it unilaterally withdrew its army to the international border. Overall, the withdrawal was not accompanied by clashes between the Israeli army and

Hizbullah fighters, with the exception of sporadic shooting. As the Israeli army and the SLA were retreating, Hizbullah's fighters entered the villages and towns that were once strongholds of the SLA and Israeli forces. The party was very careful not to turn the "victory" of the Resistance into bloodshed between Muslims and Christians, particularly in Marj'ayoun, Qliy'a, Khiam, Ain Ebil, Rmyish, and others. However, there were mass arrests of collaborators with Israel who, after interrogation by Hizbullah's security apparatus, were turned over to the Lebanese authorities.[41] More than 1,250 militiamen with their families crossed into Israel before the Is-raeli pullout was completed on May 27, 2000. The refugees, who were being housed in a camp near Lake Tiberias, complained about the squalid living conditions and expressed their anger at Israel. "Israel betrayed us. . . . We could have continued to fight Hizbullah for ten years without the Israeli army, but they handed them victory," said Etian Sakhr, known to Lebanese as "Abu Arz," the leader of the Lebanese Cedar Party.[42]

While the Lebanese people were celebrating the "liberation" of South Lebanon, squads of Hizbullah fighters began to detonate the Israeli army and SLA fortifications. Also, the guerrillas confiscated weapons, ammu-nition, and armored cars, including three Russian-made T-54 tanks abandoned in South Lebanon by Israel and the SLA. The war booty was transported to Ba'albek in a convoy greeted by delighted crowds that flocked through the villages of the Biq'a. The fifteen-hour journey to Ba'albek stopped at around twenty spots as people gathered to witness and celebrate what was described as an historic event.[43]

There is no doubt that Hizbullah's guerrilla warfare had not only produced the results desired by the party but had also made many in the Arab-Islamic world believe that Israel had suffered a major defeat at the hands of a few hundred Islamic Resistance fighters.

Contrary to speculation that Hizbullah would have no appetite to launch a military campaign across the Israeli border after Israel's with-drawal from South Lebanon,[44] the party renewed its armed struggle against Israel. In the aftermath of the withdrawal, Hizbullah set up more than twenty observations posts on Lebanon's border, stretching from the west-ern flank of Mount Hermon, near Syria, to the coastal town of Naqoura.[45] Organized in small groups of two or three, and equipped with mobile phones and concealed small arms, the Islamic Resistance fighters dressed in civilian clothes and set themselves up at former border gates between Lebanon and Israel and at newly created posts. Other members patrolled the border zone, using mainly motorbikes as their means of transportation. "We are patrolling and monitoring the Israeli movements at the border," said one Hizbullah fighter, staring at the disputed Abbad Hill near the settlement of Manara.[46]

Meanwhile the United Nations, through its secretary-general, Kofi Annan, and his Middle East assistant, Terje Rod Larson, ruled that Israel had withdrawn from southern Lebanon according to Security Council Resolution 425 of March 19, 1978. The United Nations also judged that Resolution 425 does not apply to Shebʿa Farms—an area claimed by the Lebanese government that covers 250 square kilometers (100 square miles), contains the equivalent of some fourteen farms, and has four important water resources that feed into the Jordanian basin and the Sea of Galilee.[47] The United Nations argued that Shebʿa Farms is a Syrian-held territory that was occupied by Israel in 1967. Accordingly, its status would be resolved according to Security Council Resolution 242 of June 1967.

Despite Syria's implicit acceptance of the UN ruling, the Lebanese government argued that the land was Lebanon's. For its part, Hizbullah vowed that the Islamic Resistance would continue its struggle against Israel until Israel withdrew from Shebʿa Farms, released nineteen Lebanese prisoners it was holding (released in January 2004), and stopped its aggression against civilians.[48] After the Israeli withdrawal from South Lebanon, the gap between Syria and Israel over a peace deal remained wide, and Syria held its acceptance of the UN ruling in abeyance. In fact, Syria feared such acceptance would disassociate it from the Lebanese track—an attempt by Israel that has been resisted since 1982. Instead, President Bashar al-Assad backed the Lebanese government's claim of ownership of the Shebʿa Farms by having his foreign minister, Farouk al-Sharʿa, confirm to the UN's Treje Rod Larson that the land was Lebanon's.[49]

As the Lebanese claim was being investigated by the UN, Hizbullah skillfully maneuvered its plans for Shebʿa by organizing hundreds of stone throwers and demonstrators at the border in a tactical attempt to further guerrilla warfare. Instead of outright confrontation with the Israeli army at the border, Hizbullah opted for an ambush operation. On October 7, 2000, hundreds of Palestinians and Lebanese demonstrated near the border gate, Marwahin. The demonstration turned into a bloody protest when two Palestinians were shot dead by the Israeli soldiers.[50] As the Israeli army was focused on Marwahin, Hizbullah struck in the Shebʿa Farms area. The party's guerrillas cut through the Israeli security fence of Shebʿa Farms and captured three Israeli soldiers. The soldiers were traveling along the border in a military vehicle. When they reached the south of the village of Shebʿa, they came under fire from Hizbullah's guerrillas, who were armed with rockets and machine guns. The ambush was accompanied by heavy bombardment from nearby Hizbullah artillery. The three captured Israeli soldiers were then bundled together into a waiting civilian car on the Lebanese side of the border and transferred to an unknown location.[51]

In the midst of confusion over the fate of the three Israeli soldiers, Hizbullah's External Security on October 16 kidnapped an Israeli army colonel, Elhanan Tennenbaum. As discussed in chapter 4, Hizbullah, in collaboration with Iran's intelligence service, seized him in Lebanon. Sayyid Nasrallah dedicated both operations as gifts to the detainees, the martyrs, and the wounded of the Palestinian Intifada of 2000. The United Nations and European countries, in particular Germany, France, and Russia, attempted to gain the release of the Israeli soldiers in exchange for Lebanese prisoners held in Israeli prisons, but they failed. When Sayyid Nasrallah insisted that the Israeli soldiers would be released in exchange not only for the twenty-three Lebanese detainees but for all Arab prisoners, Israel rejected Hizbullah's demands and insisted that its three captured soldiers and the colonel be released. In addition, Israel demanded information about three soldiers who had been missing since 1982 and Airman Ron Arad, whose fighter bomber crashed in Lebanon in 1986.

Despite the insistence of the two parties on their demands, the German-brokered negotiation, which started as early as 1999, succeeded in January 2004 in completing a first stage of a prisoner swap between Hizbullah and Israel. In exchange for the bodies of the three Israeli soldiers kidnapped in the Shebʿa Farms and Israeli former colonel Elhanan Tennenbaum, Hizbullah recovered at least 435 live prisoners (23 Lebanese, 12 Arabs, and 400 Palestinians) and the bodies of fighters belonging to

Hizbullah and other Lebanese leftist factions. The deal includes a second phase that is expected to include swapping Ron Arad or his body for the bodies of four Iranian diplomats killed during the Israeli invasion and for Samir Qantar, a Druze who is serving a 542-year jail sentence for killing four Israeli soldiers in 1979.[52]

Despite accepting indirect negotiations with the Israelis in 2000, the party's guerrillas stepped up attacks on the Israeli army in the Sheb'a Farms area. In November of the same year, Hizbullah's fighters detonated three roadside bombs when an Israeli armored patrol drove near Jabal al-Summaq outpost, southeast of Kfar Shuba. Three Israeli soldiers were injured as a result of the blast. The Islamic Resistance communiqué said, "In response to the party's decision to continue the path of liberation and our right in the Sheb'a Farms, Hizbullah fighters detonated several roadside bombs against a Zionist patrol, inflicting casualties and damage to the vehicle."[53] Almost two weeks later, on November 27, one Israeli soldier was killed and two wounded near Ramta in the heart of the Sheb'a Farms district, as Hizbullah's war to liberate the disputed territory intensified. Spiced with glee and shouts of victory, Hizbullah's statement said, "A unit of al-Aqsa battalion carried out an attack against an Israeli patrol to complete the liberation of the land, confident in its choice of jihad, and to recoup every inch of all occupied territory."[54] Accordingly, Hizbullah's guerrillas have continued their war against Israel since December 2001 by carrying out sporadic attacks to oust the Israelis from the Sheb'a Farms. The attacks also combined numerous flash points along the border, including Wazzani Springs, Ghajar, Abbasiyyah, and the Seven Villages. Holding Lebanon and Syria responsible for the escalation of Hizbullah attacks along the border, Israeli jet fighters raided Hizbullah and Syrian positions, including Kfar Shuba, Kfar Killa, Syrian radar sites in the Biq'a, and Ain al-Sahib, which reportedly was a training camp in Syria for Hamas and the Islamic Jihad.[55] The escalation of the conflict between Israel and Hizbullah has almost brought the whole region into a full-scale war.

Although the number of Hizbullah's guerrilla operations has been far less in comparison to operations before the Israeli withdrawal, Hizbullah has proved to be a much slyer enemy than the PLO, which has presented

Israel with a Catch-22. On the one hand, if Israel responds forcefully to Hizbullah's deadly ambushes, Israel has to pay with heavy casualties. The spectre of long-range Katyusha rockets raining down on the entire Galilee district and such major cities as Haifa, Tiberias, and Nahariya has frightened Israel into withholding a massive response to Hizbullah's guerrilla operations. According to a Tel Aviv newspaper, Hizbullah set up a belt of mobile multibarreled rocket launchers along Israel's northern flank, ready to go off the moment Israel launches a large-scale military offensive against Lebanon.[56] In addition, Fajr-3, an Iranian-manufactured third-generation Katyusha rocket with a forty-five-kilometer range was provided to Hizbullah months before Israel withdrew from South Lebanon. The fact that around ten thousand of these rockets are now stationed closer to the border constitutes a threat to the Galilee region.

On the other hand, should Israel not respond, Hizbullah guerrilla warfare will continue. There is no buffer to ward off an attack by Hizbullah, an attack that has the backing of Iran and of Syria, whose president, Bashar al-Assad, has no option now, in the absence of peace, of dealing with Israel. Although the "blue line" that the UN drew along the Lebanese-Israeli border, acknowledged by Syria and Lebanon, is meant to be a buffer to guarantee security, Hizbullah does not recognize it. "We acknowledge neither blue nor green lines. We believe in lines and decisions that bring back our occupied land in the Shebʿa Farms area and elsewhere," said Shaykh Nabil Qawok.[57] This position addresses the continuity of Hizbullah's guerrilla warfare not only in Shebʿa Farms but also in the Golan Heights, and perhaps even in all of "occupied Palestine" as described by Hizbullah.

Hizbullah thus has positioned its Islamic Resistance at the forefront, as a role model, fighting the Israeli occupation for the Arab-Islamic world. Most political decisions, especially when they are critical to the country's security, involve an element of risk, a risk that can be calculated. It is this calculation that makes a difference between a risky decision and a gamble. In the case of Hizbullah's guerrilla warfare, the worst-case scenario is that Israel abandons any balanced action, setting off a chain reaction—the very response Hizbullah and, in particular, its shrewd secretary-general, Nasrallah, are looking for. As such, the balance of terror, not a zero probability game, which Israel wants and cannot enforce at present, has permitted Hizbullah to continue its guerrilla warfare. The Palestinian resistance has followed Hizbullah's model of resistance to Israel since January 2002.

Forceful Seizure of Power

Hizbullah's militant mode also meant driving the state authorities and local rivals out of Hizbullah's areas of control. Hizbullah did not simply seek power; it sought power in order to build its Islamic order.

Aware of the favorable circumstances present in the 1980s, Hizbullah openly revolted against the Lebanese state. In fact, it was the very chaos of Lebanese politics that provided Hizbullah with the means to assert its power. In 1983 President Amin Gemayel sought to consolidate the state's power. He ordered the Lebanese army to control the eastern region between Ba'albek and Brital, Hizbullah's stronghold. Gemayel's intention was to limit Hizbullah's military activities in the region.[58] A violent battle between Hizbullah and the Lebanese army at the intersection of Taybe broke out, and many people were killed or wounded on both sides. In the end Hizbullah succeeded in keeping the area under its control, and the Lebanese army retreated to its barracks in the city of Ba'albek.[59]

However, the confrontation between the Lebanese state and Hizbullah resumed in February 1989. The Lebanese army shelled the southern suburbs of Beirut, in an attempt to eradicate Hizbullah's significant power. Nabih Berri, leader of Amal, who sought to secure his position as a principal leader of the Shi'ite community, objected to Gemayel's policies and publicly called for the Shi'ite members of the army—who made up some 60 percent of the rank and file—to resign.[60] This was followed by the nearly total collapse of the Lebanese army and the state's political apparatus.

Meanwhile, Hizbullah strengthened its positions in the southern suburbs and occupied the Lebanese army barracks in the city of Ba'albek. Reportedly, Hizbullah's fighters surrounded the barracks and requested that the army's commander capitulate. As the army was overpowered by Hizbullah fighters, the soldiers surrendered to Hizbullah, who confiscated their arms and ammunition. By turning the barracks into a military base, the whole region of Baʿalbek-Hirmil was seized by Hizbullah from the Lebanese state.[61]

Seizing power also involved armed clashes with rival movements, in particular with Amal. When Hizbullah effectively controlled the Baʿalbek-Hirmil region, it also moved to seize the southern suburbs of Beirut and South Lebanon. The struggle over power led to bloody battles from 1987 to 1989 between Hizbullah and Amal. In fact, the internecine struggle between the two goes back to 1982 when Berri refused to dissolve Amal and incorporate it into Hizbullah.[62] Furthermore, Amal led a campaign, supported by Syria, against returning to the pre-1982 status quo regarding an autonomous Palestinian presence in Lebanon. Hizbullah, in contrast, stood against this policy of forcible reduction of the Palestinian power on both ideological and political grounds. From Hizbullah's point of view, the "war of camps" led by Amal in 1985–86 tarnished the remarkable achievement of the Islamic Resistance that has always supported the Palestinian resistance against Israel.[63] At times Hizbullah actively intervened on the Palestinian side and otherwise provided the hard-pressed Palestinians with food and other supplies.

In addition, Amal's policy after Israel retreated into the security zone turned increasingly toward a pragmatic modus vivendi with Israel, in return for a tacit acceptance of the status quo. Amal's southern fiefdom of control was not to be used as a springboard for attacks on Israel.[64] Hizbullah, on the other hand, pressed for jihad against Israel under the unequivocal banner of Islam and Iran. Also, differences between the two with regard to the United Nations Interim Force in Lebanon (UNIFIL) were clear. While Amal opted for a cooperative working relationship with UNIFIL, Hizbullah considered it to be a means to protect Israel and a counter to the Islamic Resistance operations.

Differences between Amal and Hizbullah took a turning point in 1988, when U.S. Marine Lieutenant Colonel William R. Higgins, who was serving with UNIFIL, was kidnapped by al-Muqawamah al-Muʾminah (Faithful Resistance). The group is an offshoot of Amal, headed by Hajj Mustafa Dirani, who was security chief of Amal and became close to Hizbullah (see chapter 4). The subsequent kidnapping and killing of Higgins was a blow to Amal's strategy in South Lebanon and prompted a sharp offensive reaction against Hizbullah.[65]

Hizbullah's challenge to Amal and Berri's leadership complicated the Syrian-Iran alliance. On the one hand, Syria backed Hizbullah and other fundamentalist groups in their bid to oust the Western powers and Israel from Lebanon. On the other hand, Syria was not ready to stand idle as Hizbullah's power and influence in Lebanon expanded. In February 1987, after occasional clashes with Amal, the Syrian troops in Beirut clashed directly with Hizbullah, killing twenty fighters and provoking rage from Iran's top leaders, in particular then Interior Minister Ali Akbar Muhtashami.[66] Despite the Syrian-Iranian diplomatic efforts to end the crisis, the clashes between Amal and Hizbullah escalated into a large-scale war in May 1988. The fight, which erupted first in South Lebanon, permitted Amal temporarily to hold its grip on the region. Three months later, fighting erupted in the southern suburbs of Beirut, and Amal was badly defeated, virtually retreating to Shi'ite enclaves in the capital. In the fall of 1988, Hizbullah attempted again to rule out Amal in South Lebanon. This time Hizbullah fighters succeeded in eroding Amal's strongholds in Iqlim al-Tufah in South Lebanon.[67] Although several thousand Shi'ites from both sides were killed, Hizbullah has persisted in calling the fight *"fitnah"* (strife) rather than jihad.[68] The fighting, which ended in 1990, with a cease-fire mediated by Iran and Syria, paved the way for the first deployment of Syrian troops in Beirut since 1982.

Having asserted its authority in the wake of the seizure of Ba'albek-Hirmil, Beirut's southern suburbs, and Iqlim al-Tufah, Hizbullah seized the Lebanese state's institutions in these areas and forcefully imposed Islamic law. This was clearly reflected in a code of behavior that required the indoctrination of individuals, whose everyday lives are patterned after those of the Prophet and the imams as prescribed by the wali al-faqih. The party also prohibited the sale of alcohol and pork and banned illicit pleasures. The mixing of the sexes was controlled, and women were required to cover their bodies with loose garments and veil their heads, to maintain dignity and avoid the possibility of temptation. Western values and mores were replaced by strict adherence to Islam's six pillars.

Perhaps the most important mechanisms of Islamic law imposed by

Hizbullah were adjudication, arbitration, and, to some extent, mediation. Adjudication or judicial settlement is undoubtedly the best-known or preferred mechanism for bringing violators of the law to justice and settling conflicts among people. Unlike Western law, the Shari'ah does not differentiate between civil and religious obligations. As such, the Shari'ah court and the *qadi* (judge) in particular have jurisdiction that covers all fields of law. This was very much evident in the Hizbullah courts that imposed law and order in Hizbullah's areas of control (see figure 5.1).[69]

Figure 5.1 shows clearly the institutional, territorial, and jurisdictional divisions of Hizbullah's courts. Hizbullah's municipal courts are found in the regions of Beirut, the Biq'a, and South Lebanon. "The municipal court is actually less than a court. It is more of a committee headed by a judge or a delegated party official who is usually a shaykh, and who is aided by party members," according to Shaykh Qasim.[70] The jurisdiction of the mu-

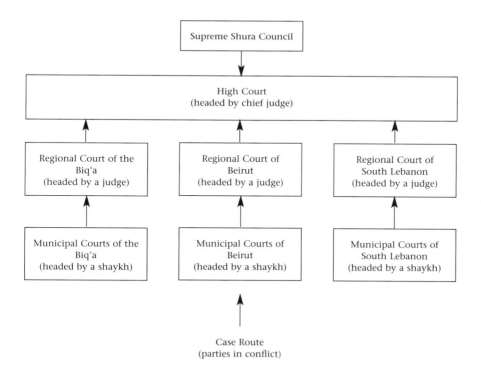

Figure 5.1. Institutional and Territorial Divisions of Hizbullah's Judicial System

nicipal court, whether in a city or a village, is over minor disputes such as family quarrels, misdemeanors, landlord-tenant disagreements, and traffic accidents. Decisions of the court are legally binding.

Complex cases such as divorce, inheritance, custody, property disputes, business contracts, trade, theft, adultery, homosexuality, prostitution, and homicide are forwarded by the municipal court to the party's regional court. This court is headed by a qadi. The chief judge of the High Court nominates judges for Hizbullah's regional courts, and the Shura Council appoints them. The judges of the regional courts should be muqallids who have demonstrated knowledge of the Shari'ah.[71] Decisions of the regional courts on complex issues or conflicts are final.

The High Court, on the other hand, is the supreme court of Hizbullah's judicial system. A chief judge, called *al-qadi al-markazi*, heads it. He is appointed by the Shura Council from among senior muqallids or high-ranking 'ulama' such as a mujtahid. The High Court has wide jurisdiction, and the chief judge may receive appellate cases from the regional courts if he is convinced that an individual has been wronged by the judgment of the court below. The High Court has specific jurisdiction over espionage, treason, and crimes committed against the party or its members. The chief judge's ruling is final because "it is religion that makes it incumbent upon every judge to enforce hukm Allah as came in the divine Shari'ah."[72] As for enforcement of Hizbullah's court decisions, they have ranged from warnings to arrest, imprisonment, and execution.[73] Hizbullah's courts rule on many cases and conflicts among disputants within Hizbullah's areas of control.[74] For example, one of the major rulings of Hizbullah's High Court was the execution of eleven people, including one woman, who were involved in detonating a car bomb on March 8, 1985, in Beir al-Abd near the home of Sayyid Muhammad Husayn Fadlallah, killing sixty people and wounding more than two hundred. After extensive investigation by the party's security apparatus, the "murderers" were put on trial before Hizbullah's chief judge, who applied hukm Allah (God's rule). The prisoners were sentenced to death, after they admitted their involvement.[75] Since that time, Hizbullah has accused the CIA and the Lebanese army intelligence of responsibility. Other examples of Hizbullah's High Court verdicts included the execution of a teenage boy who killed a woman and her two children in Ba'albek in 1995, not to mention the imprisonment of hundreds of individuals who violated the Islamic code of behavior.[76]

As for the procedures of Hizbullah's judicial system, the judge, in contrast to the common law courts, is not bound by case analogy. The judge does not have to follow precedents or decisions of previous cases. The significance of Muslim courts in general and Hizbullah's courts in particular is further highlighted by the absence of a jury system, which is a dominant feature of the common law courts. The judge applies the verdict of Allah by virtue of his knowledge of the Shari'ah. While the Sunnis commonly accept that the "door" of ijtihad is closed, the Shi'ites rely heavily on ijtihad as long as the Qur'anic text neither details nor addresses the issue at hand.[77] The mujtahid issues fatwas to interpret and enforce the Shari'ah, in the absence of clear Qur'anic text. As such, the role of the mujtahid is essential to the application of hukm Allah. However, in case the mujtahid is not present, a muqallid (a cleric who has the duty of accepting conclusions reached by a supreme marja') may preside over the application of the Shari'ah.[78] In other words, the opinion of the mujtahid is not binding upon the muqallid, only the opinion of the supreme marja'. In Hizbullah's case, both the mujtahid and the muqallid are bound by the fatawa of the wali al-faqih because he is the marja' al-taqlid, and his ruling is indisputable and irrevocable.[79]

Furthermore, disputants or the litigants need not be represented by lawyers in Hizbullah's courts. Litigants represent themselves directly and argue their cases before the judge. Most importantly, unlike the Lebanese court system and the J'afari (personal status courts of the Supreme Islamic Shi'ite Council), Hizbullah's courts offer free legal services. Such free services are provided not only to Muslims but to anyone who seeks the party's adjudication.[80] Of course, this practice is advantageous to low-income people who cannot afford the costs of lawyers in state courts.

Hizbullah also resorts to arbitration in resolving cases that are not considered to be matters of the "Rights of Allah," which include family quarrels, inheritance shares, and financial disputes. Crimes and patrimonial rights, especially guardianship over orphans, which are considered to be matters of the "Rights of Allah," are referred to the Shari'ah Court. According to Shaykh Qasim, "The Qur'an has stipulated that arbitration is not authorized in these matters, which must necessarily be referred to the Shari'ah Court."[81] Thus Hizbullah does not think of arbitration as *ilzam qanouni* (legally binding) but more as *ilzam ma'nawi* (morally binding). Equally important, ideologically Hizbullah cannot, as a Shi'ite organization, accept arbitration as legally binding because it does not accept the arbitral decision of the first conflict of political power between Imam 'Ali and Mu'awiyah, in which arbitral awards went to Mu'awiyah by giving him the right to the caliphate, a decision that has been rejected by the Shi'ites ever since. Yet, Hizbullah cannot reject arbitration completely because arbitration in family matters other than those involving the Rights of Allah are explicitly provided for in the Qur'an. Thus, the focus of Hizbullah's arbitration is on cases of everyday life such as family quarrels, reconciliation between disputants, calculation of inheritance shares, financial disputes, and neighborhood relations. Hizbullah's shaykhs and their mosques' imams have functioned as arbitrators on hundreds of such cases.[82] Their mandate, however, stops short when the issue involves the Rights of Allah, which require adjudication by a qadi. In any case, the decision of the arbitrators is binding upon the disputants only as long as they consent to it before the process starts.

Although Hizbullah's leaders and 'ulama' are aware that according to the Qur'an crimes may only be settled according to Islamic law, both Shaykh Qasim and Sayyid Ibrahim Amin al-Sayyid argue that crimes between *'asha'ir* (clans) of Ba'albek-Hirmil are settled neither by adjudication nor by arbitration, but by mediation.[83] One major reason for using the mediation mechanism for settling crimes or murders that are considered Rights of Allah is the tribal tradition or law that permits the victim's clan in "blood feuds" to pursue their vendetta on the third day of the murder and to kill in vengeance any kinsman of the killer's clan.[84] It is significant to note that in the early 1970s, Imam Musa al-Sadr, in one of his rallies in Ba'albek, had the clans swear "not to kill but the killer." In fact, the Lebanese criminal courts recognize the tribal tradition in the establishment of *musalaha* (conciliation) and *diyyah* (compensation) for the victim's family. If the murderer does not flee the scene and is handed over to the Lebanese authorities, trial and prosecution rarely proceed to the end. One major reason is that, due to mediation, the defendant and the plaintiff of both clans usually drop the legal suit after conciliation. However, in most cases, the murderer either flees the scene or is exiled and is rarely handed over to the Lebanese authorities.

The complexity of blood feuds among clans who usually prefer mediation over adjudication has led Hizbullah to use mediation, leaving to the victim's clan the right to ask for hukm Allah in Hizbullah's courts. It all depends on what the *wali al-dam* ("guardian of blood," such as a father, brother, or uncle) demands. According to al-Sayyid, "It is very rare that clans involved in a blood feud accept the judicial settlement of a court."[85] Hizbullah's mediation becomes a mechanism for restoring law and order among clans, despite the fact that it is inappropriate for application of the divine Shari'ah in the case of Rights of Allah.

Since 1984, Hizbullah has mediated more than two hundred blood feuds arising from murder cases, of which two-thirds were reported as resolved by the party's leaders.[86] It is clear from the various cases that Hizbullah's mediation involves a number of steps that lead to conciliation among feuding clans. First, Hizbullah's mediators, such as Shaykhs Qasim, al-Sayyid, and Yazbak, visit the victim's clan and ask the wali al-dam about his demands. The mediator's visit is understood as an attempt to prevent vendetta. According to al-Sayyid, "In preventing vendetta we avoid the use of force. In some conflicts, such as between al-Awad and al-Faqih clans, the vendetta was prevented and a truce was established through mediation. In other conflicts, however, such as the one between two families from al-Zu'aiter, we had to use force to prevent the vendetta."[87] In such cases, to preserve order in the community, Hizbullah will abandon mediation for the forceful imposition of a settlement on both groups.

Second, upon the agreement of both clans in conflict, Hizbullah holds the murderer. Holding the murderer does not mean imprisonment, rather, it implies keeping him in custody until the case is resolved. During this time, Hizbullah's mediator centers his efforts on resolving two main issues that are considered to be the core of the solution: the fate of the murderer, and the diyyah. As for the diyyah, it ranges from LL 20,000 ($15,000) to LL 100,000 ($67,000).[89] If the victim's family, however, forgives the murderer without demanding compensation, Hizbullah's mediator requires the granting of a diyyah to the victim's family if the murdered person left children. "Whenever the victim has children, forgiveness without diyyah is not acceptable according to the Shari'ah," noted al-Sayyid.[90] On the other hand, if the murderer or his family cannot afford part or the whole amount of diyyah demanded by the victim's family, Hizbullah has been known to contribute a certain amount of money to settle the payment of the diyyah. Without specifying the amount paid by Hizbullah, al-Sayyid notes that "out of ten diyyah cases, Hizbullah contributes to six." However, he adds, "our purpose in contributing money is social reform rather than encouraging crimes."[91]

The final step of Hizbullah's mediation culminates in conciliation between the clans in conflict. The musalaha is something of a gala event that is based on tribal as well as Islamic tradition. Speeches by Hizbullah and clan leaders are exchanged that reiterate the themes of faith, forgiveness, unity, and the shortcomings and negligence of the Lebanese authorities, the Israeli threat to Lebanon, and Western imperialism.

In conclusion, Hizbullah's militant mode has enabled it to drive out its foreign and local enemies from its controlled areas, seize power, and establish an Islamic state at the local level. True to Islamic doctrine, to enforce what is good and to prohibit what is objectionable *(al-amr bil ma'rouf wal-nahi'an al-munkar)*, the party has imposed Islamic law in bringing violators to justice and resolving conflicts among people. Throughout the 1980s, the political, social, and military structures discussed in chapter 4 were the means of upholding Hizbullah's Islamic order in its areas of control. However, with the changing circumstances of the late 1980s, Hizbullah opted to add a gradualist-pragmatic mode to complement its militant mode.

GRADUALIST PRAGMATISM

The changing political spectrum of Lebanese and regional politics by the end of the 1980s was not favorable for Hizbullah to continue its Islamist venture by relying only on a militant modus operandi. Lebanon inched toward a Syrian-guaranteed formula in the Ta'if accords of 1989. While Syria sought to maintain its traditional policy of balancing the different Lebanese factions against each other and keeping Lebanon within its direct orbit, the growth of Hizbullah as a potent militant force was problematic. On the one hand, Hizbullah formed the most effective instrument of proxy war against Israel and the United States. On the other hand, Hizbullah's project of installing Islamic order in Lebanon and its religious and ideological ties to Iran's clerics were potentially at odds with Syria's goal of pursuing its vital geopolitical and strategic interests in Lebanon. Thus, the Ta'if Agreement, which called on Syria to help Lebanon spread its authority over Lebanese territory, made Syria the key player in Lebanese politics.[92] As such, Syria's support of Lebanon's reemerging confessional system represented the antithesis to Hizbullah's militant mode. Of course, Hizbullah's leaders were very aware that the territories they held were at least logistically subject to Syria's rather than Iran's direct influence. Thus, their response to Syria's influence has been a policy of cooperation, accepting tacitly the Ta'if Agreement. However, the agreement by itself was a sufficient but not necessary condition that contributed to Hizbullah's adoption of a gradualist-pragmatic mode, which sought to operate within the confines of legality as defined by the Lebanese government.

In fact, Hizbullah gradualist pragmatism was largely tied to Iran and, in particular, the wali al-faqih, Ayatollah Ali Khamenei. The wali al-faqih can legitimately elaborate, mold, or alter the party's guiding ideology to fit the changing circumstances. The ascendance of Khamenei to the position of wali al-faqih and Hashemi Rafsanjani to the presidency, after the death of Ayatollah Khomeini in 1989, contributed to the emergence of a pragmatic course of action in Iran. This approach avoided direct confrontation with the West and leaned toward rapprochement policies with the Arab countries, without abandoning the Islamic revolutionary posture. Rafsanjani's pragmatic course, which was supported by Khamenei, clashed with that favored by Ali Akbar Muhtashami and Shaykh Hasan Kharoubi, who pushed for a more militant mode of action toward the West.[93] The differences over the mode of action, as well as the struggle for power among Iran's top leaders, were mirrored in Hizbullah's leadership as reflected in its first extraordinary conclave in 1989 in Tehran, attended by two hundred delegates.

At least two major factions were reported to be at the center of a major debate on the future of Hizbullah in Lebanon. It was reported that Shaykh

Subhi al Tufayli and Sayyid Abbas al-Musawi advocated rapprochement policies, as opposed to Sayyid Hasan Nasrallah and others who supported militant ones;[94] however, further research does not support the validity of these reports. In fact, it was Shaykh al-Tufayli and Sayyid Husayn al-Musawi who sought to keep Hizbullah in a state of perpetual jihad against all those who opposed their vision of an Islamic order. They pressed for tighter party discipline and limited contacts with outside groups. Al-Tufayli's faction seemed to represent Muhtashami, Iran's former interior minister.[95] The second faction, on the other hand, representing the major-ity of the party's cadre and led by Sayyid Abbas al-Musawi and Sayyid Nasrallah, favored, in addition to the militant mode, a gradualist-pragmatic mode. For this faction, whatever the exact modus operandi, their goal of seizing political power and establishing a society and regime governed by the Shari'ah is the same. For this group a gradualist-pragmatic mode would be parallel to the militant mode, and the use of any mode would depend on the circumstances.[96] This was a position identified with the views of Khamenei, who urged Hizbullah to seek a foothold within the Lebanese system. However, the decisions of Hizbullah's Tehran conclave were not risk free.

Although Sayyid Abbas al-Musawi's faction emerged victorious, Shaykh al-Tufayli was allowed by Khamenei to continue his term as secre-tary-general, in order to prevent dissension within the party. With the end of al-Tufayli's term in 1991, the party's Central Council elected Sayyid Abbas al-Musawi to the secretariat post at its second enclave in Beirut. De-spite al-Tufayli's resentment, he finally accepted the decision of the party, which acted under the instructions of the wali al-faqih. However, the as-sassination of Sayyid Abbas al-Musawi by Israel in February 1992 brought back the struggle over power among Hizbullah's leaders. Immediately, the party's Shura Council, instructed by Ali Khamenei, met and elected Sayyid Hasan Nasrallah secretary-general. The election of the young Hasan Nas-rallah alienated al-Tufayli, who felt that the wali al-faqih should have restored him to the secretariat position. For al-Tufayli, Nasrallah is not only young but he is also the disciple of Sayyid Abbas al-Musawi, with whom al-Tufayli had clashed over power since 1983.[97] Al-Tufayli found it extremely difficult to accept that his "sacrifices" and "devotion" to the party's cause had been ignored by Iran's top clerics. More likely, al-Tufayli did not grasp the role of the wali al-faqih and the idea that jihad is not just a one-way street limited to armed struggle but is in fact a two-way street of armed and unarmed struggle, as sanctioned by the jurisconsult.

Shaykh Subhi al-Tufayli's objection to Iran's power over Hizbullah escalated into dissension in 1992, when Sayyid Nasrallah called for participation in Lebanon's first parliamentary election after the civil war of 1975. The call by Nasrallah, which was encouraged by Ali Khamenei, supported the Iran-Syria alliance and inaugurated the beginning of the party's gradualist-pragmatic mode. Shaykh al-Tufayli reacted forcefully by calling to burn the voting centers during the elections. He categorized Nasrallah's decision as a bad one and against the nature and aim of Hizbullah.[98] To assert his power, al-Tufayli launched, on July 4, 1997, "the revolution of the hungry" *(thawrat al-jiya')*, during a rally that was banned by the Lebanese government.[99] Although the cause of his revolution was social justice for the needy people of the Biq'a, al-Tufayli's aim was to split Hizbullah and at least gain power over its constituency in the Ba'albek-Hirmil area of the Biq'a region. As he failed to attract Khamenei's attention and the party's mainstream, which followed Nasrallah, Shaykh al-Tufayli finally revolted with more than two hundred of his followers.

In January 1998, he and his followers occupied the religious hawzat of Hizbullah's Imam Khomeini, in Ba'albek. The occupation prompted a bloody conflict with the Lebanese army, which considered al-Tufayli's act a violation of law and order. At least two people died, including an army lieutenant and Shaykh Khodr Tlays, former Hizbullah Member of Parliament and son-in-law of Shaykh al-Tufayli, and many were wounded.[100] The revolt of al-Tufayli prompted Hizbullah's Shura Council to expel him from the party. Al-Tufayli, who disappeared with some followers into the mountains near his hometown of Brital, reportedly was encouraged by Syria to weaken Hizbullah's power in Lebanon.[101] However, the party has remained united behind Nasrallah, who reportedly rejected al-Tufayli's attempt at reconciliation.

Given Hizbullah's adoption of a gradualist-pragmatic mode of action, the party moved in the early 1990s to work within the confines of Lebanon's confessional system without abandoning its military organ. As

stated by Shaykh Na'im Qasim: "We are still in our armed jihad against Israel and its designs in the region. However, when the Ta'if Agreement took
place we entered the political life because every effort carried out by committed Muslims is jihad that is within the general jihad."[102]

Of course Hizbullah's jihad theory (see chapter 3) permits armed as
well as unarmed means of struggle. The nonmilitant mode is Hizbullah's
gradualist pragmatism that has been very much evident in the party's participation in elections and its opposition role in Parliament and capture of
local municipalities and councils.

Capturing Parliamentary Seats

Hizbullah, even when it enters the parliamentary elections or plays the
parliamentary game, does not believe in Western-style democracy but
rather in what Emmanuel Sivan calls "one man, one vote, one time."[103]
Despite Hizbullah leaders' occasional use of concepts such as freedom,
democracy, and human rights, God-given Shari'ah cannot be replaced by
such concepts, and *shura* (consultation) among Islamic leaders does not
equal democracy. Furthermore, being a member of a parliament does
not necessarily make one a believer in democracy. Rather parliamentary
membership for Hizbullah is a venue to seek political power and representation on the national level. The argument by some writers that "these
men [Hizbullahis] traded their camouflage uniforms for suits and ties, their
clashes for ministerial portfolios and their Qur'an for a profession in
democracy and institution" is not convincing.[104] In fact, playing the
parliamentary game is no proof of Hizbullah's support of Lebanon's confessional system. Rather, it is an opportunity to seek political power and to
protect the party's resistance in the regions under its control, while press-
ing for the elimination of the confessional system.

The decision of Hizbullah to participate in the parliamentary elections
in 1992 was symptomatic of the party's gradualist-pragmatic mode, coming to terms with its "political jihad." The party's success in 1992 signaled
its first penetration of the Lebanese Parliament.

As shown in table 5.6, in 1992 Hizbullah captured eight of the twenty-
seven seats allocated to the Shi'ites in the Lebanese Parliament, which is

Table 5.6

Distribution of Shiʿite Parliamentary Seats
by Hizbullah, Amal, and Shiʿite Zuʿamaʾ Families

Year	Hizbullah	Amal	Families	Total
1992	8	9	10	27
1996	7	8	13	27
2000	9	6	12	27

Source: Figures compiled from the election records of Lebanon's Ministry of the Interior for the years 1992, 1996, and 2000.

made up of 128 seats divided equally between Christians and Muslims. Although Amal and the Shiʿite Zuʿamaʾ families with ties to Amal leader Nabih Berri were ahead of Hizbullah and won nine and ten seats respectively, the extent of Hizbullah's success surprised Amal and its allies. In addition, Hizbullah won four other "allied" seats (two Sunni and two Christian) in the Baʿalbek-Hirmil district.[105] Together they formed a strong bloc in the Parliament of 1992. Also, Hizbullah was the first Islamist bloc in the history of Lebanon to enter Parliament. Of course, Hizbullah's success in 1992 did not occur in a vacuum. Several factors stood behind the party's success.

First, there is the presence of an ideologically committed constituency in Hizbullah's autonomous enclaves in the southern suburbs of Beirut, the Biqʿa, and South Lebanon. This constituency, under taklif al-shariʿ of the wilayat (the religious commands of the Guardianship) voted massively for Hizbullah's candidates.[106]

Second, the party's social welfare services made a difference in the life of many Shiʿites, in particular those of low socioeconomic status. Hizbullah's social, educational, and charity programs had helped not only the Shiʿites but the Muslim community in general, as well as a few Christians who had sought Hizbullah's services. Thus, it was not surprising to see many people rewarding Hizbullah by voting for its candidates and allies.

Third, the Islamic Resistance, in its fight against the Israeli occupation, has also contributed to the popularity of Hizbullah. Hizbullah's role in the resistance was properly perceived as being sincere, honest, and "heroic" in the fight with Israel, compared to the Palestinian organizations in Lebanon and Amal.

Fourth, Hizbullah's organizational structure formed the backbone of the party's campaign activities. The various organs of the party skillfully mobilized their campaign committees and their constituency to win the elections. Even when it was pressured by Syria to enter into a coalition with rival Amal in South Lebanon, Hizbullah's leadership and institutions stood firm in the face of Amal's hegemony, protecting its constituency politically and physically.

Fifth, Christians' boycott of the parliamentary election of 1992 may have contributed to the success of Hizbullah, as argued by some analysts.[107] However, Hizbullah would still have won in electoral districts with Shiʻite or Muslim majorities such as Baʻalbek-Hirmil, South Lebanon, and the southern suburbs of Beirut, even without the boycott.

The 1996 elections did not bring drastic changes in Hizbullah's representation in the Lebanese Parliament. The ratio between Hizbullah and Amal representation stayed the same in favor of the latter. Hizbullah representation dropped from eight seats to seven, and its allies dropped from four seats to two. Amal representation dropped from nine seats to eight, but its allies, Shiʻite notables, increased from ten seats to twelve. Despite the fact that Amal and its allies still have the majority of Shiʻite representation, Hizbullah's success in sustaining its representation was perceived as a great challenge by Amal leader Berri.

Gaining more political power in South Lebanon, Hizbullah demanded that the number of its candidates in the South Lebanon coalition list with Berri be increased from two to four, a demand that was rejected at first by Berri. Threatening to break up the coalition, Syria summoned both Nasrallah and Berri to a meeting in Damascus. Contrary to the belief that Syria was able to clip Hizbullah's wings, the party backed by Iran got what it wanted.[108] Syria was supposed to clip Hizbullah's wings as a sign of goodwill in its peace negotiation with Israel, and now found itself in a risky situation. The collapse of the Syrian-Israeli peace talks after Operation Grapes of Wrath in 1996, which killed more than two hundred people and forced nearly forty thousand southerners to seek refuge northward, made Syria reluctant to pressure Hizbullah, thus risking its relationship with

Iran.[109] On the contrary, Israel's Grapes of Wrath operation made Hizbullah's resistance movement more popular.

However, Hizbullah's popular appeal also sparked the formation of an anti-Hizbullah working majority outside South Lebanon and the Baʿalbek-Hirmil regions. While Hizbullah won with four candidates in South Lebanon and three candidates in Baʿalbek-Hirmil, the party lost its bid in Baʿabda district, of which the southern suburbs is a part. Christians and Druze politicians mobilized support for Shiʿite candidate Basem al-Sabaʿ; with little support from his own community, he won the election. Likewise, in Beirut, Hajj Muhammad Berjawi lost the election as Christians and Sunnis voted for a Shiʿite traditional family notable, Muhammad Yusuf Baydoun. The other Shiʿite seat in the capital was won by Amal.

Yet the 2000 parliamentary elections showed more clearly that Hizbullah was able not only to enhance its representation over Amal, nine to six, but also to perform as a first-class pragmatic player. Such political pragmatism was described by some Lebanese editorials as Machiavellian.[110] However, the fact remains that Hizbullah's political pragmatism, even if it is read as Machiavellian, provided support for the party to win and improve its parliamentary representation in a way better than those of the 1992 and 1996 elections. In addition to the party's committed constituency and its social welfare services that have contributed to Hizbullah's successes, Hizbullah has capitalized on two other factors for winning the 2000 elections.

First, the "liberation of South Lebanon" boosted Hizbullah's image as a heroic organization whose resistance paid blood and sacrifices in fighting the Israeli occupation. The Israeli withdrawal that became Hizbullah's victory made it extremely difficult for its rivals, regardless of sect, to ignore Hizbullah as a major political force. Thus, in areas controlled by Hizbullah, candidates cannot win without trading votes with Hizbullah.

Second, the June 2002 death of President Hafiz al-Assad, who had exercised influence on almost all Lebanese political factions including Hizbullah, removed an obstacle from Hizbullah's way when it came to operational choices and the freedom to act. Bashar al-Assad, who succeeded his father to the presidency, has not yet developed clout or a sphere of influence that helps him enforce his will or wishes over Hizbullah and on other Lebanese political factions. Nor has he been able to block significant Iranian moves in the Lebanese political arena. Reportedly Syria after Hafiz Assad has suffered elite fragmentation that requires its new president to spend most of his time managing his own house.[111] Furthermore, Assad inherited a deadlocked negotiation track with Israel that has further complicated his consolidation of power inside Syria and in Lebanon.

The convergence of these factors opened the way for Hizbullah and Iran to decide freely on the number of candidates, alliances, and coalitions with others. Hizbullah's unlikely alliance with Amal was the brainchild of Iran rather than Syria. Regarding the future of the region after the departure of Hafiz al-Assad, the liberation of South Lebanon, and the 2000 elections, Khamenei decreed that Hizbullah should continue its political pragmatism as well as its resistance against Israeli occupation of Arab lands.[112] On the Lebanese home front, Khamenei was very much concerned that Hizbullah's "victory" in its fight with Israel would turn into bloodshed with Amal over parliamentary seats, especially if "Western imperialism" might at a future stage provoke a conflict between the secularist Amal and the Islamist Hizbullah.

To cement the new alliance between Hizbullah and Amal, Khamenei's charities financed Amal's social welfare projects in South Lebanon and the Biq'a, including a rug factory. Sayyid Nasrallah has referred to this accommodation, saying that "the alliance marks the beginning of a new stage of cooperation. We have to teach ourselves to forget the past and look to the future where no one can eliminate the others."[113] Although Syria was content with Iran's newfound alliance, it tried to impose its will on Hizbullah's nominees. Reportedly, Damascus asked Hizbullah to nominate Husayn al-Musawi, leader of Islamic Amal, on the party's electoral list for Ba'albek-Hirmil. Although al-Musawi is considered a close affiliate of Hizbullah, his Syrian connections are much closer than Hizbullah's, which made his organization subject to Syria's interest more than Iran's. However, Hizbullah's Shura Council refused the nomination of al-Musawi, with the justification that decisions regarding election candidates are an internal party matter that only the Shura Council has the right to make.[114] Calculating benefits and costs, after Khamenei's binding decree, Hizbullah nominated nine candidates and three allies in a coalition with other Shi'ite leaders, including Nabih Berri and former speaker Husayn al-Husayni. The coalition lists also included Christians and Druze.

Despite efforts by Hizbullah and Amal to sell the alliance to their constituencies, there was considerable animosity among grassroots supporters as reflected in the crossing out of each other's candidates' names on the coalition lists. Such practice was the only way to judge who was the more popular of the two in the Shi'ite community.

Of the fourteen seats reserved for the Shi'ites in the provinces of South Lebanon and Nabatiyyah (which together are allocated twenty-three seats), Hizbullah candidate Muhammad Ra'ad received the highest number of popular votes, as shown in table 5.7, followed by Muhammad Fneish, also a Hizbullah candidate. Only Muhammad Abdul Hamid Baydoun of Amal received more votes than Hizbullah's Nazih Mansour and very slightly more than Abdullah Qasir. The latter received more votes than the rest of the Shi'ite candidates, including speaker Nabih Berri. Although Berri tried to play down the number of votes received by Hizbullah, the fact remains that Hizbullah's popular vote is indicative of an increase in the party's constituencies in South Lebanon and a great challenge to Berri's Amal and his leadership of the Shi'ite community. The difference between

Table 5.7

Distribution of Popular Vote for Representatives of Hizbullah, Amal, and Shi'ite Zu'ama' Families, 2000 Elections, South Lebanon

Hizbullah	*Popular Vote*	*Amal*	*Popular Vote*	*Shi'ite Families*	*Popular Vote*
Muhammad Ra'ad	201,901	Muhammad Abdul Hamid Baydoun	196,155	Ali Usayran	175,831
				Abdel Latif Zein	173,191
Muhammad Fneish	200,840	Nabih Berri	183,450	'Ali al-Khalil	175,155
				Yassin Jaber	170,012
'Abdullah Qasir	196,056	'Ayoub Humayid	174,190	'Ali Bazzi	166,796
Nazih Mansour	187,860	'Ali Hasan Khalil	65,278	'Ali Khries	165,960

Source: Election results obtained from Lebanon's Ministry of the Interior, September 25, 2000.

Hizbullah's candidate Muhammad Ra'ad and Nabih Berri was more than eighteen thousand votes. Ra'ad received thirty-six thousand more votes than Ali Khries of Amal, who received the lowest number of votes.

As for the remaining nine seats in the province, Sunni (three), Maronite (two), Catholics (two), Orthodox (one), and Druze (one), which are not shown in table 5.7, only Sunni Mustafa Sa'ad received a higher number of votes (211,000) than Hizbullah's candidates. One major reason is that neither Hizbullah nor Amal supporters crossed out his name in their contest for popular votes. In addition, Sa'ad, a close friend of Hizbullah, received more votes than Bahia Hariri, sister of Rafic Hariri, Lebanon's prime minister. It was said that the party's constituency crossed out her name. However, of the nine representatives who won election on the Amal-Hizbullah coalition list, only Maronite George Najm of Jezzine can be considered a member of Hizbullah's bloc in Parliament. The party's support for Najm is somehow ideological. It stems from the fact that Najm is a lawyer with a clean reputation and has been sympathetic to the party's resistance to Israel.[115] The other eight representatives of the province of South Lebanon are considered members of Berri's bloc in the Lebanese Parliament.[116]

As for the distribution of Hizbullah and Amal popular votes in Biq'a Province's Ba'albek-Hirmil district, Hizbullah candidates won three of the six seats reserved for the Shi'ites out of the ten seats allocated to the district (see table 5.8).

Table 5.8 shows that 'Ammar al-Musawi topped the coalition list that included Hizbullah, Amal, and independent candidate Husayn al-Husayni. Al-Musawi was followed by Berri's close associate Ghazi Zu'aiter and Husayn al-Husayni. Husayn al-Hajj Hasan of Hizbullah received the lowest number of the district votes. Reports indicated that despite the coalition, Husayn al-Hajj Hasan suffered the most in the battle for the popular vote. His name was crossed out more than any other candidate. More importantly, Shaykh Subhi al-Tufayli's followers opted to cross out Hizbullah's candidates, in particular Hajj Hasan, in favor of other Shi'ite independent candidates.

As for the remaining four seats of the district—Sunni (two), Catholic (one), and Maronite (one), not shown in the table—nobody received more

Table 5.8
Distribution of Popular Vote for Hizbullah and Other Shiʿite Representatives, 2000 Elections, Baʿalbek–Hirmil District

Hizbullah	Popular Vote	Other Shiʿites	Popular Vote
ʿAmmar al-Musawi	56,926	Ghazi Zuʿaiter (Amal)	52,139
Muhammad Yaghi	48,048	Husayn al-Husayni	50,625
Husayn al-Hajj Hasan	27,657	ʿAssem Qanso	40,153

Source: Figures obtained from Lebanon's Ministry of the Interior, September 20, 2000.

votes than ʿAmmar al-Musawi of Hizbullah. Of the four Sunni representatives, Ibrahim Bayan and Masʿaoud al-Hujiri are considered Hizbullah's allies and members of its bloc in the Lebanese Parliament. Interestingly, on the other hand, Hizbullah members consistently voted for Nadr Sukkar, a Maronite candidate on the coalition list and a former member of the Lebanese Forces. The decision to support Sukkar was justified by Hizbullah as purely pragmatic and in line with the party's political pragmatism and rapprochement with others.

The election results in the district of Baʿabda, which has a Christian and Druze majority with the exception of its Shiʿite southern suburbs, were favorable to Hizbullah. In a tough battle between a list supported by Hizbullah and another one supported by Druze Walid Jumblatt and the Kataʾib (Phalange) and other Christian forces, Hizbullah's ʿAli ʿAmmar won the elections. However, Amal's candidate, Yusuf al-Haraki, on the Amal-Hizbullah coalition list, lost the election. The rival list was not able to perform well without trading votes with Hizbullah. Likewise, in Beirut Hizbullah did very well, where its candidate, Muhammad Berjawi, received the highest number of votes (28,391) topping a six-candidate list for Beirut's second district. Berri, on the other hand, supported Shiʿite Nasir Qandil, nominated on Hariri's "Dignity" list. Qandil received the highest number of votes (28,887), topping the seven candidates for Beirut's third district.[117]

Despite Hizbullah success in entering the Lebanese Parliament and improving its representation, the party opted for the time being not to take a position in the Lebanese cabinet or to accept a ministerial portfolio. The rationale behind such a decision by Hizbullah is based on ideological and political considerations.

Ideologically, Hizbullah cannot accept a cabinet position or even cast a vote of confidence for a government because the party is bound by God's laws, not human laws. The only legitimate government for Hizbullah is an Islamic government that applies the Shari'ah as interpreted by the wali al-faqih. If conditions or circumstances militate against the emergence of such a government, then a government that represents the interest of the people or the majority would be a preferred second type. In the words of Shaykh Qasim: "We do not want to enter or cast a vote of confidence for a government that does not represent the interest of the people, or whose program we do not know. Our loyalty is to a government that represents and serves the people, not to cabinet spoils." [118]

The clear implication is that the Shi'ite demographic majority would like to be numerically better represented in the Lebanese government. Hizbullah hopes such representation would enhance its chances of influencing the government's decisions by having more than just one cabinet post that would be "lost among thirty cabinet members who are concerned about spoils rather than looking out after the needs of the people." [119]

Politically, Hizbullah prefers to stay out of the cabinet because it would have to defend decisions that might be unfavorable or contradictory to the party's interest. Such decisions include ending the resistance to Israel, disarming the party and its Islamic Resistance, peace negotiation and normalization with Israel, and economic policies—decisions that would not only be an embarrassment to Hizbullah but would be politically and ideologically problematic as well. Thus, the party's ideals and aspirations are considered more valuable for Hizbullah than sacrificing them for a cabinet position in a country that suffers from elite fragmentation and corruption.

As a result of these two considerations, Hizbullah has stayed out of all cabinets and refrained from giving a vote of confidence to the successive governments since 1992. Instead, the party has preferred to play the parliamentary role of opposition. Together with its allies, Hizbullah has formed a strong bloc opposing the distribution of spoil taken by the government and approved by Parliament. Although the party might not have succeeded in strongly influencing the Parliament's decisions, Hizbullah's MPs contend that they have prevented things from getting worse and have always represented the interests of the people.[120] For example, Hizbullah objected and voted no on budgets in the three successive governments of 1992, 1996, and 2000 headed by Prime Minister Hariri. From Hizbullah's point of view, Hariri's governments have treated the country like a business acquisition, simply added to Hariri's hefty portfolio. To Hizbullah, the Lebanese cabinets have acted as "boards of directors, not as a responsible government accountable to the people."[121] It opposed all the Hariri governments, which had made money in real estate, reconstruction of the country's infrastructure, and investment in treasury bonds. As a priority, Hizbullah pushed for government investment in the various sectors of the economy, in particular agriculture and industry. For Hizbullah, Hariri's governments have bankrupted the country in the name of reconstruction, whereby the public debt has exceeded $40 billion.[122]

In addition, Hizbullah has been adamant about fighting a fierce battle in the Parliament and against any government attempt to silence the Resistance and to pass acts and policies that benefit Israel or its collaborators in particular. When the government of Hariri in 1992 ordered the Lebanese troops to ban a demonstration organized by Hizbullah and its Resistance against the Gaza-Jericho agreement, Hizbullah considered that part of a hidden plan to eradicate the party.[123] The confrontation with the Lebanese army led to the killing of thirteen members of Hizbullah. Overall, Hizbullah has sent many messages warning cabinets or political leaders that the party will not be reluctant to respond promptly to any plan that seeks its eradication.

Other issues that have shaped Hizbullah's parliamentary platform and provided it with a good reputation are social welfare services and official corruption. Hizbullah can claim the high moral ground on these two issues in comparison with all other parliamentary blocs, in particular with Amal's and Hariri's followers, who have been accused of being corrupt and arrogant.

In conclusion, Hizbullah's entrance into the Lebanese Parliament has not only allowed it to have a foothold in the Lebanese political system but has also legitimized the party and added more protection to its constituency and resistance movement, a politically comfortable situation that has even gone beyond Hizbullah's expectations.

Capturing Municipal Councils

Hizbullah's gradualist-pragmatic mode was reflected even more clearly in the municipal elections than in the parliamentary elections. The 1998 municipal elections, which were held for the first time in thirty-five years, were the first local elections in which Hizbullah and other Islamist movements participated.[124] While Hizbullah's participation in the parliamentary elections since 1992 has given the party legitimacy and political clout, the municipal elections of 1998 provided the opportunity to come into power in several important cities, towns, and local governments.

Given the assumption that the nature of municipal work—the provision of social services to the community—is a fundamental tenet of faith, Hizbullah has struck at the heart of the Lebanese old and new zuʿamaʾ and their clientelism that has persisted in one form or another for more than one hundred years.[125] Equally important, the functions and powers of municipalities drew the attention of Hizbullah to the importance of subordinate-level power sharing. Although Lebanon is a unitary form of state in which municipalities or local governments do not enjoy effective autonomy as in a federal system, Lebanon is famous for its weak mechanism of central government. Furthermore, Legislative Decree 118 reinforced the concept of autonomy and decentralization, at least on paper. The law stipulates the following functions and responsibilities as being within the jurisdiction of the municipal councils: adoption of the municipality's annual budget; determination of taxes and fees; management of municipal funds; establishment of slaughterhouses; town planning and the arrangement of public transport; acceptance of gifts for the municipality; the naming of streets; development of natural resources; oversight of electrical power projects; fire and rescue services; and drafting and promulgation of laws and regulations governing employees of the municipality.[126]

The same law also stipulates that municipal functions are primarily to be financed from taxes and fees on rental values of built property; licenses for and taxes on hotels, nightclubs, cinemas, and restaurants as well as taxes on advertising fees; taxes and fees collected by the state for the municipalities, such as taxes on business profits, inheritance fees, gasoline taxes, and surtaxes and fees collected by state agencies or private concerns, such as on telephone and electricity bills or on tobacco products.[127]

Despite the elaborate infrastructure of the local administration, by virtue of control over the purse strings, the Ministry of Interior exercises considerable authority. In fact, Hizbullah and other Islamist groups, such as the Islamic Association (al-Jama'ah al-Islamiyyah), were the first to stand up and support an administrative reform bill, still awaiting the approval of the Lebanese Parliament, that grants municipal councils more effective and meaningful functions and powers.

In the municipal elections, the gradualist-pragmatic mode of Hizbullah was reflected in its programs, alliances, and campaign committees. Hizbullah sanctioned this mode under the pretext that "winning is religiously permissible" *(halal)*. As such, Hizbullah's candidates in the villages, towns, and cities of Lebanon's six provinces offered comprehensive programs of a practical rather than ideological nature.

To appeal to the voters, Hizbullah's programs placed greater emphasis on the economic, social, and developmental aspects of the various municipalities, particularly the most deprived. The party introduced its candidates on a nonsectarian basis, emphasizing honesty and seriousness in municipal work. Such an attitude was reflected clearly in Hizbullah's slogan, which declared that municipal work is a religio-legal designation that requires providing the people with the best models of services.[128] In the southern suburbs of Beirut (Ghobairi and Borj al-Barajneh), South Lebanon, Nabatiyyah, Beirut, and Biq'a, the party emphasized its experience in social welfare activities. In contrast, Hizbullah's rival, Amal, has provided neither programs nor any vision for municipal work. In brief, Hizbullah's program of action emphasized the following:

Encourage the citizen to play a more active role in the selection process of development projects;

Increase the functions and powers of municipalities in the provision of education, health care and socioeconomic affairs;

Involve qualified people in development projects;

Finance development projects from both municipal revenues and donations;

Exercise control over public works and prevent embezzlement;

Renovate the physical and administrative structures of municipalities
and provide them with computer facilities.[129]

However, Hizbullah's programs completely avoided specific statements on
services related to tourism, such as provision of alcoholic beverages, gam-
bling, and nightclubs. In Islam, these services are considered *muharamat*
(forbidden). Intentional or not, the avoidance by Hizbullah was not meant
to undermine the principle of muharamat. Rather, politics for Hizbullah is
purely utilitarian rather than ideological or religious.

The electoral lists and alliances formed by Hizbullah not only con-
firmed the adoption of a gradualist-pragmatic mode but in some instances
reflected the divide between utilitarian politics and ideological considerations. The principle of maximizing gains and minimizing losses formed
the backbone of Hizbullah's political behavior, a behavior that was essentially rational and not different from that of Western political parties.
Calculating the size and strength of all contestants, Hizbullah produced
three kinds of electoral lists. First, the party list included party members
only. Second, the mixed list included party members and friendly independents. Third, the coalition list consisted of party members and
candidates from other political parties.

Table 5.9 shows that Hizbullah's party lists were dominant in its
strongholds, in particular the municipalities of Borj al-Barajneh and
Ghobairi (known as Beirut's southern suburbs), in the district of Ba'abda,
and in the districts of Ba'albek and Hirmil, thanks to the party's strength in
these municipalities, its leading role in provision of social services, and the
widespread respect for its resistance activities against Israel. The party thus
felt that it did not need political alliances to win elections in the villages
and towns of these districts.[130] For example, Hizbullah rejected a coalition
list drawn up by Speaker Nabih Berri and Prime Minister Rafic Hariri, who
teamed up in a campaign to isolate the influence of political parties
through promoting consensus lists of largely neutral candidates, a position that was completely unacceptable to Hizbullah. As the attempt to

Table 5.9

Types of Hizbullah Lists by Municipal Electoral District in Some of Lebanon's Provinces, 1998 Municipal Elections

Type of Electoral List	Districts of the Provinces of Mount Lebanon (Southern Suburbs)		Districts of the Provinces of South Lebanon and Nabatiyyah					Province of Beirut	Districts of the Province of Biq'a	
	Borj al-Barajneh	Ghobairi	Marj'ayoun	Sidon	Tyre	Bint Jbeil	Nabatiyyah	City of Beirut	Ba'albek	Hirmil
Party lists (party members only)	+	+	–	–	–	–	–	–	+	+
Mixed lists (alliance of party members and independents)	–	–	+	+	–	+	–	–	+	–
Coalition lists (alliance of party members with other political parties):										
a) Communist Party and Kamal al Asʿad Social Democratic Party (known as Asʿadiis)	–	–	–	–	+	–	–	–	–	–
b) Communist Party and Kamal al Asʿad Social Democratic Party	–	–	–	–	–	–	+	–	–	–
c) Hariri's Future Trend, al-Kataʾib Party, Lebanese Forces, Amal, and al-Jamaʾah	–	–	–	–	–	–	–	+	–	–

Notes: + = the presence of the type of electoral list

– = the absence of the type of electoral list

Source: Author's data, compiled from various reports by Lebanese newspapers and magazines between May and June 1998.

form a joint list failed, Berri and Hariri backed an alliance list from large families such as al-Khalil, Kanj, Kazma, Farhat, and Raʿad. However, it turned out that Hizbullah had a presence in these families, which rendered the Berri-Hariri-backed list ineffective in its attempts to stand in the way of Hizbullah, which won the elections.[131]

In South Lebanon, Amal traditionally dominated, and the movement's leader, Nabih Berri, was seen as the patriarchal advocate of the Shiʿite community within Lebanon's state machine. In an attempt to curb Amal's domination, Hizbullah formed electoral lists that varied from party coalition lists. For example, the party's mixed lists were formed in the districts of Marjʿayoun, Bint Jbeil, and Sidon. However, in some front-line villages of Bint Jbeil, such as Shakra, Deir Qanoun al-Nahr, Yater, and Kafra, which were considered Islamic Resistance strongholds, Hizbullah resorted to party lists instead. But in the districts of Nabatiyyah and Tyre, where the Democratic Socialist Party of former speaker Kamal al-Asʿad (known as Asʿadiis) and the Communist Party both had some presence, Hizbullah opted for coalition lists with these parties. Likewise, in some of the party's stronghold front-line villages, such as Jbaʿa, Kfarfila, ʿArab Salim, Zoutar al-Gharbiyah, and Zoutar al-Sharqiyah, Hizbullah formed its own party lists.[132]

The tendency to form coalition lists was even greater in the city of Beirut. Hizbullah joined Beirut's Accord list, which was formed by Hariri. The list included parties who were ideologically and politically in disagreement with Hizbullah, such as Hariri's Future Trend, the Lebanese Kataʾib (Phalange) Party, the Lebanese Forces, al-Jamaʿah al-Islamiyyah, the Amal movement, al-Tashnak, and the supporters of deputy Tamam Salam. Hizbullah justified such a coalition with rivals as a way to maintain sectarian balance.[133]

As in the southern suburbs of Beirut and the district of Hirmil, Hizbullah opted for the party lists in the districts of Baʿalbek with the exception of the city itself. Nevertheless, the city of Baʿalbek has traditionally been the main bastion and focus of the party's social services network. Hizbullah's attempts to form a party list conflicted from the very beginning with the city's sectarian makeup. Besides the Shiʿite majority, the city includes Sunnis and Christians as well. Equally important, the city's dominant political groups, such as Shaykh Subhi al-Tufayli's Ansar Allah, the Syrian Social National Party, Hizb al-Ba'th, and the Amal movement, presented another major obstacle in the way of forming an alliance list. As negotiations failed between Hizbullah, the political groups, and the leading figures of large Sunni and Christian families, the party formed a mixed list that included independent Sunni and Christian candidates from small families. The deadlock faced by Hizbullah in the city had to do with the fear of many Christians and Sunnis for the future of tourism in the city. For many of them, the prospect of a Hizbullah victory at the polls meant the death knell for the local tourism industry.[134]

As in the parliamentary elections, Hizbullah's campaign committees were extremely active during the municipal elections. The party's Central Campaign Committee and its subcommittees started their work five months before the election. Their efforts to reach the electorate ranged from structuring the vote to providing services through the party's social and health institutions. Hizbullah's campaign committees consisted of six hundred full-time party members who were paid six hundred dollars each per month, and several hundred party members who served as volunteers.[135] The party finances all campaign activities. Some reports estimated that Hizbullah's spending on the local election of 1998 exceeded five million dollars,[136] an amount that is high in comparison to all other Lebanese political factions.

The 1998 municipal election ballot was the first time Hizbullah and Amal directly competed against each other. In the 1992, 1996, and 2000 parliamentary elections, both parties featured joint lists, and neither party was in existence during the municipal elections of 1963. Hizbullah, however, was able to perform very well in the 1998 municipal elections, thanks to its committed constituency and the party's social welfare services.

In the southern suburbs of Beirut (Borj al-Barajneh and Ghobairi), and in the municipalities of Mount Lebanon province, with an overwhelmingly Shi'ite population (Kayfoun, Joun, and Lasa), Hizbullah won a landslide with a total of ninety seats, in contrast to Amal, which won none (see table 5.10). This victory was not surprising in Hizbullah-controlled towns, particularly Borj al-Barajneh and Ghobairi. These two major coastal towns have been under Hizbullah's influence for more than ten years, par-

Table 5.10

Distribution of Municipalities and Seats in Some of Mount Lebanon's Shi'ite Districts by Hizbullah and Amal, 1998 Municipal Elections

Municipalities of Mount Lebanon's Districts/ No. of Seats	*Hizbullah*	*Amal*
Ba'abda (Borj al-Barajneh, 18)	18	0
Ba'abda (Ghobairi, 21)	21	0
A'ley (Kayfoun, 21)	21	0
Shouf (Joun, 15)	15	0
Jbeil (Lasa, 15)	15	0
Total	90	0

Source: Figures obtained from *Al-Ahd,* May 20, 1998, 9, 10, 11; see also *Al-Shira',* June 1, 1998, 14–15.

ticularly after Amal lost the southern suburbs to Hizbullah in 1989. More importantly, the social, educational, and health services that Hizbullah has provided to many of the families in the suburbs and other districts have made it a widely respected party. This was a position that Amal was not able to achieve during its control of the southern suburbs.

In the provinces of Nabatiyyah and South Lebanon, the results indicated in table 5.11 show that even though Hizbullah did not win overwhelmingly as in Beirut's southern suburbs, it is now a potent threat to Amal in its traditional stronghold. In fact, Hizbullah expected to win Nabatiyyah and South Lebanon after its landslide victory in the southern suburbs. However, both Amal and Hizbullah tried to put their own spin on the election results. While Speaker Berri claimed that out of seventy-five contested municipalities Amal won fifty-one, Hizbullah's deputy in the Lebanese Parliament claimed that out of sixty-eight municipalities contested by both parties, Hizbullah won thirty-three, while thirty-five went to Amal.[137] The conflicting claims centered on the fact that each party had added to its own actual gains a number of the disputed municipalities.

However, after reassessing the election results of the contested municipalities between Hizbullah and Amal, it was found that, of the ninety-seven municipalities in Nabatiyyah and South Lebanon, competition occurred only in seventy-four municipalities. The remaining

Table 5.11

Distribution of Municipalities and Seats in the Provinces of Nabatiyyah, South Lebanon, and Biqʻa by Hizbullah and Amal, 1998 Municipal Elections

Province	Hizbullah	Amal
Nabatiyyah	11 (97 seats)	12 (94 seats)
South Lebanon	11 (122 seats)	27 (231 seats)
Biqʻa	18 (224 seats)	9 (158 seats)
Total (excludes the number of seats in 11 disputed municipalities)	40 (443 seats)	48 (483 seats)

Source: Figures obtained from *Al-Ahd,* June 12, 1998, 11–12; *Al-Safir,* June 9, 1998, 9; *Al-Nahar,* June 16, 1998, 11; and unpublished reports by Hizbullah.

twenty-three are Christian municipalities where no competition occurred between Amal and Hizbullah. Out of the remaining thirteen municipalities, eleven were claimed by both of them, one was a split, and the last was won by a coalition of Communists and Nasserites. Since it was impossible to confirm either claim in the eleven disputed municipalities, the decision here was to omit them from the total number of seats and municipalities won by each group.

In the province of Nabatiyyah, as shown in table 5.11, the results show that while Hizbullah-backed lists won eleven municipalities, including the city of Nabatiyyah, Amal-backed lists won twelve municipalities. However, the number of Hizbullah and Amal seats in these municipal councils is almost equal (ninety-seven and ninety-four respectively). Such equality of seats is also indicative of the duality of power in the province of Nabatiyyah. In addition, the victory of Hizbullah in the city of Nabatiyyah meant breaking the tacit monopoly of Amal in a city that was considered to be difficult to win. In fact, the social welfare services provided by Hizbullah, in particular the services of Muʼassasat Jihad al-Binaʼ made it possible for Hizbullah to win the city's municipal council overwhelmingly. Although the majority of the municipal seats in the province of Nabatiyyah went to Hizbullah and Amal, the election results indicate that independents were present and won forty seats.

As for the province of South Lebanon, Berri's stronghold, Amal won twenty-seven municipalities with 231 seats, compared with eleven municipalities with 122 seats won by Hizbullah (see table 5.11). Although Hizbullah is a structured party with a greater mobilization capacity than Amal, the party underestimated Berri's popularity. For example, in the district of Bint Jbeil, Hizbullah-backed lists won only three municipalities. Amal-backed lists, on the other hand, won seven municipalities. As for the number of seats, Amal managed to win seventy, compared to twenty-three for Hizbullah. Similarly, election results in the district of Tyre were a disappointment for Hizbullah, which sought similar results to those in the province of Nabatiyyah. However, Hizbullah-backed lists won four municipalities with no single seat in Tyre, while Amal-backed lists won eleven municipalities with a startling victory of twenty-one seats in Tyre. As for the distribution of municipal seats in the district of Tyre, Amal was ahead of Hizbullah (eighty to sixty-three respectively). The situation for Hizbullah was no better in the district of Sidon. Despite the fact that Hizbullah's social services were significant in the district of Sidon, known as al-Zahrani, the party was not able to undermine Berri's influence there. Amal won nine municipalities and eighty-one seats, compared to four municipalities and thirty-six seats won by Hizbullah.

The election results in the province of the Biqʿa, however, show that Hizbullah is the number one Shiʿite party, with the exception of the city of Baʿalbek. Omitting from the total the disputed municipalities, the party won eighteen municipalities, in comparison to nine municipalities won by the Amal-backed list. However, Hizbullah and Amal received an equal number of seats in two municipalities. In general, the districts of the province of the Biqʿa have proved to be Hizbullah's main strongholds, with 224 seats in contrast to 158 seats for the Amal-backed list (see table 5.11). Only in the city of Baʿalbek did the results run contrary to Hizbullah's victory in the 1992 and 1996 parliamentary elections. Amal's list of notable families won sixteen out of twenty-one seats of the city's municipalities compared with five seats won by Hizbullah. Despite the fact that Hizbullah had the largest individual electoral power in the city—famous for its loyalty to the Islamic Resistance—the party had underestimated the role of the zuʿamaʾ families that contributed to Hizbullah's defeat. In other words, the party underestimated clan affiliations and the role of Sunnis who felt they were being crushed by the city's Shi'ite majority. Also, Christian voters were not convinced that Hizbullah would support the city's tourism business as it claimed. In addition, the bloody battle of Ain Bourdy in January 1998 (on the outskirts of Ba'albek city) between Shaykh Subhi al-Tufayli's faction, Ansar Allah, and Hizbullah, contributed to weakening the party in the city. As a result, al-Tufayli's supporters backed Amal's alliance in the city of Ba'albek and won the twelve seats of Brital's municipality, Shaykh al-Tufayli's home village.

As for the elections in the city of Beirut, Hizbullah's candidate, Muhammad Shirri, won his seat on Hariri's Beirut Accord list. The results were a setback for Amal's candidate, Fadi Shahrour, who lost his allocated seat. One major reason for the defeat of Amal's candidate is that Beirut's Sunni community has not forgotten Amal's manipulation of power when it controlled the city in 1984. In addition, Hizbullah's Islamic Resistance, with its clean reputation, was more favored than Amal by many of Beirut's Sunnis.

Finally, the election results also indicated that the districts of the provinces of South Lebanon and Nabatiyyah were not completely polarized between Hizbullah and Amal. Although the southern families and independents sided in the elections either with Amal or Hizbullah, none of these groups could be labeled partisan. While the major southern families recognize Berri's political influence, they did not necessarily abide by Amal's political directives. On the other hand, the independents, who felt they were being crushed by Amal's local politicians, found in Hizbullah a better ally. The results also showed that traditional Shi'ite leaders such as former speaker Kamial al-As'ad, as well as secular parties (Communist Party, Ba'th, and Syrian Social National Party), had not disappeared completely from the southern political map.

Yet the 2004 municipal elections showed more clearly that Hizbullah was not only a first-class pragmatic player but also a dominant political force within the Shi'ite community. Hizbullah did not only defeat Amal in Beirut southern suburbs and the Biq'a but also won over Amal the majority of the municipalities of the provinces of South Lebanon and Nabatiyyah.

The election results of the southern suburbs of Beirut (Borj al-Barajneh, Ghobairi and Haret Hureik) and other Shi'ite municipalities of Mount

Table 5.12

Distribution of Municipalities and Seats in Some of Mount Lebanon's Shi'ite Districts by Hizbullah and Amal, 2004 Municipal Elections

Districts/ No. of Seats	Hizbullah	Amal
Borj al-Barajneh (18)	18	0
Ghobairi (21)	21	0
Haret Hureik (18)	18	0
Kayfoun (21)	16	5
Joun (15)	10	5
Lasa (15)	15	0
Total	98	10

Source: Figures compiled from *Al-Intiqad,* May 7, 2004, 8–9.

Lebanon (Kayfoun, Joun, and Lasa), indicated in table 5.12, show that Hizbullah won a landslide victory, with a total of 98 seats, in contrast to Amal, which won only ten seats.

In Beirut's southern suburbs, Hizbullah won not only the munici-palities of Borj al-Barajneh and Ghobairi but also the municipality of Haret-Hureik in its first municipal elections. Haret Hureik, which is almost equally divided between Shi'ites and Christians, did not hold elections in 1998 because its Christian residents boycotted the elections. In 2004, however, the Christians, who had returned to Haret Hureik, decided to participate, and Hizbullah succeeded in forming a consensus list with the Christians; Amal failed to achieve a such a balanced consensus list. Hizbul-lah made sure that its backed eighteen-member list was equally divided between Shi'ites and Christians. It also provided protection to the returned Christians and their property, and both actions won it broad respect among the Christians of the area. Thus Hizbullah and its Christian allies won a landslide victory over the candidates backed by Amal.

As for other Shi'ite municipalities of Mount Lebanon, table 5.12 shows that while Amal was able to improve its representation a little in Kayfoun and Joun relative to its 1998 standing, Hizbullah won a landslide in Lasa and was still dominant in Kayfoun and Joun.

In the provinces of South Lebanon and Nabatiyyah, the 2004 mu-nicipal elections were contested between Hizbullah and Amal in 142 municipalities out of 171 Shi'ite municipalities. These numbers, which represented a considerable increase from the 75 municipalities in which the two groups contested one another in 1998, reflected the fact that the liberation of South Lebanon had allowed 67 municipalities to hold elections for the first time. Of the remaining 29 municipalities, 19 saw victories mainly by families representing neither Amal nor Hizbullah. The other 10 municipalities were won by consensus lists supported by Hizbullah, Amal, and other smaller political forces. Table 5.13 reports the election results for only the 142 municipalities contested between Hizbullah and Amal.

In the provinces of South Lebanon and Nabatiyyah, a comparison of the municipal election result in 2004 and 1998 (see table 5.13) show that Hizbullah not only enhanced its representation in 2004 but won a majority of the municipalities: 86 municipalities (61%) with 1,163 seats, compared with 55 municipalities (39%) with 613 seats in 1998. Of the seven major cities and towns in the two provinces, Hizbullah won 5 in 2004 (Nabatiyyah, Bint Jbeil, Khram, Aytaroun, and Jwaya), compared with two (Tyre and Mayes al-Jabal) won by Amal; Amal's power shrank to the city of Tyre and the district of Zahrani, while Hizbullah's power expanded considerably, dominating the districts of Nabatiyyah and Bint Jbeil—particularly cities and towns close to the northern border with Israel—and more than half the district of Tyre, particularly the town of Naqoura. In addition, Amal completely lost to Hizbullah powerful strongholds such as Jba'a, 'Ain Bouswor, Houmin al-Fouqah, Shakra, Shabiyyah, Shhoor, and Kafra. Most important, it failed to regain control of the city of

Table 5.13

Distribution of Municipalities and Seats in the Provinces of Nabatiyyah, South Lebanon, and Biq'a by Hizbullah and Amal, 2004 Municipal Elections

Province	Hizbullah	Amal
South Lebanon and Nabatiyyah	87 (1,163 seats)	55 (613 seats)
Biq'a	36 (490 seats)	2 (30 seats)
Total	123 (1,653 seats)	57 (643 seats)

Source: Figures compiled from *Al-Intiqad,* May 14, 2004, 4–9, and May 28, 2004, 4–9.

Nabatiyyah. Berri and Amal have underestimated Hizbullah's increased popularity, especially after the liberation of South Lebanon. Hizbullah now is not only a potent threat to Amal but is dominant in both South Lebanon and Nabatiyyah.

The 2004 municipal election results in the Biqʿa were a sweeping victory for Hizbullah and a complete defeat for Amal (see Table 5.13). Of the 57 Shiʿite municipalities in the Biqʿa, Hizbullah and Amal contested the elections in thirty-eight municipalities. Of these, Hizbullah won control of 36 municipalities with 490 seats, twice what it won in the 1998 elections, while Amal won control of only 2 municipalities with 30 seats. The other 19 municipalities in the province were not contested between Hizbullah and Amal; they were won mainly by families. Hizbullah's greatest victory in 2004 in Biqʿa was its regaining of control of the city of Baʿalbek, which it had lost to Amal in the 1998 municipal elections. Despite Hizbullah's large constituency in the city, Hizbullah's campaign committees did not take any risk in 2004, moving with full force to structure Hizbullah's voters and form alliances with other political groups, such as the Baʿth Party, and with Sunni and Christian families of the city. As a result, the candidates backed by Hizbullah won 21 municipal council seats, removing Amal completely from the municipal council of Baʿalbek.

In the city of Beirut in 2004, both Hizbullah and Amal candidates won their seats on a consensus list formed by Prime Minister Hariri from among a number of political forces in the city which they had not seriously consulted by a rival list.

Hizbullah's sweeping victories in the 2004 municipal elections did not come as a surprise. Whether Hizbullah is a "resistance movement," as its supporters contend or a "terrorist organization," as its foes assert, the fact remains that the party won major victories in 2004 for several reasons, most of its own making and having nothing to do with Syria and Iran.

First, Hizbullah's many social welfare services have helped the party build a solid constituency and expand its patronage. Neither state institutions nor Amal have provided the significant social services granted by Hizbullah. Second and equally important, Hizbullah's ongoing successes— its liberation of South Lebanon, its continuing fight against the Israeli army in the Shebʾa farms, and its success in securing the release of Lebanese and Arab detainees from Israeli prisons—have all received various degrees of support from Lebanon's religious committees. It is not only the issue of the resistance that has made Hizbullah popular but also—indeed most importantly—the level of commitment it has demonstrated through these actions. Third, the close connection between Hizbullah's leadership and its base has translated into political momentum on the ground. Conversely, Amal has been weakened by an internal power struggle between the upper echelons of the party and its rank and file, a struggle that has translated into a loss of momentum at the local level. Last but not least, Hizbullah's success reflects its pragmatic approach to the municipal elections, particularly its emphasis on economic, social, and developmental imperatives. The candidates or lists backed by Hizbullah in 2004 consisted mainly of individuals from professions—engineers, doctors, lawyers, and businessmen—chosen as the best qualified to understand the needs of a particular municipality.

SEPTEMBER 11 AND THE WAR IN IRAQ: A CALCULATED RESPONSE

The U.S. war on terror after September 11 and its victories over al-Qaʻida and the Taliban forces in Afghanistan and Saddam in Iraq have pushed Hizbullah further into a strategy of calculated response regarding the new political stage created by the United States in the region.[138] In fact, Hizbullah's calculated-response strategy is not completely new nor does it contradict the party's modes of action—militancy and pragmatism. The strategy complements Hizbullah's modes of action and goes beyond them to a deeper process of calculating the party's choices and their consequences. Such strategy has made the party more aware of not risking its survival.

Although Hizbullah has been included in the State Department's list of foreign terrorist organizations since 1999, the Bush administration in the immediate aftermath of September 11 excluded the party from the list, along with Syrian-backed Palestinian groups, in order to secure the backing of Arab states.[139] For the first month, the American antiterror campaign was strictly limited to the al-Qaʻida network. However, on September 24, 2001, an executive order threatened sanctions against states or financial institutions that do business with twenty-seven groups and individuals tied to Usama Bin Laden. On October 12, the Bush administration released an additional list of thirty-nine individuals, which included the former head of Hizbullah's special overseas operations, Imad Mughniyyah, along with two other members, Hasan Ezzeddine and Ali Attwah. Reportedly, the list of individuals also included Hizbullah's secretary-general, Sayyid Hasan Nasrallah, and his predecessor, Shaykh Subhi al-Tufayli. The American officials demanded that the Lebanese government freeze the assets of all listed individuals.[140]

American officials charge that Hizbullah's activities constitute "terrorist" acts and that the party is capable of staging them with global reach. The United States made two specific charges against Hizbullah: first, that top operatives from Hizbullah, including Imad Mughniyyah, and al-Qaʻida members met near the Paraguayan city of Ciudad del Este in the triborder region that includes Paraguay, Brazil, and Argentina, to plan more terrorist attacks against the United States; and, second, that Hizbullah has trained members of the Palestinian Islamist groups Hamas and Islamic Jihad, both of which are classified as terrorist groups by the Bush administration.[141]

However, Lebanese officials denied an al-Qaʻida-Hizbullah link. President Emil Lahoud has dismissed reports of a meeting in South America between al-Qaʻida and Hizbullah as Israeli-sponsored propaganda. "The media campaign, which is conducted by Israeli circles, seeks to exploit the September 11 attacks to slander the Lebanese resistance by stigmatizing it with the image of terrorism," Lahoud said.[142] Accordingly, Lebanese officials defiantly rejected U.S. demands that they freeze Hizbullah's assets in the country.

While Hizbullah officials and members rejected and condemned the U.S. accusations of terrorism, calling them lies, the party stopped short of calling for a war against the United States or for the expulsion of its ambassador in Lebanon, Vincent Battles.[143] Instead, the party opted for a war of words with the U.S. administration. Sayyid Hasan Nasrallah, during a rally in support of the Intifada, challenged the U.S. administration to provide evidence that Hizbullah's activities went beyond resistance to Israel.[144]

As the United States escalated its pressure on Hizbullah to disarm, the party threatened to respond to any attack whether by the United States or by Israel. Nasrallah declared, "The Islamic Resistance will respond to aggressors, whether they are Americans, Israelis, or Jewish Zionists." However, he added, "the resistance in Lebanon and Palestine is in defensive rather than offensive conditions."[145] Nasrallah's declaration created an extensive war of words between Hizbullah and the United States.

However, realizing the danger of leading an active war, like al-Qaʻida's against the United States, the party chose not to put its survival at risk. Equally important, Hizbullah did not want to complicate its good relations with the Lebanese and Syrian governments, to whom they made clear that Hizbullah is a resistance organization, not a terrorist organization. Although Hizbullah has considered that the United States is its enemy because of its partnership with Israel, Hizbullah is certain that the cost of leading a war against the United States after September 11 is too great for Hizbullah to undertake. Perhaps the aftermath of September 11 did not elicit expressions of fear or moderation from Hizbullah; however, it has made the party strive to distinguish itself, ideologically and politically, from al-Qaʻida and to show neither support nor sympathy for its terrorist acts. Many militant Wahhabists and Sunni Islamist movements criticized this position privately and publicly across the Arab-Muslim world. Despite the fact that the situation between the United States and Hizbullah was very tense, Hizbullah chose not to lead a war against the United States. Instead, it launched a wave of mortar and rocket offensives against Israeli outposts in Shebʻa Farms, a calculated escalation in reaction to the United States, as well as to Israel's reoccupation of the West Bank.

Hizbullah's calculated response not to lead a war against the United States was even clearer in the party's calculated reaction to the U.S. war in Iraq. Although Hizbullah positioned itself at the forefront of fighting Israeli and U.S. plans in the region, the party's reaction to the Iraqi situation has not been to urge resistance against the Americans. In fact, when the United States was preparing to invade Iraq, Hizbullah's leader, Sayyid Hasan Nasrallah, did not call for jihad against the Americans. Instead, he rejected the U.S. war and proposed an initiative of reconciliation between Saddam and the Iraqi opposition, in particular the Shiʻite opposition.[146] Nasrallah's proposal presented three major points. First, he called for no one to offer help to the Americans because such help would not be against Saddam but against the ummah. Second, the initiative called on the Arab League or the Islamic Conference Organization to sponsor a national reconciliation conference that would establish a structure for the reconciliation between Saddam's regime and the Iraqi opposition. Finally, he gave a call for elections by the Iraqi people that would result in the formation of a national government.[147] Nasrallah vowed that if such reconciliation took place, then "we would say that it is a duty on every Arab and Muslim able to carry guns to fight the Americans to defend Iraq."[148] However, such reconciliation was impossible because of Saddam's refusal to reconcile with the Iraqi opposition. More importantly, the initiative neither supported Saddam nor called for jihad against the Americans. The initiative was desperately needed in order for Hizbullah to get out of a situation that divided Shi'ites and Sunnis across the Arab-Muslim world over the war in Iraq. Nasrallah admitted such division: "If you say something against the Americans, some will understand it as a defense of Saddam, and they will clap for you, but if you criticize Saddam's regime, some will clap for you while others will accuse you of being an agent for the United States. Thus, the situation is very sensitive."[149]

While everyone in Israel, at least, expected all hell to break loose after the Americans entered Iraq and Hizbullah started shelling the northern Israeli villages, towns, and "settlements," the speculations were far off the mark. On the contrary, Hizbullah did not find benefit to that approach. The party was forthright in dismissing reports linking it to Iraq. "We have clearly said that we have not received anything from Iraq, neither now nor in the past," Nasrallah said.[150] He added, "Our opposition to war against Iraq is not in support of Saddam Hussein but is a matter of principle."[151] After all, Saddam Hussein's persecution of the Iraqi Shi'ite community did little to endear the Iraqi leader to Hizbullah. By the same token, Hizbullah cannot forgive Saddam Hussein for the 1980–88 war against Iran. Thus, there seemed little or no benefit to Hizbullah to jeopardize its own existence by attacking Israel in support of someone they despised and who would be dethroned regardless of any action that the party undertook. However, Hizbullah escalated the stream of its rhetoric and battle of words against the U.S. war in Iraq. "We tell the United States, don't expect that the people of this region will welcome you with roses and jasmine. The people of this region will welcome you with rifles, blood, and martyrdom operations. We are not afraid of the American invaders, and we will keep saying 'death to America,' " Nasrallah said during the commemoration of ʿAshuraʾ.[152]

Yet such battle of words by Hizbullah has not been accompanied by action on the ground either before the war or after Saddam's regime was toppled. Although Nasrallah in a number of statements stressed that resistance is the only strategy for fighting the Israeli and American occupations, he said that Muslims in each state know more how to run their own affairs. Speaking at the Urgent Conference of Arab and Islamic Political Parties in Beirut convened to discuss the Iraqi crisis after Saddam, Nasrallah said, "Your real and right way is the resistance, to liberate your land with possible and available means, but you choose the time and place."[153]

However, the call for resistance by Saddam's Baʿth members and Sunni Islamists, in particular the al-Qaʿida network, against the Americans did not find great support among the absolute majority of Iraqi and Iranian Shiʿite clerics. There has been a fear that such resistance will bring back another Saddam whose persecution of Shiʿites has not been forgotten yet. A future regime dominated by a Sunni minority has become unacceptable to the Iraqi Shiʿites, who make up 70 percent of the population. Likewise, despite Iran's rejection of the American occupation and its continued differences with the United States over the status of Jerusalem and Palestinian rights, Iran's Khamenei opted, for strategic reasons, not to call for resistance against the Americans. Similarly to the Iraqi Shiʿites, Iran does not wish to see a Sunni Islamist system, with a radical Wahhabi-Salafi ideology, denouncing the Shiʿites emerging in its backyard. Equally important, Iran hopes to use its influence over the majority of Iraqi Shiʿite clerics—notably Abdel Aziz al-Hakim of the Supreme Council of the Islamic Revolution in Iraq (SCIRI), Kazim al-Haʾiri of the Daʿwah, and Muqtada al-Sadr, leader of a militia known as the Army of the Mahdi (the expected Messiah)—to alter the United States' negative image of its political system and to gain recognition of its strategic interest in the region. In addition to these two reasons, Iran is more interested in maintaining indirect talks with the United States through its ally the United Kingdom than in leading a deadly confrontation that will not pay off in the end.

While Saddam's remaining Ba'th members, Sunni Islamists, and al-Qa'ida formed their own resistance, the absolute majority of Iraqi Shi'ite leaders, despite denial of the occupation, cooperated in one way or another with the American administration for Iraq. The SCIRI and the Da'wah of al-Ha'iri, which are known for their loyalty to Ali Khamenei, have accepted participation in Iraq's Transitional Governing Council, formed by the Americans. Compared to the Sunnis, Kurds, Turkmans, and Christians, the Shi'ites have the highest representation in the council. The SCIRI is represented by Sayyid Abdel Aziz al-Hakim, who became the head of the SCIRI after the assassination of his brother Ayatollah Sayyid Muhammad Baqir al-Hakim in August 2003. Reportedly, the charismatic Baqir al-Hakim, who was loyal and close to Ali Khamenei, was assassinated by loyal members of Saddam's Ba'th party and by al-Qa'ida cells in Iraq.[154]

As the Iraqi resistance against the Americans assumed more of a Sunni Islamist stature, Hizbullah again found itself reaffirming that Muslims in each state are allowed to run their own affairs, a calculated response to division between Shi'ite and Sunni Islamists over the resistance in Iraq. Speaking at the fourteenth anniversary of the kidnapping of Shaykh Abdel Karim Obeid, a Hizbullah leader, Sayyid Hasan Nasrallah reaffirmed that "the resistance is a choice of unity, not of division or betrayal. When, for example, the Palestinians escalate, fight, or stop the resistance, it is their right because they know their own affairs. Nobody has the right to put the mujahiddin in the circle of accusation. This is the logical and the brotherly way."[155]

Despite the increased high level of tension between the United States and Hizbullah, in particular after the Syrian Accountability and Lebanese Sovereignty Restoration Act endorsed sanctions against Syria for supporting "terrorism,"[156] Hizbullah has maintained a calculated response to the U.S. pressure. It has neither called for a large-scale war against the Americans, like al-Qa'ida, nor urged for resistance in Iraq, similar to Iran. In an interview with CNN, Nasrallah said, "The American administration's problem with us is that the party fights Israel. If we stopped fighting the Israelis there is a great possibility that the U.S. administration would take us off the terrorist organization list." He added, "We don't want a war with America, but if any person attacks us we will answer him in the same way and it is our right to defend ourselves." [157] However, it appears that a war between Hizbullah and the United States is still possible if emotions and idealism get in the way and substitute for calculated responses. A war would have a direct impact on Iran and accordingly on the situation in Iraq.

In conclusion, Hizbullah's operational choices—militancy and gradualist-pragmatic modes—sanctioned by its ideology as "armed" and "unarmed" struggle—give the party a choice to act according to the circumstances. This is why Hizbullah has fluctuated between militancy that sought to conquer the state from the top down and political gradualism that strove to conquer the state from the bottom up. The fact remains that whatever the exact modus operandi applied by Hizbullah, the aim—seizing political power and establishing a regime governed by the Shariʿah—is the same.

6

Conclusion

Hizbullah's Islamist Venture

For almost two decades Hizbullah's vision of Islamic order and its regional role has not receded from view. The persistence of crisis conditions in Lebanon and the Middle East has given Hizbullah the freedom to act according to the circumstances and has rendered the Lebanese regime in particular vulnerable to the party's challenges. The triumph of Hizbullah's Islamic order, or at least Shi'ite majoritarianism in Lebanon, and the liberation of occupied Arab lands, in particular Jerusalem, all seem more real to Hizbullah than ever. Has Hizbullah succeeded in setting the framework of its future Islamic order in Lebanon and its role in the region?

FUTURE OF THE ISLAMIC ORDER

In 2004, no one could deny that Hizbullah's goal—establishing an Islamic order or republic—has become a real possibility in Lebanon. Hizbullah never expected to turn Lebanon into an Islamic republic in a short period of time, but it has fought its way into the hearts and minds of as many as half of Lebanon's politically active Shi'ites as well as some Sunni Muslim sympathizers.

Hizbullah has had the ideological, organizational, and operational means to seize opportunities to get closer to its aim. The party's ideology, in particular the wilayat al-faqih, has provided flexibility in the face of changing political circumstances. The essential role of the wali al-faqih or the mujtahid to elaborate, mold, or alter the party's ideology to fit changing circumstances has given Hizbullah leeway to fluctuate between

142

militant and gradualist-pragmatic modes that are closely related to a parallel apparatus to deal with them. Whatever the exact modus operandi, the aim—seizing political power and establishing the Islamic order—has remained the same.

Hizbullah's militant mode—"armed jihad"—has served the party's aim in capturing power in its controlled areas. The militant mode has played an instrumental role in driving foreign forces out of Lebanon and in tirelessly pursuing continued guerrilla warfare against Israel, even after the latter's withdrawal from South Lebanon. The party has defeated its Shi'ite and non-Shi'ite rivals in one battle after another. And above all, the party has applied Islamic law in its controlled areas in the name of Islam under Khomeini's and Khamenei's guardianship of the jurisconsult, thus gradually delegitimizing both the traditional Shi'ite establishment and the Lebanese state institutions.

When political circumstances changed in the late 1980s, Hizbullah, like Iran, opted for political pragmatism without abandoning its militant Islamist posture. Hizbullah's gradualist-pragmatic mode has been equally instrumental in securing the party's aim and its members. The party tacitly accepted the Syrian-backed Ta'if Agreement, moving from confrontation to participation within the confines of the Lebanese political system. It entered the Lebanese parliament and has played the parliamentary game in opposition. It has also participated in municipal elections and come into power in several important cities and towns in Lebanon. And above all, Hizbullah has acquired legitimacy as a political party whose leaders, members, and constituency have the right of freedom of expression and association like all political parties in the country.

Writers and critics may argue that Lebanon's reemerging confessional system prevents any of Lebanon's communities or parties from becoming a dominant political power. Thus, Hizbullah's future Islamic republic is not seen as feasible, and, it is argued, the party eventually will be co-opted into the system. Such arguments may be understandable, but Lebanon's confessional system seems not to be working effectively to block the party's plans of creating an Islamic republic. The ineffectiveness of Lebanon's confessional system is attributed to a paradox inherent in the system itself. On the one hand, the Lebanese confessional system has failed to create national cohesion among the various communities. Sectarian loyalties have constantly undermined the democratic aspect of the system, and accordingly the nation-state building model was transformed into sectarian regional loyalty. On the other hand, the Ta'if Agreement, which amended Lebanon's Constitution, changed the confessional formula of power distribution from a six-to-five ratio in favor of Christians to a five-to-five ratio of equitable distribution of power between Christians and Muslims. To complicate matters further, the Ta'if accord decreed the elimination of political confessionalism for power distribution. Although the Ta'if Agreement did not provide a timetable for the elimination of confessionalism, Hizbullah has been pushing hard to implement it as soon as possible.

In a way it is this dilemma of the Lebanese confessional system that one has to understand in assessing the future of Hizbullah's Islamic republic. Although Hizbullah realizes that suitable conditions for its Islamic order are not present now, in the meantime the party is very well aware of the Lebanese political dilemma and bases its plans on it. By keeping the confessional system as is, Hizbullah will benefit by winning a number of parliamentary seats on a sectarian basis. So far, neither Berri's Amal nor its allies of Shi'ite bourgeois families have been able to undermine Hizbullah's strength in the Shi'ite community. On the contrary, Hizbullah, through its social services and commitment to its constituency, has been able to attract Amal's members and other neglected forces in the Shi'ite community. This is even more problematic on the municipal or local government level where the party is in actual power of several important municipalities. In these autonomous enclaves, the party has created an Islamic order within the artificial presence of the state institutions in these areas.

On the other hand, the elimination of political confessionalism from the system opens up greater possibilities on the national or state level for Hizbullah's plans for an Islamic republic. After all, eliminating the confessional system and substituting it with majoritarian rule would open the way for a Shi'ite president and perhaps a Shi'ite majority in the Parliament. These would be important positions in Hizbullah's bid for power. Hizbullah, since its inception, has demanded a general referendum on the question of the Islamic state. While the Sunnis might object to an Islamic state patterned after Iran's Islamic Republic and on the theory of wilayat al-faqih, the Christians and the Druze have absolutely rejected such a state. Although an anti-Hizbullah majority of Christians, Druze, and mainstream Sunnis would prevent the creation of Hizbullah's Islamic order on the state level, Hizbullah bids on the Shi'ite demographic majority for the realization of its aim. The Shi'ite population is expected to double in the coming five years because of high birth and low emigration rates relative to those of Sunnis, Druze, and Christians, whose birthrates are lower and emigration rates higher. (Of the three, the Christians have the lowest birthrate and the highest emigration rate.) The Shi'ites also differ from the other three groups in that Shi'ites who emigrate are more likely to return to Lebanon. Accordingly, the Shi'ites would grow from being the largest single community to being a clear majority in the country. As such, the establishment of Hizbullah's Islamic state will depend on the freedom of choice of this Shi'ite majority whom Hizbullah plans to capture. Should Hizbullah survive the massive winds of change in the region and continue as a dominant political force into the future of the Shi'ite community, then the party will reach its goal on the state level. Even if Hizbullah is unable to capture the Shi'ite majority, it seems that the country is demographically destined toward a Shi'ite majority. Nothing then will prevent the establishment of a state dominated by Shi'ites, or Hizbullah from using the state apparatus for the realization of its Islamic order.

Fear of Hizbullah's Islamic order, whether achieved forcibly or through demographic majoritarianism, has prompted a reaction from the Christian leaders, in particular the Maronite patriarch, Cardinal Sfair. The Christians have considered that, while Hizbullah is in almost total control of the land, Berri with his Amal is in control of the political and administrative decisions of the state. As such, from the Christian leaders' view, "Nothing will prevent the emergence of a Shi'ite state in the coming twenty years."[1] The concerns of the Christian leaders were expressed immediately after Hizbullah held the biggest-ever military parade on December 2001, celebrating "Jerusalem Day." The parade featured an estimated two hundred thousand trained members, many of whom are determined to die for the aims of the party in the long run.[2]

However, until the circumstances of the Islamic order mature, Hizbullah stresses that the creation of the Islamic order should rely on the free choice of the people rather than force. In Shaykh Na'im Qasim's words, "The text of the 'Open Letter' is clear in calling for the creation of an Islamic state based on the free choice of the people if they desire and will that." He further stated, "It is not right for anybody to cancel any idea of it [faith/Islamic State], or create a new model violating the text or object to the conviction of the rightful Allah's order over others." For practical performance, however, Shaykh Na'im Qasim said, "Our duty is to call for Allah's religion by wisdom and good preaching."[3] Accordingly, Hizbullah's calculation for creating an Islamic order, whether by *da'wah* or by jihad, has not been given up and still might be feasible. After all, the party has achieved some results within the actual circumstances, some of which it has created, while others await the passage of time.

ROLE MODEL FOR RESISTING ISRAEL

Praising the "victory" of Hizbullah's Islamic Resistance and the people of Lebanon, Ayatollah Khamenei puts Hizbullah's future role in the region in perspective: "Hizbullah is the front line of the Islamic world in its fight with the Zionist enemy. The liberation of occupied Palestine is the prime goal for the jihad against the Zionist entity. This last victory has facilitated the way for the new Palestinian generation to lead its struggle and resistance against the Zionist entity that has usurped the sacred Jerusalem."[4]

Responding to Khamenei's decree, Nasrallah answered, "As you are *wali amr al-Muslimin* (guardian of the Muslims), the resistance will continue its path of jihad until the liberation of all occupied land."[5] It is to be noted, however, that all occupied land does not mean the disputed Sheba'a Farms. Rather, it means occupied Palestine and in particular Jerusalem.

It is beyond any doubt that Hizbullah's future role in the region as well as in Lebanon will be determined by Iran. Although Syria under Hafiz al-Assad had called the shots and limited Hizbullah's activities to some extent, the present Syrian regime seems unable to exercise the influence of the past. The fragmentation of the Syrian political elite, the deadlock of peace talks with Israel, and the increase in anti-Syrian elements, in particular among Christians in Lebanon, have rendered Syria's influence weak over Hizbullah. Syria has found itself in need of both Iran and Hizbullah to support its policies, particularly in Lebanon. Although both Iran and Hizbullah have avoided confrontation with Syria over its peace talks with Israel, the two consider the peace process between Syria and Israel dead. In addition, the collapse of the peace process between Israel and the Palestinian Authority following the onset of the Intifada of October 2000 has contributed to weakening Syria and strengthening Iran's position further.

Such conditions have made Hizbullah, and behind it Iran, the key players in the politics of the region. As such, Hizbullah's path of jihad against Israel will continue into the future. Hizbullah thus sets Jerusalem and the furnishing of assistance to the Palestinian people to liberate their land at the core of its future regional role. Such a regional role has considerable support among Sunni Muslims, in particular Sunni Islamic movements, despite their negative attitude toward Shi'ism.

To show its commitment to the common cause of Palestine, Hizbullah has translated its regional role into a role model that is not only involved in supporting the struggle of the Palestinians but is totally involved in the Intifada as well. The party has provided military training, social welfare services, and logistic support, in particular to the Palestinian Islamic Jihad and Hamas, to ensure the continuation of the resistance in the West Bank and Gaza. Of course, important financial matters and support of weaponry were handled directly between leaders of the Palestinian Islamists and Khamenei's office or assistants.

On January 30, 2001, at the opening ceremony of a major conference on Jerusalem organized by Hizbullah, Hamas, Islamic Jihad, and al-Jama' al-Islamiyyah of Lebanon, Sayyid Nasrallah stressed the issue of complete involvement in the Intifada. "If we want to discuss how to regain Jerusalem, we must be completely involved in the Intifada and resistance. This means at all levels, from fighting normalization, to popular mobilization, to armed struggle."[6]

The conference was attended by many distinguished Islamist leaders, including Shaykh Yusuf al-Qaradawi, ideologue and chief of the Islamic National Conference; Hujjat al-Islam Ali Akbar Muhtashami, Khamenei's representative; Shaykh Husayn Ahmad, the amir of Pakistan's al-Jama'ah al-Islamiyyah; Shaykh Abdel Rashid Turabi, the amir of Kashmir's *al-Jama'ah al-Islamiyyah*; Yasin Omar al-Imam, Hasan al-Turabi's representative; Shaykh Faisal al-Mawlawi, secretary-general of Lebanon's Islamic Association; Liath Shibaylat, spokesman of the Islamic Association of Jordan; Khalid Mash'al, head of Hamas's Politburo; and Abdullah Ramadan Shallah, secretary-general of the Islamic Jihad, as well as others from Syria, Yemen, Kuwait, Saudi Arabia, and Algeria. These leaders have come to believe in Hizbullah's role model of resistance and that Israel has suffered a major defeat at the hands of Hizbullah's fighters and that Jerusalem is not only a Palestinian but also an Arab-Muslim cause. In the words of Ali Akbar Muhtashami: "The resistance against the occupation in South Lebanon should serve as a lesson to all Muslims and to the Palestinian people."[7]

In a more explicit way, the chief of the Islamic National Conference, Shaykh Yusuf al-Qaradawi of Egypt, forbids Muslims from giving up Jerusalem. He said, "Jerusalem is not only a Palestinian and Arab cause, but also a Muslim cause. Arabs and non-Arabs, Sunnis and Shi'ites are forbidden to give up any inch of Jerusalem, and we are ready to fight until the last breath in us."[8]

This warning by Shaykh al-Qaradawi, who is highly respected and followed by many Sunni Islamist movements—in particular the Islamic Association of Lebanon and their counterparts in Egypt, Algeria, and the Gulf—should be heeded as a call on all Islamists to be ready for the battle of Jerusalem. Furthermore, Abdullah Ramadan Shallah, secretary-general of the Islamic Jihad, has revealed Islamic Jihad's coordination with Hizbullah's Islamic Resistance. In his words: "The conflict with Israel today is not about the streets and neighborhoods that are measured by centimeters or inches. It is a conflict over possessing the history and future of the region. Our struggle in Palestine would not have achieved success if it were not for the support of the experience of Hizbullah's Islamic Resistance and the party's leadership."[9]

Similarly, many in the Arab-Muslim world have already concluded that armed jihad, when applied with adequate tenacity, as Hizbullah has done, will win surrender to Arab-Muslim demands. The Palestinians—not only Hamas and Islamic Jihad but the militant faction of Fateh' as well, took a leaf out of Hizbullah's book of jihad and followed its model of resistance. Since October 2001 the confrontation with Israel has evolved from stone throwing to martyrdom operations to guerrilla warfare, taking a big toll on both Palestinians and Israelis. This kind of resistance is modeled precisely on Hizbullah's example, despite the Palestinians' long experience in their fight with Israel. Hizbullah has become not only the bridge between Shi'ism and Sunnism, Iran and the Arabs, but also a project of the Arab-Islamic world in its fight with Israel. Although in principle Hizbullah is more likely to continue its resistance against Israel in the Sheba'a Farms or in support of the Palestinians, the party forges a sense of realism with regard to changing after the war in Iraq. Keeping the party's options open for all possibilities indicates such realism. "The issue is not related only to what the Resistance has decided, but related to a number of regional developments, which will leave the door open for all possibilities." [10] The party is well aware that an Israeli withdrawal from Sheba'a Farms might limit the activities of the resistance and even bring it to a halt. Also, preparing for "the battle of Jerusalem," a core issue that is more likely than any other addressed in Islamic history to unify Islamists, requires more than Hizbullah's resistance alone, more, even, than support from Hamas and Islamic Jihad; it requires a wider resistance belt around Israel involving Syria, Jordan, and Egypt—a condition that has not yet been met.

Despite the conclusion of the first stage of the prisoner swap with Israel, which somehow removes another element upon which Hizbullah has justified its continued resistance, the party resistance is continuing. "Nothing has changed," Nasrallah said. "Hizbullah is Hizbullah. There are still detainees in prison. The land is still occupied. The daily Israeli violations are still there. The Israeli threat is still there and Hizbullah's main task is still valid." [11] To that extent, Hizbullah has somehow redefined its role. The party will continue supporting the resistance of the Palestinians and remain a role model for them, but its main task is to defend Lebanon's national sovereignty by striking a balance of terror through its proven guerrilla warfare and substantial armory. Given this goal, it will continue its resistance more as a defensive force along the border with Israel than as an offensive force marching to "liberate Jerusalem."

TRENDS AND PROSPECTS

It is not at all certain that, in its present configuration, Hizbullah has reached the final stage of its project of creating an Islamic order in Lebanon or of its wider regional goal of leading the resistance against Israel. It is certain, however, that the Lebanese government is unable to overcome the difficulties and challenges posed by Hizbullah without significant help from Syria and Iran. Nevertheless, Hizbullah's long-term fate is likely to be affected by at least two additional factors: the evolution of the Arab-Israeli conflict and the relations between Iran and the United States. Clearly, a Syrian-Israeli peace settlement—unlikely at present—would seriously undermine Hizbullah's resistance activities and undoubtedly threaten Hizbullah's role as a political force in Lebanon. Despite the mounting pressure by the United States on Syria—in particular the Syrian Accountability and Lebanese Sovereignty Restoration Act, which calls for evicting all "terrorist" and foreign forces from southern Lebanon, including Hizbullah and the Iranian Revolutionary Guards—Syria has refused to eradicate Hizbullah as a political force in Lebanon.[12] At least two reasons for this refusal seem likely: fear of adding to the already growing opposition to Syria in Lebanon, particularly among Christians, and reluctance to endanger Syria's strategic relationship with Iran, which would strenuously resist any decision to eradicate Hizbullah or its resistance. Hizbullah's leaders have refused to consider even the possibility of eradicating the party or its resistance. According to Shaykh Naʿim Qasim, "The resistance has become an undivided part of the stable Syrian politics of President Dr. Bashar al-Assad."[13] In fact, Hizbullah and Syria both appear determined to keep their relations nonconfrontational. "The options for cooperation between Hizbullah and Syria are wide open, no matter what the difficulties are."[14] Given this, it is doubtful that halting the resistance would prompt Syria to dismantle the party. Moreover, a protracted conflict between Syria and Israel or Syria and the United States would be bound to polarize the region and provoke an increase in resistance activities. A confrontation between Iran and the United States would likewise cause a resurgence of militancy against the United States in Lebanon and the region. And even if the regime in Iran were to collapse, Hizbullah has reached a stage now where it can easily exist.

Beyond these external factors, the future course of Hizbullah will depend on the ability of the Lebanese state to accommodate both Muslim and Christian interests under the Ta'if formula, and to bring some measure of economic prosperity to all social classes, in particular the poor classes, regardless of sectarian affiliation.

Notes

Glossary

Bibliography

Index

Notes

1. THE HIZBULLAH COMPLEX

1. Hala Jaber, *Hezbullah: Born with a Vengeance* (New York: Columbia Univ. Press, 1997); Magnus Ranstorp, *Hizb'allah in Lebanon: The Politics of the Western Hostage Crisis* (New York: St. Martin's Press, 1997); Marius Deeb, *Militant Islamic Movements in Lebanon: Origins, Social Basis, and Ideology* (Washington, D.C.: Center for Contemporary Arab Studies, Georgetown Univ., 1986); Shimon Shapira, "The Origins of Hizbullah," *Jerusalem Quarterly* 46 (spring 1988): 116–25; Amal Saad Ghorayeb, *Hizbu'llah: Politics and Religion* (London: Pluto Press, 2002).

2. Augustus Richard Norton, *Hizbullah of Lebanon: Extremist Ideals vs. Mundane Politics* (New York: Council on Foreign Relations, 1999).

3. Elizabeth Picard, "The Lebanese Shi'a and Political Violence," Discussion Paper 42 (United Nations Research Institute for Social Development [UNRISD], 1993); As'ad Abu Khalil, "Ideology and Practice of Hizbullah in Lebanon: Islamization of Leninist Organizational Principles," *Middle Eastern Studies* 27, no. 3 (July 1991): 390–400; Eyal Zisser, "Hizbullah in Lebanon: At the Crossroad," *Terrorism and Political Violence* 8, no. 2 (summer 1997): 90–106.

4. Waddah Sharara, *Hizbullah: Dawlat al-Mujtama' al-Mahali* (Hizbullah: The state of local society) (Beirut: Dar al-Nahar Press, 1997); Martin Kramer, "Hizbullah: The Calculus of Jihad," *Bulletin of the American Academy of Arts and Sciences* (May 1994): 36–52.

5. Ahmad Nizar Hamzeh, "Lebanon's Hizbullah: From Islamic Revolution to Parliamentary Accommodation," *Third World Quarterly* 14, no. 2 (spring 1993): 321–36; Ahmad Nizar Hamzeh and R. Hrair Dekmejian, "The Islamic Spectrum of Lebanese Politics," *Journal of South Asian and Middle Eastern Studies* 16, no. 3 (spring 1993): 25–42.

6. For insightful analysis of crisis environment see R. Hrair Dekmejian, *Islam in Revolution: Fundamentalism in the Arab World*, 2d ed. (Syracuse: Syracuse Univ. Press, 1995), 1–3, 23–30.

7. For other attributes discussed by Dekmejian, see ibid., 6.

2. CRISIS CATALYSTS TO THE EMERGENCE OF HIZBULLAH

1. For further treatment of crisis environment see Dekmejian, *Islam in Revolution,* 23–35. See also John Esposito, *Islam and Politics* (Syracuse: Syracuse Univ. Press, 1991); Emmanuel

Sivan, *Radical Islam* (New Haven, Conn.: Yale Univ. Press, 1985); R. Stephen Humphreys, "The Contemporary Resurgence in the Context of Modern Islam," in *Islamic Resurgence in the Arab World,* ed. Ali E. Hillal Dessouki (New York: Praeger, 1982); and Ali E. Hillal Dessouki, ed., *Islamic Resurgence in the Arab World* (New York: Praeger, 1982).

2. See Fouad Ajami, *The Vanished Imam: Musa al-Sadr and the Shia of Lebanon* (Ithaca, N.Y.: Cornell Univ. Press, 1986); Augustus Richard Norton, *Amal and the Shi'a: Struggle for the Soul of Lebanon* (Austin: Univ. of Texas Press, 1987); Juan R. I. Cole and Nikki R. Keddie, eds., *Shi'ism and Social Protest* (New Haven, Conn., and London: Yale Univ. Press, 1986); Helena Cobban, *The Making of Modern Lebanon* (London: Hutchinson, 1987); Theodor Hanf, *Coexistence in Wartime Lebanon: Decline of a State and Rise of a Nation,* trans. John Richardson (London: I. B. Tauris, 1993); Elizabeth Picard, *Lebanon, a Shattered Country: Myths and Realities of the Wars in Lebanon,* trans. Franklin Philip (New York: Holmes and Meier, 1996); Charles Winslow, *Lebanon: War and Politics in a Fragmented Society* (New York: Routledge, 1996); William W. Harris, *Faces of Lebanon: Sects, Wars, and Global Extension* (Princeton, N.J.: Markus Wiener, 1997); Farid Khazen, *The Breakdown of the State in Lebanon, 1967–1976* (Cambridge, Mass.: Harvard Univ. Press, 2000).

3. For a thorough analysis of psychological factors, see Erik H. Erikson, *Identity, Youth, and Crisis* (New York: W. W. Norton, 1968); Emile Durkheim, *Suicide: A Study in Sociology* (Glencoe, Ill.: Free Press, 1951); Dekmejian, *Islam in Revolution,* 26–27.

4. Muhammad Baqir al-Sadr, *Nash'at al-Shi'ah wal-Tashaya'* (The emergence of the Shi'ite and Shi'ism) (Beirut: Al-Ghady Publication, 1999), 113–28.

5. Ibid.

6. For a good introduction to Islam, see Fazlur Rahman, *Islam* (Chicago: Univ. of Chicago Press, 1979).

7. Abdulaziz A. Sachedina, "Activist Shi'ism in Iran, Iraq, and Lebanon," in *Fundamentalism and the State: Remaking Politics, Economics, and Militance,* ed. Martin E. Marty and R. Scott Appleby (Chicago: Univ. of Chicago Press 1993), 422–23.

8. For further analysis of the idea of the Mahdi, see Abdulaziz A. Sachedina, *The Idea of the Mahdi in Twelver Shi'ism* (Albany: State Univ. of New York Press, 1981).

9. Dekmejian, *Islam in Revolution,* 15.

10. For the pattern of the Lebanese Shi'ite settlements, see Kamal Salibi, *A House of Many Mansions* (London: I. B. Tauris, 1988), 3–14; Philip Hitti, *Lebanon in History: From the Earliest Times to the Present* (London: Macmillan, 1967); Wajih Kawtharani, *Al-Itijahat al-Ijtima'iyyah wa al-Siyassiyyah fi Jabal 'Amil* (The political and social trends of Mount Amil) (Beirut: Bahsun Press, 1994), 55–139; Ahmad Rida, "Al-Mutwali al-Shi'i fi Jabal 'Amil," *Al-'Irfan* 2 (June 1910): 15; William Roe Polk, *The Opening of South Lebanon, 1788–1840* (Cambridge, Mass.: Harvard Univ. Press, 1963), 81–82.

11. Salibi, *Many Mansions,* 3–14; Iliya Harik, "The Ethnic Revolution and Political Integration in the Middle East," *International Journal of Middle Eastern Studies* 13, no. 2 (fall 1972): 313–14.

12. Polk, *Opening of South Lebanon,* 81.

13. Salibi, *Many Mansions,* 126.

14. Rida,"Al-Mutwali al-Shi'i," 15; Polk,*Opening of South Lebanon,* 15.

15. Albert Hourani, *Minorities in the Arab World* (Oxford: Oxford Univ. Press, 1947), 21; Leila Meo, *Lebanon, Improbable Nation: A Study in Political Development* (Bloomington: Indiana Univ. Press, 1965), 60; Harik, 272–73.

16. Muhsin al-Amin, *Khitat Jabal 'Amil* (Plans of Mount Amil) (Beirut: Dar al-Ilmiyyah, 1983), 126.

17. Meir Zamir, *The Formation of Modern Lebanon* (London: Croom Helm, 1985), 85–86.

18. 'Ali al-Amin, *Sadiq Hamza al-Fa'aur* (Beirut: Asia Publishing Company, 1985), 72–73; Hussein M. Gharbieh, "Political Awareness of the Shi'ites in Lebanon: The Role of Sayyid Abd al-Husain Sharaf al-Din and Sayyid Musa al-Sadr," (Ph.D. thesis, Univ. of Durham, 1996), 88–92.

19. Kawtharani, 314–15.

20. Hanf, *Coexistence in Wartime Lebanon,* 583.

21. Ralph Crow, "Confessionalism, Public Administration, and Efficiency in Lebanon," in *Politics in Lebanon,* ed. Leonard Binder (New York: John Wiley and Sons, 1966), 171–72.

22. See Salim Nasr, "Beyrouth et le conflit libanais: Restructuration de l'espace urbain," in *Politiques urbaines dans le monde arabe,* ed. J. Metral and G. Mutin (Lyons: Maison de l'Orient, 1984), 287–305.

23. Rania Maktabi, "The Lebanese Census of 1932 Revisited: Who Are the Lebanese?" *British Journal of Middle Eastern Studies* 26, no. 1 (May 1999): 219–41.

24. Karl W. Deutsch, *Politics and Government: How People Decide Their Fate* (New York: Houghton Mifflin, 1970), 89.

25. Picard, "The Lebanese Shi'a," 5.

26. Norton, "Hizbullah of Lebanon," 5.

27. Amal Sa'ad, "Political Mobilization of the Lebanese Shi'ites" (M.A. thesis, Department of Political Studies, American Univ. of Beirut, 1996), 96.

28. For details of status discrepancy, see Thomas H. Greene, *Comparative Revolutionary Movements* (Englewood Cliffs, N.J.: Prentice Hall, 1984), 200–204; Dean G. Pruitt and Jeffrey Z. Rubin, *Social Conflict: Escalation, Stalemate, and Settlement* (New York: Random House, 1986), 13–14.

29. Greene, *Comparative Revolutionary Movements,* 154; Dekmejian, *Islam in Revolution,* 28.

30. Ritchie Ovendale, *The Origins of the Arab-Israeli Wars,* 2d ed. (London: Longman, 1992), 232–33; Norton, "Hizbullah of Lebanon," 6.

31. Cited in Gharbieh, "Political Awareness," 125.

32. Norton, *Amal and the Shi'a,* 53.

33. Robin Wright, "Lebanon," in *The Politics of Islamic Revivalism,* ed. Shireen T. Hunter (Bloomington and Indianapolis: Indiana Univ. Press, 1988), 63.

34. Ovendale, *Origins of the Arab-Israeli Wars,* 233.

35. Hussein J. Agha and Ahmad S. Khalidi, *Syria and Iran: Rivalry and Cooperation* (London: Pinter, 1995), 14–15.

36. Ibid., 17.

37. Ibid.

38. Greene, *Comparative Revolutionary Movements,* 174.

39. Ibid., 175.

40. Chibli Mallat, *Shi'i Thought from the South of Lebanon* (Oxford: Center for Lebanese Studies, 1988), 6–7; Shapira, 116–17.

41. Dekmejian, *Islam in Revolution,* 122–23.

42. Kramer, "Calculus of Jihad," 543.

43. Agha and Khalidi, *Syria and Iran,* 7.

44. Hamzeh and Dekmejian, "The Islamic Spectrum," 36–37.

45. For a biography of Musa al-Sadr, see the Supreme Islamic Shi'ite Council, *Samahat al-Imam Musa al-Sadr* (His Eminence Imam Musa al-Sadr) (Supreme Islamic Shi'ite Council, n.p., n.d.), 1–2; see also Ajami, *The Vanished Imam,* 33–35; Norton, *Amal and the Shi'a.*

46. See Hamzeh and Dekmejian, "The Islamic Spectrum," 26–27.

47. For further analysis of the Supreme Islamic Shi'ite Council, see *Samahat al-Imam,* 4–5; Hamzeh and Dekmejian, "The Islamic Spectrum," 27–28.

48. *Samahat al-Imam,* 31–32; Ajami, *The Vanished Imam,* 115–17.

49. *Samahat al-Imam,* 12; Ajami, *The Vanished Imam,* 168.

50. *Samahat al-Imam,* 8–10; Norton, *Amal and the Shi'a,* 47–49.

51. Ajami, *The Vanished Imam,* 118–19.

52. For further details of Al-Sadr's disappearance, see Ajami, *The Vanished Imam,* 180–94.

53. Dekmejian, *Islam in Revolution,* 167.

54. Shaykh Na'im Qasim, *Hizbullah* (Ghobairi, Beirut: Dar al-Hadi, 2002), 20–22.

55. Muhammad Husayn Fadlallah, *Al-Islam wa mantiq al-quwwah* (Islam and the logic of power) (Beirut: Al-Mu'assasat al-Jam'iyyah, 1981), 247–49.

56. Hamzeh and Dekmejian, "The Islamic Spectrum," 35–37.

57. Ibid., 40.

58. See Ahmad al-Musawi, "Min Antum Hizbullah" (Who are you, Hizbullah?), *Al-Shira'a,* no. 2 of five parts (Apr. 10, 2000): 23–24.

59. Shaykh Subhi al-Tufayli, interview by author, Beirut southern suburbs, Apr. 10, 1995.

60. See Al-Musawi, "Man antum Hizbullah?" no. 1, Apr. 3, 2000, 24–25.

61. Ibid.

62. Ibid.

63. Al-Musawi, "Man antum Hizbullah?" no. 2, Apr. 10, 2000, 23–25.

64. See John L. Esposito, ed., *The Iranian Revolution: Its Global Impact* (Miami: Florida International Univ. Press, 1990), 116–37; Daniel Pipes, *In the Path of God: Islam and Political Power* (New York: Basic Book, 1983).

65. Agha and Khalidi, *Syria and Iran,* 18–20.

3. ISLAMIC JURISTICAL IDEOLOGY

1. For emphasis on Hizbullah's "Open Letter," see Marvin Zonis and Daniel Brumberg, *Khomeini, the Islamic Republic of Iran, and the Arab World* (Cambridge, Mass.: Center for Middle Eastern Studies, Harvard Univ., 1987); Jaber; Norton, "Hizbullah of Lebanon."

2. Shaykh Naʿim Qasim (Hizbullah's deputy secretary), interview by author, Beirut southern suburbs, Jan. 25, 2001.

3. See "Nass al-risalah al-maftuha alati wajjahah Hizbullah ila al-mustadʿafin fi Lubnan wa al-ʿalam" (Text of the open letter addressed by Hizbullah to the downtrodden in Lebanon and the world), Lebanon, Feb. 16, 1985, 48.

4. For the concept of God's just society see Sayyid Hasan Nasrallah, "Al-Jamaʿh al-bashariyyah wal-risalah wal-wilayah" (The human group and the message and the guardianship), lecture, *Al-Ahd,* July 16, 1997, 4–6; also see Ali Khamenei, *Al-Imamah wal-wilayah* (The rightful successor and the guardianship) (Beirut: Markaz Baqiyat Allah al-ʿAzzam, 1999).

5. Nasrallah, "Al-Jamaʿh al-bashariyyah," 4; Khamenei, 19.

6. Qasim, interview by author, Nov. 27, 2000; see also Nasrallah, "Al-Jamaʿh al-bashariyyah"; and Ruhallah Khomeini, *Al-Hukumah al-islamiyyah* (The Islamic government) (Beirut: Dar al-Taliya, 1979), 27–28.

7. Nasrallah, "Al-Jamaʿh al-bashariyyah," 4.

8. Qasim, interview by author, Jan. 25, 2001; see also Qasim, *Hizbullah,* 38–39.

9. "Hizbullah: Identity and Goals," www.hizbollah.org.

10. Hanf, *Coexistence in Wartime Lebanon,* 28.

11. Ibid.

12. Qasim, interview by author, Jan. 25, 2001.

13. Sayyid Hasan Nasrallah, "Min wilayat ʿAli ila wilayat al-faqih" (From the guardianship of Ali to the guardianship of the jurisconsult), *Al-Ahd,* May 26, 1995, 27.

14. For further detail, see Said Amir Arjomand, *The Shadow of God and the Hidden Imam: Religion, Political Order, and Societal Change in Shiʿite Iran from the Beginning to 1890* (Chicago: Univ. of Chicago Press, 1984).

15. Sachedina, "Activist Shiʿism," 428–29.

16. Qasim, interview by author, Nov. 27, 2000; see also Khomeini, *Al-Hukumah al-islamiyyah,* 49.

17. Arjomand, *Shadow of God,* 238.

18. Dekmejian, *Islam in Revolution,* 125.

19. Khomeini, *Al-Hukumah al-islamiyyah,* 43, 69, 81, 84, 114.

20. Ibid., 49.

21. Ibid., 76–79; see also Nasrallah, "Al-Jamaʿh al-bashariyyah," 4.

22. Khomeini, *Al-Hukumah al-islamiyyah,* 47–49; see also Nasrallah, "Al-Jamaʿh al-bashariyyah," 4.

23. Nasrallah, "Min wilayat ʿAli," 27; see also Khamenei, 73–88.

24. Nasrallah, "Min wilayat ʿAli," 27.

25. Ibid.

26. Nasrallah, "Al-Jamaʿh al-bashariyyah," 4.

27. Nasrallah, "Min wilayat ʿAli," 27.

28. Qasim, interviews by author, Nov. 27, 2000, and Jan. 25, 2001; see also Qasim, *Hizbullah,* 67–68.

29. Ibid.

30. Ibid.; Sayyid Hasan Nasrallah, interview, *Al-Wasat,* Mar. 3, 1996, 31.

31. See *Al-Hayat,* Dec. 2, 1993, 18; *Al-Wasat,* Mar. 18, 1996, 37.

32. *Al-Wasat,* Mar. 18, 1996, 37.

33. Nasrallah, "Min wilayat ʿAli," 27; also, Nasrallah, "Al-Imamah wal-wilayah," unpublished lecture delivered in Beirut southern suburbs—Qaʿat al-Jinan, June 2, 1997.

34. For such emphasis see Jaber, 63–65; Norton, "Hizbullah of Lebanon," 15–16.

35. Nasrallah, "Al-Jihad," lecture delivered on the seventh night of ʿAshuraʾ, Beirut southern suburbs, May 6, 1998; see also Shaykh Muhammad Yazbak, "Dawr al-jihad fi hayat al-ummah" (The role of the jihad in the life of the community), in *Muatamar al-jihad wal-nahda* (Conference on the jihad and the awakening) (Beirut: Khomeini's Committee, 2000), 83–94.

36. Qasim, interview by author, Nov. 27, 2000; also see Qasim, *Hizbullah,* 44–56.

37. Nasrallah, "Al-Jihad," 4–5.

38. Qasim, interview by author, Nov. 27, 2000.

39. Nasrallah, "Al-Jihad," 9.

40. Qurʾan, verse 193, chapter 2 or surat, 2.

41. Ibid., verse 33, chapter 9 or surat, 9.

42. Qasim, interview by author, Jan. 25, 2001.

43. Ibid.; see also Yazbak, 89; Nasrallah, "Al-Jihad," 11.

44. Nasrallah, "Al-Jihad," 11–12.

45. Ibid., 4.

46. Qasim, interview by author, Nov. 27, 2000; Yazbak, 85.

47. "Hizbullah: Goals and Identity," www.hizbollah.org.

48. Cited in Ahmad Sayyid Rafʿat, "Al-Imam wa Filastin" (The Imam and Palestine), in *Muʾatamar al-jihad wal-nahda* (Beirut: Khomeini's Committee, 2000), 435.

49. Ibid., 435.

50. Nasrallah, *Al-Ahd,* Aug. 4, 2000, 4.

51. Nasrallah, *Al-Nahar,* June 1997, 5.

52. Nasrallah, *Al-Ahd,* Aug. 4, 2000, 5.

53. Nasrallah, interview, *Al-Mushahid al-Siyyasi,* May 14, 2000, 15.

54. Nasrallah, interview, *Al-Wasat,* June 29, 2000, 15.

55. *Al-Nahar,* May 19, 1997, 8.

56. *Al-Nahar,* Dec. 23, 2000, 7; *Al-Ahd,* Dec. 29, 2000, 1–2.

57. Nasrallah, interview, *Al-Mushahid al-Siyassi,* May 7, 2000, 7.

58. Qasim, interview by author, Jan. 25, 2001; *Al-Ahd,* June 6, 1997, 5.

59. For discussion of the similarity of Hizbullah ideology to Leninist theory, see Abu Khalil, 390–403.

60. Qasim, interview by author, Jan. 25, 2001.

61. Ibid.

4. CLERICAL LEADERSHIP AND HIERARCHICAL STRUCTURE

1. See Norton, "Hizbullah of Lebanon"; Jaber; Ranstorp; Picard, "The Lebanese Shi'a"; Zonis and Brumberg; Esposito, *Islam and Politics.*

2. Nasrallah, interview, *Al-Wasat,* May 13, 2000, 11; see also "Hizbullah: Identity and Goals," www.hizbollah.org (accessed Sept. 6, 2000).

3. See Hamzeh, "Lebanon's Hizbullah," 328.

4. Qasim, interview by author, Nov. 27, 2000. See also Qasim, *Hizbullah,* 85–86.

5. Qasim, interview by author, Nov. 27, 2000.

6. Ibid.

7. For further detail on Iran's Assembly of Experts, see Said Amir Arjomand, "Shi'ite Jurisprudence and Constitution Making in the Islamic Republic of Iran," in *Fundmentalism and the State,* ed. Martin Marty and Scott Appleby (Chicago: Univ. of Chicago Press, 1993), 94–95.

8. Qasim, interview by author, Nov. 27, 2000.

9. All information is derived from Mu'assasat Jihad al-Bina', in particular, *Jihad al-Bina: Its Twelfth Spring: 1988–2000* (Beirut: Jihad al-Bina, 2000); *The Generous Hand: Six Years of Work and Construction 1988–1994* (Beirut: Jihad al-Bina, 1994) and *Nashat al-mu'assasah li 'aam 1995* (1995 annual activities report; Beirut: Jihad al-Bina, 1995). See also UN ESCWA, "Rural Community Development: Two Case Studies from Lebanon," (paper; Beirut: UN-ESCWA, May 21, 1999), 16–66.

10. Mu'assasat Jihad al-Bina', *Its Twelfth Spring,* 7; *The Generous Hand,* 2.

11. UN-ESCWA, "Rural Community Development," 16.

12. Jihad al-Bina': *Its Twelfth Spring,* 39; UN-ESCWA, "Rural Community Development," 65.

13. Ibid., Mu'assasat Jihad al-Bina': *Its Twelfth Spring.*

14. Mu'assasat Jihad al-Bina': *Its Twelfth Spring; Nashat,* 5–6.

15. See Mu'assasat al-Shahid (Martyrs Foundation), *Nashat al-mu'assasah li 'aam 1999* (1999 annual activities report); see also UN-ESCWA, "Rural Community Development," 16.

16. Mu'assasat al-Shahid, 1.

17. Ibid., 2.

18. See Mu'assasat al-Jarha (Foundation for the wounded), *Nashat al-mu'assasa li 'aam 2000–2001* (2000–2001 annual activities) (Beirut: Hizbullah, 2001), 1–3.

19. Ibid., 2.

20. http://almashriq.hiof.no/Lebanon/300/320/Hizbullah/Emdad Committee.

21. Ibid.

22. See Al-Hay'a al-Suhiyyah al-Islamiyyah (Islamic health society), *Al-Takrir al-thanawi li 'aam 2000,* 1–3.

23. Ibid.

24. See Al-T'abi'a al-Tarbawiyyah (Education Enforcement Office), "The 2000–2001 Annual Report," in *Al-Ahd,* Nov. 24, 2000, 9.

25. Ibid.

26. *Al-Ahd,* Aug. 25, 2000, 5.

27. See Shaykh Hani Fahas, "Al-Dawlah al-lubnaniyyah wa al-dawlah al-mutawaziyyah" (The Lebanese state and the parallel state), *Al-Hayat,* June 25, 1996, 19.

28. *Daily Star,* Jan. 3, 2001, 4.

29. Ibid., Oct. 30, 2003, 2; Hajj Hason Ezzedine, interview by author, Beirut southern suburbs, Oct. 31, 2003.

30. Fahas, "Al-Dawlah al-lubnaniyyah," 19.

31. Ibid.

32. Ibid.

33. Hajj Yusuf Mer'i, interview by author, Beirut southern suburbs, May 21, 1996.

34. Ibid.

35. Hajj, 'Ali Fayyad, interview by author, Beirut, Jan. 10, 2001.

36. Nasrallah, interview, *Al-Mushahid al-Siyassi,* May 7, 2000, 12–13.

37. Ibid., 13.

38. Ahmad Nizar Hamzeh, "Islamism in Lebanon: A Guide to the Groups," *Middle East Quarterly* 5, no. 3 (Sept. 1997): 48.

39. Arjomand, "Shi'ite Jurisprudence," 99.

40. Nasrallah, *Al-Mushahid al-Siyassi,* May 7, 2000, 13.

41. Ibid.

42. Ibid.

43. Fahas, "Al-Dawlah al-lubnaniyyah," 19.

44. See Haya't Dam al-Muqawamah al-Islamiyyah (Association for the Support of the Islamic Resistance), *Al-Takrir al-sanawi li 'aam 1999* (The 1999 annual report), 1–3.

45. Ahmad Nizar Hamzeh, "Lebanon's Islamists and Local Politics: A New Reality," *Third World Quarterly* 21, no. 5 (spring 2000): 48.

46. Jeffrey Goldberg, "In the Party of God," *The New Yorker,* October 14, 2002 and October 21, 2002, 183.

47. Ahmad Nizar Hamzeh, "The Role of Hizbullah in Conflict Management Within Lebanon's Shi'ite Community," in *Conflict Resolution in the Arab World,* ed. Paul Salem (Beirut: American Univ. of Beirut, 1997), 103.

48. Norton, "Hizbullah of Lebanon," 23.

49. *Al-Ahd,* June 1996, 2.

50. Shaykh Muhammad Kawtharani, interview by author, Ras al-Nab'a, Beirut, Dec. 14, 2000.

51. Ibid.

52. Nasrallah, interview, *Al-Wasat,* May 29, 2000, 15.

53. Nasrallah, interview, *Al-Shira'a,* Dec. 18, 2000, 7.

54. Ibid.

55. Hamzeh, "Islamism in Lebanon," 48.

56. See Qasim, *Hizbullah,* 87.

57. Ibid.

58. Ibid., 86.

59. *Wijhat Nazar* 2 (Aug. 2000): 25.

60. Ibid.

61. See interview with Thai'r, Hizbullah's fighter, *al-Diyyar,* June 6, 1999, 3.

62. Ibid.

63. Information based on some of Hizbullah's Islamic Resistance operations published in Hizbullah, *Safahat 'Izz fi kitab al-ummah* (Glorious pages in the book of the ummah) (Beirut: Hizbullah, 1999), 558–76.

64. Nasrallah, interview, *Al-Wasat,* Mar. 18, 1996, 10–13.

65. See *Al-Watan al-Arabi,* Oct. 20, 2000, 36; *Al-Hawadith,* Oct. 27, 2000, 19.

66. See Hizbullah, *Safahat 'Izz,* 563–76.

67. *Al-Hawadith,* Oct. 27, 2000, 22.

68. Ibid.

69. Nasrallah, interview, *Al-Mushahid al-Siyassi,* May 27, 2000, 17–18.

70. *Al-Hawadith,* Nov. 27, 2000, 21.

71. Ibid.

72. Ibid.

73. *Al-Ahd,* Oct. 20, 2000, 3.

74. Ibid.

75. Ibid. See also *Daily Star,* Oct. 17, 2000, 2.

76. See Hamzeh, "Lebanon's Hizbullah," 328.

77. Nasrallah, interview, *Al-Wasat,* Mar. 18, 1996, 3.

78. See Hamzeh, "Islamism in Lebanon," 48.

79. On the difference between cadre and mass parties, see Maurice Duverger, *Political Parties: Their Organization and Activity in the Modern State,* (London: Methuen, 1978); Giovanni Sartori, *Parties and Party Systems* (Cambridge: Cambridge Univ. Press, 1979).

80. See Nasrallah, *Al-Mushahid al-Siyassi,* May 7, 2000, 4.

81. For further details of Hizbullah's culture, see Ali al-Kurani, *Tariqat Hizbullah fi al-'aml al-islami* (Hizbullah's method in Islamic work) (Beirut: Al-Mu'assasah al-Alamiyyah, n.d.), 107–10.

82. Ibid., 165–81.

83. Ibid.

84. I conducted field observations in Beirut's southern suburbs, the South, and the Ba'albek-Hirmil region between July and September 2000.

85. Nasrallah, interview, *Al-Mushahid al-Siyassi,* May 7, 2000, 11.

86. For further details, see Hamzeh and Dekmejian, "The Islamic Spectrum," 40–41.

87. See Hamzeh, "Lebanon's Islamists," 51.

88. Ibid., 52.

89. Ibid.

90. See Hizbullah, *Safahat 'Izz,* 305.

5. OPERATIONAL CHOICES: BETWEEN MILITANCY
AND GRADUALIST PRAGMATISM

1. For the distinction between moderate and extremist modes of action, see Daniel Pipes and John Esposito, "Symposium: Resurgent Islam in the Middle East," *Middle East Policy* (Aug. 1994): 1–21; Mumtaz Ahmad and William Zartman, "Symposium: Political Islam: Can It Become a Loyal Opposition?" *Middle East Policy* (Jan. 1997): 68–74.

2. Agha and Khalidi, *Syria and Iran,* 17–18.

3. Qasim, interview by author, Jan. 25, 2001. For revolutionary movements' techniques, see also Greene, *Comparative Revolutionary Movements,* chap. 8.

4. Agha and Khalidi, *Syria and Iran,* 19.

5. See in particular Al-Musawi, "Man antum Hizbullah?" no. 1, Apr. 3, 2000, 26.

6. Ibid., 27.

7. Ibid., 29.

8. Ibid., 28

9. Kramer, "Calculus of Jihad," 45.

10. See Al-Musawi, "Man antum Hizbullah?" no. 1, Apr. 3, 2000, 29.

11. Qasim, interview by author, Jan. 25, 2001.

12. Greene, *Comparative Revolutionary Movements,* 132.

13. See Hamzeh, "Lebanon's Islamists," 51.

14. Ibid.

15. Ibid.

16. Al-Musawi, "Man antum Hizbullah?" no. 5, May 22, 2000, 6.

17. Kramer, "Calculus of Jihad," 45.

18. Nasrallah, interview, *Al-Wasat,* Mar. 3, 1996, 30.

19. See Agha and Khalidi, *Syria and Iran,* 24–25.

20. Greene, *Comparative Revolutionary Movements,* 133.

21. See Hizbullah, *Safahat 'Izz,* 305–7.

22. Greene, *Comparative Revolutionary Movements,* 136.

23. Al-Musawi, "Man antum Hizbullah?" no. 2, Apr. 10, 2000, 20.

24. Ibid., 19.

25. *Al-Shira'a,* June 5, 2000, 17–24.

26. See Hamzeh, "Lebanon's Hizbullah," 322.

27. www.hizbollah.org (accessed June 2, 2001); see also *Al-shira',* June 5, 2000, 26.

28. Shaykh Nabil Qawok, interview, *Daily Star,* Oct. 7, 2000, 2.

29. Hizbullah, *Safahat 'Izz,* 14.

30. *Al-Shira'a,* Apr. 3, 2000.

31. *Jerusalem Post,* Mar. 1, 1999, 1.

32. *Al-Shira'a,* Apr. 3, 2000, 27.

33. *Al-Ahd,* Feb. 15, 2000, 1.

34. Ibid., 2.

35. Ibid.

36. Norton, "Hizbullah of Lebanon," 27.

37. *Al-Shira'a,* June 5, 2000, 26.

38. For details of complaints filed by Hizbullah and Israel, see Hizbullah, *Safahat 'Izz,* 207–27.

39. Amos Harel, "Time to Go," www.hizbollah.org (accessed June 15, 2001).

40. *Al-Nahar,* Oct. 14, 1999, 1.

41. *Al-Shira'a,* June 5, 2000, 9–10.

42. Agence France Press, www.moqawama.org (accessed May 25, 2000).

43. *Al-Ahd,* June 15, 2000, 2–4.

44. See Norton, "Hizbullah of Lebanon," 30.

45. Author's field trip to the South—Kfar Shuba to Naqoura, along the Lebanese-Israeli border—Sept. 9, 18, 2000.

46. Ibid., Sept. 20, 2000.

47. Agence France Press, www.moqawama.org (accessed May 25, 2000).

48. *Al-Ahd,* July 7, 2000, 1–2.

49. *Daily Star,* Sept. 29, 2000, 1–2.

50. *Al-Ahd,* Oct. 13, 2000, 1–2.

51. *Daily Star,* Oct. 9, 2000, 1.

52. *Daily Star,* Jan., 30, 2004, 1–2.

53. *Al-Ahd,* Oct. 17, 2000, 1, 3.

54. Ibid., Dec. 1, 2000, 3; *Daily Star,* Nov. 27, 2000, 1–2.

55. *Al-Nahar,* Mar. 16, 2001, 1; *Daily Star,* Nov. 18, 2002, 2, and Oct. 28, 2003, 1.

56. *Al-Nahar,* Feb. 21, 2001, 1, 3.

57. Shaykh Nabil Qawok, interview, *Al-Ahd,* Dec. 1, 2000, 3.

58. See Al-Musawi, "Man antum Hizbullah?" no. 2, Apr. 10, 2000, 26.

59. Ibid.

60. Zonis and Brumberg, 60.

61. Al-Musawi, "Man antum Hizbullah?" no. 3, Apr. 17, 2000, 21.

62. Ibid.; see also *Al-Shira'a,* May 22, 2000, 13–14.

63. See Agha and Khalidi, *Syria and Iran,* 21–22.

64. Norton, "Hizbullah of Lebanon," 9.

65. Ibid., 30.

66. See Al-Musawi, "Man antum Hizbullah?" no. 3, Apr. 17, 2000, 23.

67. Ibid.

68. Qasim, interview, Jan. 25, 2001.

69. All information is derived from Hamzeh, "Role of Hizbullah," 99–114. It is worth noting also that this study was based on interviews conducted with Shaykh Na'im Qasim in March and April 1993 and with Sayyid Ibrahim Amin al-Sayyid in March and May 1993. All interviews took place in Hizbullah's offices in the southern suburbs of Beirut.

70. Ibid., 101.

71. Ibid., 102.

72. Ibid., 103.

73. Ibid.

74. Ibid.

75. Ibid., 104.

76. Ibid.

77. Ibid., 105.

78. Qasim, interview by author, Jan. 25, 2001.

79. Hamzeh, "The Role of Hizbullah," 105.

80. Ibid., 106.

81. Ibid., 107.

82. Ibid., 108.

83. Ibid., 109.

84. Ibid., 110.

85. Ibid., 111.

86. Ibid., 112.

87. Ibid., 113.

88. Ibid., 114.

89. Ibid., 113.

90. Ibid.

91. Ibid.

92. Elie Salem, *The Ta'if Agreement* (Beirut: Lebanese Center for Policy Studies, 1992); Augustus Richard Norton, "Lebanon after the Tai'f: Is the Civil War Over?" *Middle East Journal* (summer 1991): 471–73.

93. See Hamzeh and Dekmejian, "The Islamic Spectrum," 38.

94. See *Al-Hayat,* Feb. 1990, 8.

95. Al-Musawi, "Man antum Hizbullah?" no. 2, Apr. 10, 2000, 25.

96. Ibid., 26.

97. *Al-Shira'a,* Apr. 10, 2000, 24.

98. *Al-Shira'a,* Aug. 10, 1992, 13.

99. *Al-Safir,* July 5, 1997, 1, 3.

100. Ibid., 3; Norton, "Hizbullah of Lebanon," 23.

101. Norton, "Hizbullah of Lebanon," 23.

102. Qasim, interview by author, Jan. 25, 2001.

103. See Emmanuel Sivan, "The Holy War Tradition in Islam," *Orbis* 4, no. 2 (spring 1998): 17–22.

104. See Picard, "The Lebanese Shi'a," 41.

105. For further details of the 1992 Lebanese parliamentary elections, see Hamzeh, "Lebanon's Hizbullah," 329–35.

106. Ibid., 322; *Al-Safir,* Sept. 9, 1992, 3.

107. *Al-Safir,* Sept. 9, 1992, 3.

108. Graham Usher, "Why Have Hizbullah's Wings Been Clipped?" *Middle East International,* Oct. 4, 1996, 18–19.

109. See Patrick Seale, "The Address Is Syria," in *Lebanon on Hold,* ed. Rosemary Hollis and Nadim Shehadi (Oxford: Royal Institute of International Affairs and the Center for Lebanese Studies, 1996), 21–22.

110. See *Al-Shira'a,* Sept. 11, 2000, 19–21.

111. See *Al-Watan al-Arabi,* June 30, 2000, 7; *Al-Ahd,* July 7, 2000, 1, 3.

112. *Al-Ahd,* July 7, 2000, 1, 3.

113. See Nasrallah's speech on reconciliation with Amal in *Al-Ahd,* Sept. 1, 2000, 3.

114. Ahmad Nizar Hamzeh, interview, *Daily Star,* Sept. 1, 2000, 3.

115. *Daily Star,* Aug. 16, 2000, 3.

116. For details see *Daily Star,* Sept. 5, 2000, 3.

117. Ibid.

118. Qasim, interview, *Al-Ahd,* Nov. 6, 2000, 6.

119. Ibid.

120. Hajj Muhammad Ra'ad, interview, *Al-Ahd,* Nov. 6, 2000, 3.

121. *Al-Ahd,* Nov. 6, 2000, 6.

122. Ibid.

123. *Ha'aretz,* Oct. 19, 1995, 1; *Al-Wasat,* May 2, 1994, 15.

124. Most information is derived from Hamzeh, "Lebanon's Islamists," 739–59.

125. For further discussion of clientelism, see Ernest Gellner and John Waterbury, eds., *Patrons and Clients in Mediterranean Societies* (London: Duckworth, 1977).

126. Hamzeh, "Lebanon's Islamists," 744.

127. Ibid.

128. Ibid.

129. Ibid., 745.

130. Ibid., 746.

131. Ibid.

132. Ibid.

133. Ibid.

134. Ibid., 748.

135. Ibid., 750.

136. *Al-Shira'a,* June 8, 1998, 14.

137. See *Daily Star,* June 4, 1998, 2.

138. Reference to the strategy has been made many times by the party's top leadership—Sayyid Hasan Nasrallah, Shaykh Na'im Qasim, and others. See *Al-Intiqad,* 2001–2002.

139. See Gary C. Gambill, "Has American Pressure Sidelined Hizbullah," *Middle East Intelligence Bulletin,* www.meib.org (accessed Dec. 2001).

140. *Al-Safir,* Oct. 18, 2001, 1.

141. *Daily Star,* Nov. 11, 2002, 2.

142. Ibid.

143. *Al-Intiqad,* Sept. 13, 2002, 4.

144. Ibid.

145. Ibid., 145. See Nasrallah's speech on the International Day of Jerusalem, *Al-Intiqad,* Nov. 29, 2003, 13.

146. *Al-Intiqad,* Feb. 10, 2003, 5.

147. Ibid., 6.

148. Ibid.

149. Ibid., 4.

150. Sayyid Hasan Nasrallah, interview by NBN (National Broadcasting Network), Jan. 5, 2003, 8:00 P.M.

151. Ibid.

152. See Nasrallah's speech on 'Ashura', *Al-Intiqad,* Mar. 14, 2003, 13–14.

153. *Al-Intiqad,* May 5, 2003, 12.

154. *Al-Intiqad,* Sept. 9, 2003, 6.

155. *Al-Intiqad,* Aug. 1, 2003, 7.

156. *Daily Star,* Oct. 22, 2003, 5.

157. Sayyid Hasan Nasrallah, interview for CNN, Jan. 24, 2003, 8:00 P.M.

6. CONCLUSION: HIZBULLAH'S ISLAMIST VENTURE

1. *Al-Watan al-Arabi,* Jan. 1, 2001, 18.

2. Ibid.

3. Qasim, *Hizbullah,* 39–40.

4. See Ayatollah Ali Khamenei's speech to the ummah after the withdrawal of Israel from South Lebanon in *Al-Ahd,* July 7, 2000, 3.

5. See article regarding Nasrallah's meeting with Khamenei in Tehran, ibid., 1, 3.

6. *Al-Ahd,* Feb. 2, 2001, 3.

7. Ibid.

8. Ibid.

9. Ibid.

10. Qasim, *Hizbullah,* 383.

11. See Nasrallah's speech celebrating the return of the prisoners, *Al-Intiqad,* Jan. 30, 2004, 4–5.

12. *Daily Star,* Oct. 22, 2003, 6.

13. Qasim, *Hizbullah,* 381.

14. Ibid., 383.

Glossary

'adalah al-ijtima'iyyah: social justice

ahbar: men of religion, clerics

'ahd: divine covenant

ahl al-kitab: literally, "people of the book," that is, Christians and Jews, who are also known as *ahl al-dhimmi,* or "protected people"

akhirah: heavenly world

amn al-hizb: Party Security

amn al-khariji: external security

amn al-muddad: encounter security

amr bil ma'rouf: enforcing virtue

amr shari': legitimate enforcement in accordance with Islamic law

'ashira', pl. 'asha'ir: clan

ayatollah: literally, "Ayat-Allah," or "sign of Allah"; an important Shi'ite leader; Shi'ite religious rank

caliph: earthly representative of God; the Prophet's successor as spiritual head and temporal ruler of the Islamic state but lacking Muhammad's gift of prophecy

caliphate: successorship, succession

da'm: support

da'wah: literally, "call"; propagation of the faith; religious propaganda

dawlah: state

din: religion, faith

diyyah: compensation

fatwa, pl. fatawa: juridical opinion or legal opinion

fitna: situation of discord, strife, and trial

faqih, pl. fuqah'a: jurist

al-gha'ibah al-kubra: the great occultation of the (Shi'ite) imam

hajj: pilgrim; one who has made pilgrimage to Mecca

halal: religiously permissible

harakat: movement

harb al-dam: war of blood

hawzat al-ʿilmiyyah (sing. and pl.): circle(s) of learning; Shiʿite seminaries

hayʾa: commission or society

hizb: party

hujjat: proof

hujjat al-Islam: "Proof of Islam"; Shiʿite clerical rank

hukm Allah: God's rule or authority

huquq al-Sharʿiyyah: legitimate Islamic rights

ʿibadah: worship or religious observance; submission to God

ijmaʿ: consensus

ijtihad: authoritative interpretation in Islamic law

ilzam maʿnawi: morally binding

ilzam qanouni: legally binding

imam: religious leader; for the Shiʿites, the rightful successor to the Prophet

al-imam al-ghaʾib: the Hidden Imam

imam al-qaʾid: religious leader

imdad: support; social welfare support

intizam: discipline

irtibat: engagement

Islamiyyah: Islamic

istishadiyyun: martyrs

jaʿfariyyah: school of jurisprudence established by Imam Jaʿafar al-Sadiq

jamʿiyyah: society, association

jarha: wounded

jihad: holy struggle

jihad al-akbar: the greater holy struggle; involves the struggle of the soul against evil

jihad al-asghar: the lesser holy struggle; involves armed and unarmed struggle against enemies

jihad al-difaʿi: defensive holy struggle; defending the people and the land of Islam

jihad al-ibtidaʾi: elementary struggle; holy war to spread Islam worldwide

jihad al-nafs: spiritual holy struggle

khiriyyah: philanthropy; charity

khums: dues of one-fifth of annual income paid by believers to the mujtahid or marja'

lujnat: committee

mabarat: charitable organizations

Mahdi al-muntazar: anticipated messianic imam— the twelfth imam, the expected messiah for the Shi'ites

majlis: council

majmu'ah: group

marja' al-taqlid, pl. **maraji' al-taqlid:** source of imitation for religious practice among Shi'ites

marja', pl. **maraji':** highest religious authority among Shi'ites

marj'iyyah: Shi'ite supreme religiious authority

markazi: central

ma'sum: infallible, sinless

mawt: death

mu'assasat: foundation

mu'minah: faithful, believer

mufti: jurisprudent who issues *fatawa*; highest Sunni religious rank

muharamat: acts forbidden under Islamic law

mujahiddun: holy strugglers; those waging jihad

mujtahid: authoritative interpreter in Islamic law who has the right to issue *fatawa*; qualified jurisprudent

mujtama' al-'adl al-illahi: God's just society

munazzamat: organization

muqallid: a follower of a mujtahid; a cleric who has the duty of accepting conclusions reached by a supreme marja'

muqawamah Islamiyyah: Islamic resistance

murshid al-ruhi: spiritual guide

musalahah: conciliation

mustad'afin: downtrodden; the oppressed or the disinherited

mustakbirin: arrogant; those who consider themselves above others

Mutwali, pl. **Mutwalis:** Shi'ites

nabi, pl. **nabiyyun:** prophet

nafy: exile

nahi'an al-munkar: to prohibit what is objectionable; prohibiting vice

nahiyah: small district

qadi, pl. **qudat:** judge

qadi al-markazi: chief judge

qaʾid: leader

qaʿida: base; headquarters for fighter

qital: fighting

quwat al-taʿah: power of obedience

rabbaniyun: godly men

sanjak district(s)

sarrayah: brigade

Sayyid: title for a descendant of one of the Shiʿite imams

shahadah: martyrdom; a particularly Shiʿite definition that involves jihad and that
usually means profession of faith

shahid: martyr

Sharʿ Allah: God's Law

shariʿah: Islamic law

shaykh: religious teacher; tribal chief

shura: consultation

suhhiyyah: health

Sunnah: traditions of the Prophet as legally binding precedents

taʿbiaʾ: enforcement

tahkim: arbitration

tajammuʿ: assembly or association

taklif shariʿ: religious command or legitimate empowerment of the guardianship

tansiq: coordination

tarbawiyyah: educational

thawriyyah: revolutionary

ʿulamaʾ, pl.; sing. **ʿalim:** Islamic scholars

ummah: community of believers; the Islamic community

usrat: family

wahda: unit of a department

wahi: revelation

wajib: duty; religious duty

wakil: representative

wali al-amr: guardian

wali amr al-Muslimin: guardian of the Muslims

wali al-dam: guardian of blood such as father or brother

wali al-faqih: jurisconsult

wilayat al-faqih: guardianship of the jurisconsult

wilayat al-i'tibariyyah: participation in the final revelation of the word of God

wilayat al-takwinniyyah: personal covenant with Allah

zakat: alms giving

zu'ama': bosses, leaders

Bibliography

BOOKS AND ARTICLES

Abu Khalil, As'ad. "Ideology and Practice of Hizbullah in Lebanon: Islamization of Leninist Organizational Principles." *Middle Eastern Studies* 27, no. 3 (July 1991): 390–400.

Agha, Hussein J., and Ahmad S. Khalidi. *Syria and Iran: Rivalry and Cooperation.* Chathan House Papers. London: Pinter Publisher, 1995.

Ahmad, Mumtaz, and William Zartman. "Symposium: Political Islam: Can It Become a Loyal Opposition?" *Middle East Policy* (Jan. 1997): 68–74.

Ajami, Fouad. *The Vanished Imam: Musa al Sadr and the Shia of Lebanon.* Ithaca, N.Y.: Cornell Univ. Press, 1986.

Al-Amin, 'Ali. *Sadiq Hamza al-Fa'ur.* Beirut: Asia Publishing Company, 1985.

Al-Amin, Muhsin. *Khitat Jabal 'Amil* (Plans of Mount Amil). Beirut: Dar al-Ilmiyya, 1983.

Arjomand, Sa'id Amir. *The Shadow of God and the Hidden Imam: Religion, Political Order, and Societal Change in Shi'ite Iran from the Beginning to 1890.* Chicago: Univ. of Chicago Press, 1984.

———. "Shi'ite Jurisprudence and Constitution Making in the Islamic Republic of Iran." In *Fundamentalism and the State,* ed. Martin Marty and Scott Appleby. Chicago and London: The University of Chicago Press, 1993.

Binder, Leonard, ed. *Politics in Lebanon.* New York: John Wiley and Sons, 1996.

Chartouni-Dubarry, May. "Hizbullah: From Militia to Political Party." In *Lebanon on Hold: Implications for Middle East Peace Process,* ed. Rosemary Hollis and Nadim Shehadi. Oxford: Royal Institute of International Affairs and Center for Lebanese Studies, 1996.

Cobban, Helena. *The Making of Modern Lebanon.* London: Hutchinson, 1987.

Cole, Juan R. I., and Nikki R. Keddie. *Shi'ism and Social Protest.* New Haven, Conn.: Yale Univ. Press, 1986.

Crow, Ralph. "Confessionalism, Public Administration, and Efficiency in Lebanon." In *Politics in Lebanon,* ed. Leonard Binder. New York: John Wiley and Sons, 1966.

Deeb, Marius. *Militant Islamic Movements in Lebanon: Origins, Social Basis, and Ideology.* Washington, D.C.: Center for Contemporary Arab Studies, Georgetown University, 1986.

Dekmejian, R. Hrair. *Islam in Revolution: Fundamentalism in the Arab World.* 2d ed. Syracuse, N.Y.: Syracuse Univ. Press, 1995.

Dessouki, Ali E. Hilal, ed. *Islamic Resurgence in the Arab World.* New York: Praeger, 1982.

Deutsch, Karl W. *Politics and Government: How People Decide Their Fate.* New York: Houghton Mifflin, 1970.

Durkheim, Emile. *Suicide: A Study in Sociology.* Glencoe, Ill.: Free Press, 1951.

Duverger, Maurice. *Political Parties.* London: Cambridge Univ. Press, 1964.

Erikson, Erik H. *Identity, Youth, and Crisis.* New York: W. W. Norton, 1968.

Esposito, John. *Islam and Politics.* Syracuse, N.Y.: Syracuse Univ. Press, 1991.

———, ed. *The Iranian Revolution: Its Global Impact.* Miami: Florida International Univ. Press, 1990.

Fadlallah, Muhammad Husayn. *Al-Islam wa mantiq al-quwwa* (Islam and the logic of power). Beirut: Al-Mu'assasah al-Jam'iyyah, 1981.

Fahas, Shaykh Hani. "Al-Dawlah al-lubnaniyyah wa al-dawlah al-mutawaziyyah" (The Lebanese state and the parallel state). *Al-Hayat,* June 25, 1996.

Gambill, Gary C. "Has American Pressure Sidelined Hizbullah?" *Middle East Intelligence Bulletin,* www.meib.org (accessed Dec. 2001).

Gellner, Ernest, and John Waterbury. *Patrons and Clients in Mediterranean Societies.* London: Duckworth, 1977.

Gharbieh, Hussein M. "Political Awareness of the Shi'ites in Lebanon: The Role of Sayyid Abd al-Hussein Sharaf al-Din and Sayyid Musa al-Sadr." Ph.D. thesis, Univ. of Durham, UK, 1996.

Ghorayeb, Amal Saad. *Hizbu'llah: Politics and Religion.* London: Pluto Press, 2004.

Goldberg, Jeffrey. "In the Party of God." *New Yorker,* October 14, 2002, and October 21, 2002, 188–195.

Greene, Thomas H. *Comparative Revolutionary Movements.* Englewood Cliffs, N.J.: Prentice Hall, 1984.

Gurr, Ted. *Why Men Rebel.* Princeton, N.J.: Princeton Univ. Press, 1969.

Hamzeh, Ahmad Nizar. "Islamism in Lebanon: A Guide to the Groups." *Middle East Quarterly* 5, no. 3 (Sept. 1997): 47–53.

———. "Lebanon's Hizbullah: From Islamic Revolution to Parliamentary Accommodation." *Third World Quarterly* 14, no. 2 (spring 1993): 321–26.

———. "Lebanon's Islamists and Local Politics: A New Reality." *Third World Quarterly* 21, no. 5 (spring 2000): 739–59.

———. "The Role of Hizbullah in Conflict Management Within Lebanon's Shi'ite Community." Chapter 6 of *Conflict Resolution in the Arab World*, ed. Paul Salem. Beirut: American Univ. of Beirut, 1997.

Hamzeh, Ahmad Nizar, and R. Hrair Dekmejian. "The Islamic Spectrum of Lebanese Politics." *Journal of South Asian and Middle Eastern Studies* 14, no. 3 (spring 1993): 25–42.

Hanf, Theodor. *Coexistence in Wartime Lebanon: Decline of a State and Rise of a Nation.* Trans. John Richardson (from German). London: I. B. Tauris, 1993.

Harik, Iliya. "The Ethnic Revolution and Political Integration in the Middle East." *International Journal of Middle Eastern Studies* 13, no. 2 (fall 1972): 303–23.

Harris, William W. *Faces of Lebanon: Sects, Wars, and Global Extensions.* Princeton, N.J.: Markus Wiener, 1997.

Al-Hay'a al-Suhiyyah al-Islamiyyah (Islamic Health Society). *Al-Takrir al-thanawi li 'aam 2000* (The 2000 annual report). Beirut: Hizbullah, 2000.

Hitti, Philip. *Lebanon in History: From the Earliest Times to the Present.* 3d ed. London: Macmillan, 1967.

Hizbullah. "Hizbullah: Identity and Goals" (in English). www.Hizbollah.org.

———. *Mu'atamar al-jihad wal-nahda* (Conference on the jihad and the awakening). Beirut: Khomeini's Committee, 2000.

———. "Nass al-risalah al-maftuha alati wajjahah Hizbullah ila al-mustad'afin fi Lubnan wal-'alam" (Text of the open letter addressed by Hizbullah to the downtrodden in Lebanon and the world). Lebanon, Feb. 16, 1985.

———. *Safahat 'Izz fi kitab al-ummah* (Glorious pages in the book of the ummah). Beirut: Hizbullah, 1999.

Hollis, Rosemary, and Nadim Shehadi, eds. *Lebanon on Hold: Implications for Middle East Peace Process.* Oxford: Royal Institute of International Affairs and Center for Lebanese Studies, 1996.

Hourani, Albert. *Minorities in the Arab World.* Oxford: Oxford Univ. Press, 1947.

Hudson, Michael. *The Precarious Republic: Political Modernization in Lebanon.* New York: Random House, 1968.

Humphreys, R. Stephen. "The Contemporary Resurgence in the Context of Modern

Islam." In *Islamic Resurgence in the Arab World,* ed. Hilal Dessouki. New York: Praeger, 1982.

Hunter, Shireen T., ed. *The Politics of Islamic Revivalism.* Bloomington: Indiana Univ. Press, 1988.

Jaber, Hala. *Hezbullah: Born with a Vengeance.* New York: Columbia Univ. Press, 1997.

Haya't Da'm al-Muqawamah al-Islamiyyah (Association for the Support of the Islamic Resistance). *Al-Takrir al-sanawi li 'aam 1999* (The 1999 annual report). Beirut: Haj'at D'amal-Muqwneh allamiyyah, 1999.

Kawtharani, Wajih. *Al-Itijahat al-ijtima'iyyha wal-siyassiyyah fi Jabal 'Amil* (The political and social trends of Mount Amil). Beirut: Bahsun Press, 1994.

Kazemi, Farhad. "Iran, Israel, and the Arab-Israeli Balance." In *Iran since the Revolution,* ed. B. Rosen. Social Science Monographs. New York: Columbia Univ. Press, 1985.

Khalidi, Walid. *Conflict and Violence in Lebanon: Confrontation in the Middle East.* Cambridge, Mass.: Center for International Affairs, Harvard Univ., 1979.

Khamenei, Ali. *Al-Imamah wal-wilayah* (The rightful successor and the guardianship). Beirut: Markaz Baqiyat Allah al-'Azzam, 1999.

Khazen, Farid. *The Breakdown of the State in Lebanon, 1967–1976.* Cambridge, Mass.: Harvard Univ. Press, 2000.

Khomeini, Ruhallah. *Al-Hukumah al-islamiyyah* (The Islamic government). Beirut: Dar al-Tali'ah, 1979.

Kramer, Martin. "Hizbullah: The Calculus of Jihad." *Bulletin of the American Academy of Arts and Sciences,* May 1994: 36–52.

Al-Kurani, Ali. *Tariqat Hizbullah fi al-'amal al-islami* (Hizbullah's method in Islamic work). Beirut: Al-Mu'assasah al-Alamiyyah, n.d.

Lewis, Bernard. "Islam and Liberal Democracy." *The Atlantic,* Feb. 1993: 894–98.

Lipset, Seymour Martin. *Political Man: The Social Bases of Politics.* Baltimore: Johns Hopkins Univ. Press, 1981.

Maktabi, Rania. "The Lebanese Census of 1932 Revisited: Who Are the Lebanese?" *British Journal of Middle Eastern Studies* 26, no. 1 (May 1999): 219–41.

Mallat, Chibli. *Shi'i Thought from the South of Lebanon.* Oxford: Center for Lebanese Studies (May 1988). Monograph.

Marty, E. Martin, and R. Scott Appleby, eds. *Fundamentalism and the State: Remaking Politics, Economics, and Militance.* Chicago: Univ. of Chicago Press, 1993.

Meo, Leila. *Lebanon, Improbable Nation: A Study in Political Development.* Bloomington: Indiana Univ. Press, 1965.

Metral, J., and G. Mutin, eds. *Politiques urbaines dans le monde arabe.* Lyons: Maison de l'Orient, 1984.

Mu'assasat al-Jarha (Foundation for the wounded). *Nashat al-mu'assasah li 'aam 2000–2001* (2000–2001 annual activities). Beirut: Hizbullah, 2001.

Mu'assasat Jihad al-Bina' (Holy Struggle Construction Foundation). *The Generous Hand: Six Years of Work and Construction: 1988-1994* (in English).

———.*Jihad al-Bina: Its Twelfth Spring: 1988–2000* (in English). Beirut: Jihad al-Bina, 2000.

———. *Nashat al-mu'assasa li 'aam 1995* (1995 annual activities).

Mu'assasat al-Shahid (Martyrs Foundation). *Nashat al-mu'assasah li 'aam 1999* (1999 annual activities).

Al-Musawi, Ahmad. "Man antum Hizbullah?" (Who are you, Hizbullah?) *Al-Shira'a,* no. 1 (Apr. 3, 2000), no. 2 (Apr. 10, 2000), no. 3 (Apr. 17, 2000), no. 5 (May 22, 2000).

Nasr, Salim. "Beyrouth et le conflit libanais: Reconstruction de l'espace urbain." In *Politiques Urbaines dans le monde arabe,* ed. J. Metral and G. Mutin (Lyon: Maison de l'Orient, 1984): 287–305.

Nasrallah, Sayyid Hasan. *Al-Imamah wal-wilayah* (The rightful successor and the guardianship). Unpublished lecture given on June 2, 1997, Beirut.

———. "Al-Jama' al-bashariyah wal-risala wal-wilaya" (The human group, the message, and the guardianship). Lecture given on July 16, 1997, Beirut. *Al-Ahd,* July 16, 1997.

———. "Al-Jihad." Unpublished lecture delivered on May 6, 1998, the seventh night of 'Ashura'. Beirut southern suburbs.

———. "Min wilayat 'Ali ila wilayat al-faqih" (From the guardianship of Ali to the guardianship of the jurisconsult). Speech published in *al-Ahd,* May 26, 1995.

Norton, Augustus Richard. *Amal and the Shi'a: Struggle for the Soul of Lebanon.* Austin: Univ. of Texas Press, 1987.

———. *Hizbullah of Lebanon: Extremist Ideals vs. Mundane Politics.* New York: Council on Foreign Relations, 1999. Monograph.

———. "Lebanon after the Ta'if: Is the Civil War Over?" *Middle East Journal* (summer 1991): 471–73.

Oliver, Roy. *The Failure of Political Islam.* Cambridge, Mass.: Harvard Univ. Press, 1994.

Ovendale, Ritchie. *The Origins of the Arab-Israeli Wars.* 2d ed. London: Longman, 1992.

Picard, Elizabeth. *Lebanon, a Shattered Country: Myths and Realities of the Wars in*

Lebanon. Trans. Franklin Philip (from French). New York: Holmes and Meier, 1996.

———. "The Lebanese Shiʿa and Political Violence." Discussion paper 42. United Nations Research Institute for Social Development (UNRISD). Geneva, 1993.

Pipes, Daniel. *In the Path of God: Islam and Political Power.* New York: Basic Books, 1983.

Pipes, Daniel, and John Esposito. "Symposium: Resurgent Islam in the Middle East." *Middle East Policy,* Aug. 1994: 1–21.

Polk, William Roe. *The Opening of South Lebanon, 1788-1840.* Cambridge, Mass.: Harvard Univ. Press, 1963.

Pruitt, Dean G., and Jeffrey Z. Rubin. *Social Conflict: Escalation, Stalemate, and Settlement.* New York: Random House, 1986.

Qasim, Shaykh Naʿim. *Hizbullah.* Ghobairi, Beirut: Dar al-Hadi, 2002.

Rafʿat, Ahmad Sayyid. "Al-Imam wa Filastin" (The imam and Palestine). In *Muatamar al-jihad wal-nahda* (Conference on the jihad and the awakening). Beirut: Khomeini's Committee, 2000.

Rahman, Fazlur. *Islam.* Chicago: Univ. of Chicago Press, 1979.

Ranstorp, Magnus. *Hizb'allah in Lebanon: The Politics of the Western Hostage Crisis.* New York: St. Martin's Press, 1997.

Rida, Ahmad. "Al-Mutwali al-Shiʿi fi Jabal ʿAmil" (The Shiʿi partisan in Mount Amil). *Al-ʿIrfan,* Vol. 2. June 1910: 10–25.

Saad, Amal. "Political Mobilization of the Lebanese Shiʿites." M.A. thesis, Department of Political Studies, American Univ. of Beirut, 1996.

Sachedina, Abdulaziz A. "Activist Shiʿism in Iran, Iraq, and Lebanon." In *Fundamentalism and the State: Remaking Politics, Economics, and Militance,* ed. E. Martin Marty and R. Scott Appleby. Chicago: Univ. of Chicago Press, 1993.

———. *The Idea of the Mahdi in Twelver Shi'ism.* Albany: State Univ. of New York Press, 1981.

Al-Sadr, Baqir Mohammad. *Nash'at al-Shiʿah wal-Tashayaʿ* (The emergence of Shiʿite and Shiʿism). Beirut: Al-Ghady Publications, 1999.

Salem, Elie. *The Ta'if Agreement.* Beirut: Lebanese Center for Policy Studies, 1992. Monograph.

Salem, Paul, ed. *Conflict Resolution in the Arab World.* Beirut: American Univ. of Beirut, 1997.

Salibi, Kamal. *A House of Many Mansions.* London: I. B. Tauris, 1988.

Sartori, Giovanni. *Parties and Party Systems: A Framework for Analysis.* New York: Cambridge Univ. Press, 1976.

Seale, Patrick. "The Address Is Syria." In *Lebanon on Hold,* ed. Rosemary Hollis and Nadim Shehadi. Oxford: Royal Institute of International Affairs and Center for Lebanese Studies, 1996.

Shapira, Shimon. "The Origins of Hizbullah." *Jerusalem Quarterly,* no. 46 (spring 1988): 116–25.

Sharara, Waddah. *Hizbullah, Dawlat al-mujtama' al-mahali* (The state of local society). Beirut: Dar an-Nahar, 1997.

Sivan, Emmanuel. "The Holy War Tradition in Islam." *Orbis* 4, no. 2 (spring 1998): 17–22.

———. *Radical Islam.* New Haven, Conn.: Yale Univ. Press, 1985.

Supreme Islamic Shi'ite Council. *Samahat al-Imam Musa al-Sadr* (His Eminence Imam Musa al-Sadr). Supreme Islamic Shi'ite Council: n.p., n.d.

Al-T'abi'a al-Tarbawiyyah (Education Enforcement Office). "Al-Takrir al-thanawi li 'aam 2000" (The 2000 annual report). In *Al-Ahd,* Nov. 24, 2000.

United Nations Economic and Social Commission for Western Asia (UN-ESCWA). "Rural Community Development: Two Case Studies from Lebanon." Paper. Beirut: UN-ESCWA, May 21, 1999.

Usher, Graham. "Why Hizbullah's Wings Have Been Clipped?" *Middle East International* Oct. 4, 1998: 18–19.

Winslow, Charles. *Lebanon: War and Politics in a Fragmented Society.* New York: Routledge, 1996.

Wright, Robin. "Lebanon." In *The Politics of Islamic Revivalism,* ed. Shireen T. Hunter. Bloomington: Indiana Univ. Press, 1988.

Yazbak, Muhammad. "Dawr al-jihad wal-nahda fi hayat al-ummah" (The role of the jihad in the life of the community). In *Mu'atamar al-jihad wal-nahda* (Conference on the jihad and the awakening). Beirut: Khomeini's Committee, 2000.

Zamir, Meir. *The Formation of Modern Lebanon.* London: Croom Helm, 1985.

Zisser, Eyal. "Hizbullah in Lebanon: At the Crossroad." *Terrorism and Political Violence* 8, no. 2 (summer 1997): 90–106.

Zonis, Marvin, and Daniel Brumberg. *Khomeini, the Islamic Republic of Iran, and the Arab World.* Cambridge, Mass.: Center for Middle Eastern Studies, Harvard Univ. Press, 1987.

JOURNALS AND NEWSPAPERS

Al-Ahad (Beirut).
Al-Bilad (Beirut).

Daily Star (in English, Beirut).

Al-Diyar (Beirut).

Al-Ghadir (Beirut).

Al-Hawadith (London, Beirut).

Al-Hayat (Beirut).

Al-Intiqad (Beirut).

Al-'Irfan (Beirut).

Al-Muntalaq (Beirut).

Al-Mushahid al-Siyassi (London, Beirut).

Al-Nahar (Beirut).

Al-Sabil (Beirut).

Al-Safir (Beirut).

Al-Sharq al-Awsat (London).

Al-Shira'a (Beirut).

Al-Wasat (London, Beirut).

Al-Watan al-'Arabi (London, Beirut).

Wijhat Nazar (Beirut).

AUTHOR'S INTERVIEWS

Ezzedine, Hajj Hasan (head of Hizbullah's press office). Beirut southern suburbs, Oct. 31, 2003.

Fayyad, Hajj Ali (director of Hizbullah's Consultative Center for Documentation and Research). Beirut southern suburbs, Jan. 10, 2001.

Kawtharani, Shaykh Muhammad (former head of Hizbullah's Politburo Cultural Committee). Ras al-Nab'a, Beirut, Dec. 14, 2000.

Meri', Hajj Yusuf (head of Hizbullah's External Relations Unit). Beirut southern suburbs, May 21, 1996.

Qasim, Shaykh Na'im (Hizbullah's deputy secretary). Beirut southern suburbs, Nov. 27, 2000, Jan. 25, 2001.

Al-Tufayli, Shaykh Subhi (Hizbullah's former secretary-general). Beirut southern suburbs, Apr. 10, 1995.

Index